Transitions Through Homelessness

Transitions Through Homelessness

Lives on the Edge

Carol McNaughton
University of York, UK

First published 2008 by
PALGRAVE MACMILLAN
Houndmills, Basingstoke, Hampshire RG21 6XS and
175 Fifth Avenue, New York, N.Y. 10010
Companies and representatives throughout the world

PALGRAVE MACMILLAN is the global academic imprint of the Palgrave
Macmillan division of St. Martin's Press, LLC and of Palgrave Macmillan Ltd.
Macmillan® is a registered trademark in the United States, United Kingdom
and other countries. Palgrave is a registered trademark in the European
Union and other countries.

ISBN 13: 978–0–230–20162–0   hardback
ISBN 10: 0–230–20162–8   hardback

This book is printed on paper suitable for recycling and made from fully
managed and sustained forest sources. Logging, pulping and manufacturing
processes are expected to conform to the environmental regulations of the
country of origin.

A catalogue record for this book is available from the British Library.

A catalogue record for this book is available from the Library of Congress.

10   9   8   7   6   5   4   3   2   1
17 16 15 14 13 12 11 10 09 08

Transferred to Digital Printing 2011.

Contents

Acknowledgements

Thanks go to all the people who assisted in the research and development of this book, including: the people who allowed their lives to be studied, of course; the agency that assisted with the research and without whom it would not have been possible; the many academic influences that I have been lucky to have over the years, and especially, to the memory of Robina Goodlad.

On a personal note, this is for those with the keys to my home: my family, friends and TL.

With thanks.
w.

Glossary

Divestment passages: Occur when transitional events (such as going to prison) lead to what is perceived to be a failure or the wrong outcome. They may lead to a separation from status or rupturing of narrative identity.

Edgework: Actions and events that involve negotiating at the edge of normative behaviour. In this analysis this applies to voluntary and non-voluntary risks that require people to negotiate difficult circumstances and may involve a rupturing of, or escape from, material reality. These acts can involve drug use, violence, or suicide attempts. Going over the edge (such as becoming an addict, committing suicide) occurs when these risky actions are not managed.

Emplotment: Through a process of 'emplotment', actual 'events' that occur, and how people present them and make sense of them, as part of their 'story' of life, become interwoven subconsciously by them, over time. This creates a narrative identity.

Integrative passages: Transitional stages that maintain an individual's integration to society over their life course. They adhere to the norms of society, such as moving from parental home to student accommodation.

Material reality: The actual 'here and now' of time and space that people experience in the circumstances they are in. For example this may be constituted by the actual room in a hostel someone is in, the sounds, people and smells there, the street and city there.

Narrative identity: Through emplotment people can maintain a sense of narrative identity over time – they are the 'same' person today as yesterday, the same person as ten years ago, however much their external circumstances change. By constructing a cohesive internal narrative of the different events that have occurred in their life, they can maintain ontological security and a sense of identity, despite changes in the context this occurs in.

Rationale of irrational behaviour: Actions that can be understood as rational when the motivations for them and the material reality they occur within are taken into account. They may not appear rational to avoid risk but can be viewed as rational from within the micro-level context they occur within.

Resources: Collectively, resources here refer to the different forms of human, social, cultural, material, or economic capital that people have access to.

Social welfare system: Collectively the services (voluntary and statutory) that are funded through a broad government framework to provide assistance to people, and other resources (such as Benefits) from the state, often in a non-direct way.

Stressed perspective on homelessness and causation: (The term is an amalgamation of structuration, realism, and edgework). Asserts that it is the resources that people have that provide a buffer to outcomes such as homelessness occurring in their lives, despite the same acts of edgework occurring (drug use, for example). With these resources they can generate resilience to manage the stress of life, and engage in edgework effectively. It is not this edgework that is the cause of homelessness, but the inability to manage it, due to the context it occurs within and resources individuals have.

Targeted populations: Groups that are particularly conceptualised as being in need of support or interventions from agencies funded as part of the welfare system to assist them resolve the problems they represent. This includes the homeless, unemployed, and addicts.

Introduction

The homeless person is an evocative social character of late modernity. Homelessness encapsulates many things: destitution, displacement, poverty, criminality, fear, pity, crisis, anomie, (Fooks & Pantazis, 1999; Somerville, 1992). The homeless are archetypal 'outsiders', and, even in a modern world that apparently celebrates plurality and difference, it remains that 'homelessness is distinguished by a lack of social status, invisibility, as a 'problem' to others, with the homeless being seen as outcast and rejected, at the bottom of the social scale, disreputable and nicheless' (Somerville, 1992:532). Homelessness is a social problem that has been a key focus of recent policy developments and of 'targeting' by the state (Dean, 1999), particularly in the UK. This indicates the strong currency that homelessness has as a discursively understood phenomenon (Anderson, 2004; May, Cloke & Johnsen, 2005). There has been much research and debate into homelessness in recent years (for example, Anderson, Kemp & Quilgars, 1993; Kennett & Marsh, 1999; Jacobs, Kemeny & Manzi, 1999; Fitzpatrick, Kemp & Klinker, 2000) and sophisticated development of knowledge about why homelessness occurs and how it can be understood. However there has been little exploration of *transitions through* homelessness, over time, with a focus on the *experiences of the individuals* making these transitions that ties them to broader theoretical frameworks.

This book begins to address this and presents a perspective on homelessness in late modernity, developed using biographical case studies narrated by twenty-eight people who were or had recently been homeless. What happened to them as they made transitions through homelessness for a year was then explored in a series of in-depth interviews conducted with each.

Far-reaching changes have taken place in the social and political context that these individuals operate within over recent years, on a global scale. Technological developments, the overarching success of global capitalism, changing welfare states, ecological crisis, new patterns of family life, relationships, employment, markets, mass migration, transnationality, and the emergence of 'new' national terrorist threats, encapsulate these changes. These are themselves recognised as being the (sometimes unintended) consequences of the process of modernity. This is a time of late, reflexive, modernity (Beck, 1992; 1999), distinct, but following on from, first modernity, as the structures of full employment, the nuclear family, clear class, gender, and national identities, become increasingly fragmented and fluid (Giddens, 1991; 2002). This has affected individuals and how their actions are perceived in profound ways and discursively fed into the institutions and mechanisms used to govern society, as well as the individual lives of those interacting with and creating these mechanisms.

With this as the social context, this study provides new insight into how individual factors and structural contexts interact and lead to homelessness, for some people, in some circumstances – and how they then experience this. Contacts with key institutional mechanisms developed to address and regulate homelessness are also assessed, as is how a sense of ontological security is affected by being homeless. Finally, the lives of some of the people who made a transition out of homelessness are presented, to go full circle in this study of lives, trapped at the edge.

Outline of the book

In the first chapter the empirical and theoretical context for the study is set. In Chapter 2 the key concepts used to develop a new perspective on homelessness in late modernity are outlined. A clear definition of agency and structure is also provided. The research process and the characteristics of the people studied are then outlined. In Chapter 3, the people who are studied biographies and their transitions into homelessness are analysed. In Chapter 4, the actual transitions through homelessness they took over the course of the research are presented. Three transitional routes are identified and discussed. The findings are then brought together to present a new perspective on homelessness, causation, and individual actions – the 'stressed' perspective.

In Chapter 5 the role of the social welfare system, and the micro-level interactions that the people studied engaged in as they negotiated with this system, are analysed, to assess the role that this system played in constraining or enabling changes in their lives. In Chapter 6, their sense of identity, the day-to-day interactions they engaged in, and the sense of ontological security they had, as they made these transitions over time, is explored. The findings are brought together, in Chapter 7, to provide an overview of these transitions through homelessness, the key mechanisms that affected them and the theoretical assertions.

This book is about how homelessness is experienced within the conditions of late modernity – as the reader will see, it is about real lives, lives negotiating on the edge perhaps, but an edge that many of us negotiate at points in our lives. It is about the motion of lives, lived in late modernity, as experienced by one group, all homeless for a time.

1
In the Absence of Home: Understanding Homelessness

The dance on the periphery may not be leading anywhere, but at least it celebrates a refusal to sleep; a resistance to arrest; a mode of motion turns out to be a way, perhaps the only way, of life.

(Cohen & Taylor, 1992:236)

1. Constructions of homelessness

A burgeoning of research into homelessness throughout the 1990s (encapsulated in a comprehensive UK summary, Fitzpatrick et al, 2000) and increasingly sophisticated academic analysis (in edited collections by Hutson & Clapham, 1999; Burrows, Pleace & Quilgars, 1997; and Kennett & Marsh, 1999 for example) has led to a body of academic work constituting 'homelessness studies'.

A key element of this work has been the identification of the constructed nature of homelessness as both a phenomenon and circumstance (Jacobs et al, 1999). This approach asserts that social problems are *'formed by the power of identifiable groups in society to define a certain issue as a 'problem' that needs tackling in a particular kind of way'* (Jacobs et al, 1999:13). With this in mind, definitions of homelessness have been identified as falling into minimalist or maximalist accounts (Jacobs et al, 1999). Minimal homelessness is applied in a narrow sense to those who lack the most minimal of homes – a spatial dwelling, and is often associated with individual failing or actions such as drug use and illness, that have caused this a lack of a home. Maximal homelessness relates to range of circumstances that could be construed as homelessness, and has attributed this to the structural macro-level forces such as housing and employment systems that operate within a power dynamic to construct this outcome (Hutson, 1999). Increasingly sophisticated reviews of this dichotomy recognise

3

that the two sides may not be mutually exclusive (Clapham, 1999), both macro-level forces and individual actions interact in complex ways to lead to homelessness (Fitzpatrick, 2005, explored in more detail in the Section 2). This interaction is embedded within a wider material and social world consisting of many structures, and characterised, perhaps, by a risk society (Clapham, 1999; Marsh & Kennett, 1999). However there has been little engagement with this theory in empirical studies of homelessness, or uncovering of the subjectivities of transitions through homelessness that moves on from the constructivist accounts that have come to dominate (Neale, 1997). This book aims to begin to address this.

Defining homelessness

Defining homelessness is a surprising contested and complex issue. There has been ongoing debate about how homelessness should be defined, often relating to how minimalist or maximalist these accounts intend to be (Speak, 2004; Tipple & Speak, 2005; Jacobs et al, 1999; Pleace, Burrows & Quilgars, 1997). Four intersecting but distinct dimensions can be identified from the literature, encapsulated here as:

1. 'Absolute' minimal homelessness – having no shelter at all, rough sleeping;
2. Homelessness pertaining to the nature or quality of the housing someone has;
3. Homelessness as it is subjectively experienced;
4. Homelessness as it relates to statutory definitions, or the welfare entitlement that exists surrounding housing in a given locale or time.

'Absolute' homelessness – no shelter

This form of homelessness may relate to those who are destitute or without any shelter due to war, natural disaster, or other such external causes. However in industrial western contexts it is this form of homelessness that has become synonymous with rough sleeping and associated with the individual characteristics or vulnerabilities associated with a pathology of homelessness – addiction, mental illness or criminality. This is the homelessness most prevalent in popular imagination – this is the image of the homeless person as the tramp, as someone sleeping on park benches, begging in stations, for example (Fooks & Pantazis, 1999; Pleace, 2000).

Rough sleeping manifests a particularly extreme and visible form of homelessness – rendering real the imagined character of the 'homeless person' that exists in popular discourse (Fooks & Pantazis, 1999) and is an indication that 'the social system is functioning inadequately' (Marsh & Kennett, 1999:2). Throughout the 1980s and 1990s (for a range of economic and social reasons (see Jacobs et al, 1999; Marcus, 2005)) visible street homelessness increased, and became high on the political and public agenda (Anderson, 2004; Pleace, 2000; O'Connell, 2003). In the US the McKinney Homeless Assistance Act, passed in 1987, set aside one billion dollars for research and support programmes to help the homeless (Marcus, 2005). In the UK, the Rough Sleepers Initiative was implemented by the government in 1990, to address street homelessness, first in London and then across the country. Specific policy measures to tackle and address rough sleeping were developed and implemented, in an attempt to end street homelessness. Whether through targeted outreach services or through the implementation of anti-social behaviour legislation (Fitzpatrick & Jones, 2005; May, Cloke & Johnsen, 2005) this highlights the continued problematisation of the actions, lifestyles, and circumstances of the 'homeless' as street dwellers.

Furthermore, as is explored in the next section, many people experiencing homelessness are not necessarily without shelter – they may have a room in a hostel, or be staying with friends, for example. Some people who are *perceived* to be rough sleepers, such as those begging on the street, are not necessarily without housing or some form of accommodation (Fitzpatrick & Kennedy, 2000). And as this study (and others, Fitzpatrick, 2000; Anderson & Tulloch, 2000) have shown, episodes of rough sleeping may often be one aspect of lives lived at the margins of society – a situation that people 'churn' in and out of, alongside other insecure housing circumstances.

Hidden homelessness and housing conditions

So homelessness can be placed along a continuum of housing need and circumstance (Bramley, 1988; Watson & Austerberry, 1986) relating to the nature or quality of the accommodation someone has. This continuum goes from 'absolute homelessness' to circumstances that include living in temporary accommodation, such as hostels or Bed & Breakfasts; sharing accommodation with friends or relatives, because no other form of housing is available; or living in overcrowded conditions. This can make charting the empirical pathways (Clapham, 2002) taken through homelessness particularly problematic for research. In a recent US study (Tsemberis, McHugo, Williams, Hanrahan & Stefancic, 2007) a time line inventory was used to demarcate where participants had slept each night over six-month periods. Sleeping in places not normally for human habitation, such as cars, doorways, and also in emergency shelters, was classed as literal homelessness. Temporary and institutional accommodation such as staying with friends, or in hospital or rehabs was then added to this to create a broader distinct category of 'functional homelessness'. These nested definitions were intended to accurately measure the length of time participants were 'homeless' whilst also acknowledging the diversity of circumstances that it can refer to. Even then there still had to be acknowledgment of the fluidity of this – people in long term supported accommodation were classed as in stable accommodation although they did not have their own legal tenure.

Homelessness relating to housing circumstance merges into an exploration of hidden homelessness. There has been increasing recognition in homeless literature that there may be a large 'dark' figure of people experiencing hidden homelessness (Webb, 1994) and that this may affect certain groups, such as women, in particular (Smith, 1999; Greve & Currie, 1990). Webb (1994) defines visible homelessness as: rough sleeping in a public place that can be observed; being in contact with statutory or voluntary services designed to assist people who are homeless or being accommodated in housing for the homeless; and, therefore, being counted in statistics on homelessness such as the statutory homeless figures, or counts by agencies that work with people experiencing homelessness, such as the number accommodated in a hostel.

Those who are part of a hidden homeless therefore may be experiencing some form of homelessness along the continuum of housing need outlined above but are not in contact with agencies to assist them with this. They may be staying with friends, for example, but are invisibly homeless, as they have no contact with the welfare system to resolve this. There is a complex intersection of forms of homelessness that makes a single definition of homelessness difficult to apply universally. People experiencing homelessness may also be in an ongoing cycle of changing housing circumstances (Fitzpatrick, 2000; Hall, 2001), on a day-to-day basis – making it difficult, and perhaps futile to attempt to place one single definition of homelessness onto fluid housing circumstances. For example, someone may have their own tenancy, but be accessing agencies that work with homeless people due to the threat of eviction they face – are they visibly homeless, despite being housed? Someone may be staying with friends, unable to move into their own accommodation, and not view this as problematic, how meaningful is it to define them as homeless?

What may be viewed as overcrowded or unsuitable housing by one person, in one country, may not be in another (Tipple & Speak, 2005).

To construct a universal definition of homelessness risks the formation of an inadequate one and a form of housing essentialism – whose definition should be used to judge how much homelessness exists in any one place at any one time, or the nature of that homelessness? If effective real understanding of homelessness is to be developed, the very range of circumstances, and context bound relativity of the concept, has to be acknowledged. And this also relates to philosophical, subjective accounts of the meaning of home.

Homelessness and subjectivity

Clearly in literal semantic terms homelessness refers to being without a home – but this then opens up the problem of defining what 'home' refers to. There has been much written in housing literature about the meaning of home (such as Depres, 1991; Somerville, 1997; Mallet, 2004). 'Home' may be a material space (Saunders, 1990) however the concept also clearly has emotional, psychological and subjective elements (Padgett, 2007; Kearns et al, 2000), elements that make a material space a 'home' (Giuliani, 1991; Somerville, 1997). The term also can apply to broad socio-spatial locations with which someone has a subjective attachment of belonging or history, such as the country someone is from. People may have multiple senses of what home means to them.

Somerville (1992) in his analysis of the meaning of home, argues that signifiers of 'homelessness' are the converse of what is valued about the ideological construct of 'home' (based on the study by Watson & Austerberry, 1986). The seven signifiers of home that Somerville (1992:533) identifies are shelter, hearth, heart, privacy, abode, roots, and paradise. Homelessness therefore may involve a lack of material shelter, lack of privacy, lack of comfort, lack of the citizenship rights, lack of ownership over space, and also merges into subjectivities: lacking a space to develop intimate relationships; lacking a sense of belonging, and with it a secure sense of identity. At the most extreme subjective form, homelessness signifies ontological crisis, anomie, and purgatory, being 'cast out' of the paradise of belonging to society, being 'outside' on both objective and subjective levels.

How homelessness is perceived will also be relative to the context it occurs within and the perceived cause. For example, someone who is homeless due to natural disaster will be viewed as, and may experience their homelessness, very differently from someone who is rough sleeping in a park, who has recently been released from prison with no where to go, or someone living in a hostel, with an addiction to heroin, or a woman staying in a friend's spare room after separating from a violent partner. Yet all could be viewed as homeless. This has long been recognised in homelessness research as the previous discussion of maximalist – minimalist accounts introduced (Jacobs et al, 1999). It can be both pathological, individually generated *and* at the same time, is about a lack of housing and exclusion caused at macro-level forces. Pathology does not confer blame, for as will be asserted in this study, individual actions and problems are generated within existing social worlds, created by many structures through the interactions and understanding of individual agents (Giddens, 1984).

Homelessness and welfare entitlement

Homelessness, how it is perceived, defined, responded to, in every country, will to some degree be affected by the government response to it that exists and the welfare entitlement citizens of that country have (Tipple & Speak, 2005). Depending on the definition of homelessness used, the number of people experiencing it, or the nature of homelessness, it will also be perceived differently in public and political discourse. This response to, and understanding of, homelessness also changes over time (Somerville, 1999), as is explored in more detail in Section 3. For example, in the UK huge increases in statutory homelessness and visible street homelessness at the end of the 1980s galvanised a government response to this (Pleace, 2000; Anderson, 2004).

In the UK a single definition does exist in the form of statutory homelessness, however this can be viewed as a 'tool for rationing social housing' rather than encapsulating anything about what it *means* to be homeless (Fitzpatrick et al, 2000: 8). Indeed it has also been asserted that this definition is a key mechanism in the construction of homelessness occurring among certain groups, and to how these groups are perceived (Anderson, 1999).

The statutory definition of homelessness outlines who, and in what circumstance, the government has a responsibility to accommodate. This responsibility is highly contingent on people fitting certain criteria, namely that they can be shown to have no other alternative and be in genuine 'need' – they are not intentionally homeless, and have some vulnerability such as having dependent children or pregnancy, that defines them as in priority need. In Scotland, the details of the statutory definition differ but operate to filter social housing in a similar way. It is important to be clear that statutory homelessness is a narrow legal definition used in the UK to ration social housing. It is quite different from the multi-faceted definitions of homelessness outlined above, and should not be confused.

There are then many meanings attached to homelessness despite, at the most basic common-sense level, it being perceived to be about someone lacking their own housing. 'Homeless people' are often associated with pathological vulnerability or deviance and conceptualised as beggars, criminals, addicts, as an underclass or a new poor that poses a threat to mainstream society (Fooks & Pantazis, 1999; Forrest, 1999; Bauman, 1998; Pleace, 2000; Speak & Tipple, 2006). This study engages with the fact that a tension exists between homelessness as an objective phenomenon relating to housing circumstance or need, and as something that is *also* understood and experienced discursively and subjectively and that may be generated and caused by both simultaneously. What is particularly important to understanding homelessness is a consideration of what *causes* it. Liddiard (1999) highlights that the perceived 'cause' of someone being 'without a home' will shape the support they can access to resolve it, and how their homelessness is perceived, by themselves and others.

2. Causes of homelessness – structure, agency and the 'new orthodoxy'

So as already noted, knowledge on what causes homelessness has historically dichotomised into explanations that either focus on structural forces (such as housing supply; unemployment, housing policy) or on the individual actions, attributes or circumstances of the person involved (such as addiction, mental illness, relationship breakdown) (Fitzpatrick, 2005). Attitudes to homelessness, and political responses to it, have shaped and been shaped by, whichever account in this dichotomy dominates in an ongoing oscillation (Fitzpatrick et al, 2000; Marsh & Kennett, 1999; Pleace, Burrows & Quilgars, 1997; Kemp, Lynch & Mackay, 2001; Anderson & Tulloch, 2000; Anderson, 2004).

Attempts to develop this dualism of agency and structure have been made in recent years (Neale, 1997). This has led to a new academic orthodoxy stating that homelessness is caused by a complex interrelation of societal and individual factors, occurring in certain circumstances, to certain people (Fitzpatrick, 2005; May, 2000; Pleace, 2000; Pleace et al, 1997). This interrelation was summed up by Fitzpatrick, Kemp & Klinker (2000) in their comprehensive review of UK homelessness research. They identified housing trends; family fragmentation; and poverty and unemployment as key structural trends that underpin homelessness. They also identified individual risk factors that precipitate homelessness including: experiences of sexual or physical abuse;

family disputes and instability; having been in care or prison previously; drug or alcohol misuse; mental health problems; school exclusions; lack of qualifications; and poor physical health. Therefore within certain conditions, changes in circumstance over the life course coupled with these risk factors, lead to episodes of homelessness for some people. Trigger points for this include: leaving the parental home after an argument; bereavement; leaving care or prison; deterioration of mental or physical health; and, increased alcohol or drug use. What is clear from the many studies conducted into homelessness (Anderson & Tulloch, 2000; Fitzpatrick & Clapham, 1999; Rosengard, Laing, Jackson & Jones, 2002) and will also be illustrated in more detail here, is that complex factors interact and lead to a transition into and through homelessness. And these factors can exacerbate or sustain this situation.

The new orthodoxy

To summarise then, the key assertion of this new orthodoxy is that:

- *structural factors create the conditions within which homelessness will occur; and*
- *people with personal problems are more vulnerable to these adverse social and economic trends than others; therefore*
- *a high concentration of people with personal problems in the homeless population can be explained by their susceptibility to macro-structural forces rather than necessitating an individual explanation of homelessness.* (Fitzpatrick, 2005:4)

This approach still lacks any 'clear conceptualization of causation' (Fitzpatrick, 2005:5) however, or clarity on how and why such individual personal factors as drug addiction, domestic violence, relationship breakdown, mental illness, occur. In fact this analytically sidesteps the fact that what is structural, such as increased family fragmentation, is also simultaneously experienced as individual (such as relationship breakdown or domestic violence). How agency, or structure, are actually defined and conceptualised in research is rarely clear however. Fitzpatrick (2005), citing the work of Neale (1997) has proposed that structuration theory (Giddens, 1984) is used within an epistemological framework underpinned ontologically by realism to address this. She argues that this theoretical approach, applied to empirical research into homelessness, may assist in developing this new orthodoxy and beginning to unpack these relationships of causation. The study presented in this book aims to do so, by examining not only the factors that may lead to or sustain homelessness, but also how they may be explained. This is grounded in an ontological approach acknowledging that whilst structures are generated by actions, actions are in turn constrained and constituted by those structures, in an ongoing hermeneutical cycle, compatible with both critical realism (Bhaskar, 1979) and structuration theory (Giddens, 1984).

In Chapter 2 how structure and how agency are conceptualised, and the epistemological framework used in this study, are outlined in detail. In the remainder of this chapter, key theoretical 'building blocks' are introduced and discussed. These key factors pertain to: firstly, providing clarification of how inequality and poverty are conceptualised here, using different forms of 'capital'; secondly, an exploration of the individual problems identified as causing homelessness and how they can be conceptualised; and thirdly, the role of governance and social policy to this. These three elements represent key tenets used here to understand and explain transitions into and through homelessness in late modernity.

Stratification, resources and forms of capital

Poverty (or at least having relatively few resources) is usually a key cause of homelessness identified throughout the literature (Fitzpatrick et al, 2000; Pleace, 1998; Anderson, 1999). Different cleavages of stratification exist in society that affect the 'life chances' people have (Breen & Rottman, 1995). This stratification also relates to the resources their position within this social system provides them with. 'Resources' here refers to the range of cultural, human, social, material and economic capital that someone may have, such as education, qualifications, networks, contacts, knowledge, possessions (Bourdieu, 1986; Coleman, 1988; Halpern, 2005; Baron, Schuller & Field, 2000). These different forms of capital intersect to influence the life chances that an individual has. These forms of capital are defined here as economic capital (financial resources or income); material capital (material resources of value, such as property or equipment); human capital (their skills, education and knowledge); cultural capital (skills, knowledge and ideas they use to interact with others) and social capital (their social networks and the resources they allow access to). Taken together these forms of capital are used to refer to and explore resources (or lack of resources) and how they affected the experiences of the people studied.

The use of these different concepts of capital is not unproblematic, and the value or meaning of social capital in particular remains contested (Baron et al, 2000; Halpern, 2005; Portes, 1998). In this study, social capital, is used in a narrow sense, defined as the *resources* that individuals' social networks (broadly defined as the people they have contact with, interact with and know) allow them access to. This parallels how the concept was developed in the work of Bourdieu, and highlighted by Edwards & Foley (1998). Social networks are organised around the norms and sanctions of different groups (Coleman, 1988; Halpern, 2005) and may generate negative as well as positive outcomes. Social networks may not necessarily act to generate more capital and can actually act to deplete it in certain circumstances (Portes, 1998) such as when social obligations operate without any real reciprocity operating. It is well documented that homelessness may rupture social networks (Lemos, 2000) but experiences of homelessness are also affected by the nature of the social networks that remain or are then generated. Both the positive and negative effects of social networks are explored here.

So resources, as they are referred to here are conceptualised as the access to various forms of capital (cultural, economic, material, social, and human) that is available to people, due to their family, social networks, employment, education, and their material social situation. This availability may stem from birth and family background, but can change over time. Power dynamics that intersect with these cleavages of stratification are also important to recognise (Lukes, 1974). This refers to the power that groups, individuals or institutions have to determine, protect, or allocate who has access to which resources. Therefore individual life chances, whilst stemming from the access to resources someone has, are also underpinned by the power groups have to protect or promote this access over time.

Returning to the risk and trigger factors that are seen to cause homelessness – low educational attainment, long-term unemployment, for example – it is clear that people experiencing homelessness often lack some or all of these resources of human, social, cultural, and economic capital (and therefore may lack a degree of power within the society they operate within). This lack of resources, and lack of power, may lead to some form of exclusion from all or some of the activities of society. In recent years the term 'social exclusion' has been used to describe the outcome a poverty of resources may lead to. Forrest (1999:17) argues that homelessness can be viewed as a *'general metaphor for severe and typically multi-faceted experiences of marginality and exclusion from mainstream society'*. Homelessness was a particular target of New Labour government in their attempt to tackle 'social exclusion', and Pleace (1998) has argued that homelessness should be reconceptualised as a product of the processes of social exclusion. It has been argued that social exclusion as a concept allows for the dynamic and multi-faceted dimensions of inequality to be explored in a way that a focus on material poverty does not (Burchard, Le Grand & Piachaud, 2002). However social exclusion remains a contested and unstable concept, and so is not explicitly used here. Using different forms of capital to understand the resources that the people studied had instead allows for a more complex analysis, than using the term 'exclusion' or 'inclusion' alone, to conceptualise their material situation.

Clearly no one factor (such as economic poverty) however important, is usually enough to explain why certain outcomes occur or to illustrate the complex relationships that lead to certain outcomes (Sayer, 2000; Bassett, 1999). For example, if someone can only afford or only access housing through the state in areas with a high concentration of social problems, or where the conditions of the housing is poor, this may also impact on their health, well-being, and lifestyle. This may in turn erode the different forms of capital they have further, in a complex relationship (Smith, Easterlow, Munro & Turner, 2003). Some people may experience homelessness even when they have access to housing, or have enough financial resources to obtain housing. This homelessness may have occurred for a variety of reasons, and not necessarily a lack of economic capital. The value of using different concepts of capital is that they illustrate the multi-dimensional relationships and resources that interact and impact on the life chances people have, and the transitions they make, within an 'open' social system. In this open system it is recognised that one factor may not directly cause another to occur, but instead a complex set of mechanisms operate, in certain circumstances, to underpin and trigger the opportunities, actions, and outcomes that actually occur (Sayer, 2000). This epistemological framework of critical realism used here is outlined in more detail in Chapter 2 and these different levels of resources can be seen as paralleling key causal mechanisms in the generation of homelessness Fitzpatrick (2005) identifies – economic, interpersonal, housing and individual attributes.

In a society with a social welfare system that is supposed to filter access to essential services and resources for those individuals that need them most, another layer of complexity as to why some people (even with few resources) become homeless and others do not, is added. Often it is individual factors – addiction, mental illness – cited as causing homelessness that are emphasised in accounts of homelessness and causation that people provide, as is shown here. What is rarely questioned however in these accounts of homelessness, and remains central, is a sociological understanding of how these problems (addiction, violence, mental illness) are generated, and come to affect some people's lives in such a way as they become homeless, whilst not others. These problems are real, they do exist and cause real suffering and conflict – but what generates them?

Individual factors and homelessness – edgework

Recent empirical studies into causes and processes of marginality and vulnerability have continued to highlight how individual factors identified as the risk and trigger factors precipitating homelessness interact and compound each other (For example, Van Der Poel & Van De Mheen, 2006; Tyler & Johnston, 2006; Martijn & Sharpe, 2006; Mallett, Rosenthal & Keys, 2005; Crane & Warnes, 2006). These studies identify drug or alcohol use; mental illness; and relationship and family conflict, as key problems that can lead to and interact with homelessness. For example, once someone becomes addicted to heroin they may be more likely to become homeless. Once they are homeless they are more likely to be unable to cease their drug use, and so an obvious cycle is created (Tyler & Johnston, 2006). This cycle is also what much of the services of the welfare system that target key problems groups (Dean, 1999) are engaged in managing, and are attempting to break.

Highly traumatic incidents and abuse having occurred in the life histories of people who experience homelessness are also prevalent factors (Buhrich, Hodder & Teesson, 2000; Collins & Phillips, 2003; Hyde, 2005). These traumatic incidents include sexual abuse, violence, or witnessing fatal or near fatal incidents. Once people become homeless they also often face extreme vulnerability and trauma, and homeless people are far more likely to be the victims of crime and violence (from both other homeless and non-homeless people) than the general population (Newburn & Rock, 2005; Lee, 2005). There are high rates of suicide among people who are homeless (Baker, 1997; Molnar, Shade, Kral, Booth & Watters, 1998) and more subjectively, high levels of social isolation and loneliness (Lemos, 2000). The American Psychiatric Association's definition of trauma is that a person must have experienced, witnessed or been confronted with actual threatened death or serious injury, or threat to physical integrity of self or others (APA, 2000). As will be shown here, and has been found in many of the studies cited in this chapter, people who are homeless may often be negotiating with experiences of extreme trauma. This cannot help but affect the emotional landscape from which they go on to negotiate their ongoing life course and the choices and actions taken.

Clearly then, a life history characterised by the individual factors identified as causing or occurring alongside homelessness is often one characterised by trauma, difficulty, and a lack of resources, as stressed in minimalist accounts of homelessness. But why these individual problems occur, and the relationship of causation inherent to this – why they only lead to homelessness in some cases and not others – remains relatively unexplored. Just recognising these factors prevail, without actually moving forward in understanding *why* they occur, or how they may lead to homelessness in some cases and not others, means that understanding about homelessness and marginality will not move on either. Sometimes it is individual acts that lead to homelessness (as Crane & Warnes, in their 2006 study of homelessness among older people, identify) but this does not necessarily mean it *always* is, nor remove the significance of the structural context that this has occurred within. Individual problems and situations may be the objective *reasons* cited by someone as why their homelessness occurs, but this does not actually provide a relationship of causation. What actually caused that social context, at that moment, to lead to homelessness for one individual, when they may have already been negotiating with a range of difficult situations (poverty, drug use etc) prior to it?

To examine this aspect of homelessness, the individual problem factors (such as mental illness; drug use; traumatic incidents) the concept of 'edgework' (Lyng, 1990; 2005a; 2005b) is used and adapted. Stephen Lyng (1990; 2005a; 2005b) developed the concept of edgework to define voluntary risk taking, encapsulating actions that involve negotiating on the 'edge' of normative social actions.

Edgework refers to actions that may involve negotiating, for example: '*the boundary between sanity and insanity, consciousness and unconsciousness, and the most consequential one, the line separating life and death*' (Lyng, 2005a:4). In this study, this concept of edgework is adapted and used broadly, to conceptualise any events or actions that carry clear risk *and* involve the negotiation of boundaries of normative behaviour. These actions encapsulate events whereby day-to-day life and 'normality' has been ruptured or transcended. This can be used to bring together the disparate individual factors often prevalent in the lives of people experiencing homelessness, into one conceptual whole. Edgework associated with homelessness and explored here (such as mental illness, violence, or addiction) may not be 'voluntarily' undertaken, and may be a manifestation of 'going over the edge' rather than negotiating it, however it still is something that clearly prevails in the lives of people who are homeless – and profoundly affects their actions and transitions. These acts and experiences include suicide attempts, drug and alcohol use, engaging in or being the victims of violence, mental illness, sudden breakdown in relationships due to violence or conflict. These events involve negotiating the edge of normative social behaviour, and a rupturing of 'normal' routine life that will be experienced subjectively and involve some degree of agency to negotiate (this is discussed in more detail in Chapter 2). Many people experiencing homelessness whose lives are explored here were also engaging in extreme edgework – engaging in actions that may be perceived as voluntary risk taking, such as substance use, or experiencing situations of extreme risk that have to experientially (and sometimes physically) be negotiated with, such as violence and mental illness.

Sometimes it is individual acts that lead to homelessness but this does not remove the significance of the structural context that this has occurred within (Fitzpatrick, 2005). Individual problems and situations may be the objective *reasons* cited by someone as why their homelessness occurs, but this does not actually provide a relationship of causation. What actually caused that social context, at that moment, to lead to homelessness for one individual, when they may have already been negotiating with a range of difficult situations (poverty, drug use and so on) prior to it? Why for other individuals does the apparent same situation not lead to homelessness?

There is also another, third, aspect to understanding homelessness and why it occurs that is examined here. And this is how the mechanisms of the state operate to respond to and address homelessness.

Governance, welfare states, and homelessness

As has been extensively recognised in previous studies, the social welfare system in place in a given locale provides the key institutional context to how people negotiating with homelessness may (or may not) access resources to resolve it, and how they experience accessing these resources at micro-levels (Pleace, 1998; Tipple & Speak, 2005; Fitzpatrick et al, 2000; Crane & Warnes, 2006; Evans, 1999). Policy responses to social problems such as homelessness also play a role in the ideological construction of these issues, and how they should be responded to (Clapham, 2002; 2003; Anderson, 2004; Kennett, 1999; Jacobs et al, 1999; Pleace et al, 1997; Pleace & Quilgars, 2003).

Pleace (1998) for example argues that it is the inability to negate the (structurally generated) effect of a lack of resources through an individual's access (or lack of access) to state support that some people have, that explains why homelessness occurs. He asserts that homelessness is not a 'discrete social problem' but what occurs due to the '*inability of a section of the socially excluded population to access welfare services and social housing'* (1998:50). In the context of the UK it is the model of neo-liberal governance, within the framework of *'unfettered capitalism'* that has led to a situation whereby some people who lack resources do not have access to the *'state support and other welfare services that prevent most of the socially excluded population of the UK from experiencing (...) homelessness'* (Pleace, 1998:54). However it could also be argued that the effect of capitalism is not 'unfettered' in the UK, and various levels operate through the welfare state to provide some protection for different groups with the least resources.

Furthermore, the welfare system is an important focus of analysis because in the UK homelessness is often one aspect of a life course characterised by intense contact with the social welfare system (Fitzpatrick et al, 2000): being in care as a child; contact with the criminal justice system; reliance on national health services to address poor physical or mental health, or addictions; long-term unemployment; and a reliance on unemployment or disability Benefits for income.

So a major influence on peoples' transitions when they are negotiating with homelessness can be the services of the social welfare system that exists to address it and some of these interactions are explored in this study. To the individual experiencing homelessness, homelessness policy will be negotiated with through the micro-level interactions with statutory and voluntary sector services and agencies they have. These agencies may be not for profit and part of the voluntary sector but much of their work is now funded and managed as part of a broad government framework, underpinned by political ideology (Kennett, 1999). To contextualise these interactions, typical homeless services people negotiating with homelessness in the UK may encounter are briefly described below. Much of this has been described at various levels in previous studies (such as Anderson et al, 1993; Hutson, 1999; Harvey, 1999; Neale, 1997, and for a critical overview see Fitzpatrick et al, 2000:37–44). They are outlined here to contextualise the type of services referred to in this study, and the role they may have play in these transitions through homelessness.

Examples of homeless services

Contact with the statutory homeless system is typically made by an individual or family going to a central local authority office or venue and presenting as 'homeless' (Evans, 1999). It may also be that people who are already receiving some support from social services, or are already housed in institutions, such as prison, residential rehabilitation services, or hospitals, are referred to homelessness services once their circumstances change. Some may also refer themselves to agencies that assist people who are homeless, by phoning them for example, and asking for advice. They may then be able to access temporary accommodation, usually funded through Housing Benefit. Therefore people have to be eligible for Housing Benefit to be able to stay there. Those who are not will not be able to access accommodation for homeless people even if they are literally without shelter of any kind. Some forms of temporary accommodation, such as Bed & Breakfasts or hostels, provide literally just a room with a bed, and access to a bathroom and perhaps cooking facilities or a canteen. Studies into the conditions of such accommodation (and as will be illustrated here) often find that it is poor quality and people accommodated there feel threatened or 'abandoned' (Hutson, 1999; Rosengard, 2001). Some temporary accommodation is provided in the form of furnished flats, in a block of flats, managed by a housing authority and this is generally perceived as quieter and more adequate by residents (Hutson, 1999).

Supported accommodation usually involves being provided with accommodation (such as a bedroom or self-contained flat in a shared project) and being allocated a support worker also based there. These workers assist people address individual problems that they have, usually through the implementation of a structured Care Plan. The idea is that they will be assisted to obtain and move into their own housing in the future, and their room in the temporary accommodation will then be made available to another person. Sometimes there is a time limit to how long someone can be accommodated in temporary accommodation and they may have to move elsewhere when this is up. Often people will move to supported accommodation from institutions such as drug or alcohol rehabilitation centres, or psychiatric hospitals.

Soup kitchens, cafes, and drop-in's also operate, to provide food and facilities for people on the 'margins'. The people who use drop-in's may be perceived to be rough sleepers, but they are not always homeless (Fitzpatrick & Kennedy, 2000). Some are living in a hostel or have their own tenancy but access these services for the resources and social contact provided there. Often these drop-in services are not funded through the social welfare system but through Christian organisations. The opening hours for such services may be limited with some only open once a week or for a few hours a day but also may constitute important additions to the services people can access (May, Cloke & Johnsen, 2006), operating as they do outside of the funding frameworks that many voluntary sector agencies are now bound by (Kennett, 1999). There is also some debate however that the existence of such services act to perpetuate homelessness and street cultures (Fitzpatrick & Jones, 2005).

Outreach street workers actively locate and make contact with people who are rough sleeping (sometimes through the drop-in's described above) and focus on 'crisis intervention' to provide food, clothing and advice to them (Randall & Brown, 1995). These workers will then assist them to gain accommodation through the social welfare system, such as a bed in an emergency shelter. They will also encourage them to access other resources and services (such as health care) they may need.

Housing, resettlement or tenancy sustainment workers provide one-to-one advice and assistance to individuals to assist them obtain their own tenancy, often whilst they are currently living in temporary accommodation. They are allocated to work with an individual after an initial referral and assessment is made. They will then help them to apply for a socially rented or privately let tenancy through different housing authorities, to complete the application forms, and make contact with the agency processing the application, for example. Once people are offered a tenancy their worker may visit it with them to ensure it is 'suitable'. Once people move into their own tenancy their worker will provide practical advice and assistance to help them 'settle' there, such as setting up electricity and gas supplies to the property; information on where to obtain furniture and ensuring 'payment plans' for utility bills and rent are in place. Resettlement and housing support workers may work with people for short or long term periods, although the funding limit for many is two years. Tenancy sustainment workers may take over from resettlement workers to advise and assist people once they have moved into their tenancy, for a longer period of time. They may also work with people to prevent them becoming homeless when they are having problems paying their bills or coping with living in their own tenancy. This is usually funded through government schemes that the people supported have to be eligible for to access this service and is commonly known as 'floating support'.

Employability projects have also recently developed to assist homeless people develop their skills and access training and employment (Randall & Brown, 1999b). Other services may provide training on 'life skills', 'anger management' or 'personal development' (Jones, Quilgars & Wallace, 2001). There are also training services that focus on resettlement rather than employment, providing training courses and advice on moving into housing, cooking and budgeting, for example, for people who are homeless (a need recognised in previous research, such as

Franklin, 1999). These courses sometimes run over a period of set weeks, and the tutors may also act to provide some support and advice to the people who attend. They may refer them to other agencies that can assist them with problems such as addiction, or access to housing. Some agencies also now provide Service User Forums, or may have volunteer programmes that operate. These provide service users and 'ex-homeless' people who have used homeless services the opportunity to comment on the services they are accessing and how they are managed. People who have used these services may also work as volunteers to advise other people experiencing homelessness and there has been an increasing emphasis on this among service providers (Rosengard & Ogg, 2004). Many people accessing some of the services outlined above will also be accessing services for support for other specialist issues, such as having an addiction councillor they see; or day centres for people with mental health problems. Therefore their day-to-day lives and interactions are often inexorably bound up within the structures of the welfare state. Services such as those described above may be provided by third sector 'voluntary' organisations. However this is usually funded by through the state as part of a broad welfare provision available for those most 'in need'.

Overall there has been a marked shift over the last two decades, with the recognition that people making a transition out of homelessness (and other marginalised groups, (McNaughton & Sanders, 2007)) require support just as much as housing to be able to do so (Franklin, 1999). This has been underpinned by rafts of robust research (such as Anderson et al, 1993; Randall & Brown, 1996) and has fed into the services that exist for people who are homeless, and how they operate. There has also been increased reflexivity and service user involvement. Again perhaps, this can be seen broadly as reflecting wider social trends (Forrest, 1999) in the more reflexive and fluid context of the risk society (Beck, 1992).

3.   Homelessness, policy and governance

So the social welfare system is an important aspect to transitions through homelessness. Whilst there is no scope for a rigorous analysis here, and the focus of this study is the individual experiences of those researched, homeless policy that exists in the UK, and how it developed, is outlined briefly, below.

Political ideology and changing responses to homelessness

Three eras of welfare are used here to summarise how homelessness policy has developed in the last 60 years in the UK (originally outlined by Anderson, 2004). These are post-war social democracy (1945–1979); Conservatist neoliberalism (1979–1997); and Labour's 'Third way' (1997–2007?).

Social democracy and post-war welfarism

The modern welfare provision to address homelessness stems from the introduction of the 1977 Housing (Homeless Persons) Act, which was introduced towards the end of the social democratic post-war era of high welfarism. The first piece of homelessness legislation, the 1948 National Assistance Act was also introduced towards the beginning of this period. What was distinct about the 1977 Act was that it created a statutory definition of homelessness for the first time. This statutory definition meant that local authorities had a duty to house people if they were deemed to be 'unintentionally' homeless, in 'priority need' of housing (such as families with children, or pregnant women) and had a 'local connection' to the area they wished to be housed in. This represented a 'major step forward in provision for homeless people' (Fitzpatrick & Stephens, 1999:415). This was in a time of high employment, with a post-war welfare state that had been developed to 'insure' those who were particularly vulnerable in society against risk, on the assumption they had or would contribute to the state through their employment and related taxes if they could. During this period, public opinion on homelessness also began to be underpinned by a 'structuralist' perspective, with the screening of the film 'Cathy Come Home' in 1966, and the setting up of the housing campaigning organisation Shelter, both of which stressed homelessness could 'happen to anyone' and was due to structural forces, such as poverty and housing supply, rather than individual lifestyle, choice, or deviance (Jacobs et al, 1999; Pleace et al, 1997).

However it could also be argued that the 1977 legislation hardened and reinforced the ideology that there are two 'types' of homeless people, defined by their circumstances and the reason they are homeless (Anderson, 2004). People who do not meet the statutory criteria of homelessness became defined as 'single homeless people'. They may be without housing, but through the application of the 1977 Act were not perceived to be 'deserving' of state support to access housing. Those not defined as statutorily homeless may have few means to resolve homelessness through the welfare system, with short term temporary accommodation, such as a bed in a hostel, often the only provision made for them, if any is at all. This Act also heralded a key shift in social housing policy, basing the allocation to those deemed homeless, to that based on individual's need and vulnerability rather than 'desert' of housing in their area, as had previously been the case (Fitzpatrick & Stephens, 1999). Finite resources such as housing do have to be distributed by the state in relation to some criteria however, and whether this is needs based or not, the fundamental issue in the allocation of housing is the extent to which the distribution of social housing is done in a fair and just way.

Thirty years on the 1977 act has been identified (by Fitzpatrick & Stephens, 1999) as one of the drivers in the residualisation (and increasing stigmatisation) of social housing (others are explored in the next section) – due to this there has been a *'tendency for the sector to house even greater concentrations of the poorest and most disadvantaged households'* (Fitzpatrick & Pawson, 2007:170). Those viewed as the most vulnerable in society (and often those with fewest resources) have become concentrated in areas of social housing, and this has also contributed to an ensuing spatial segregation and stigmatisation associated with this form of housing. As housing constitutes a key component of the material reality someone is embedded within, this residualisation is an important consideration to understand the lived reality of people making a transition into and out of homelessness, and the housing they can and have accessed over their life. Some of the other drivers for this are explored below.

Conservative welfare reform

In the next 'era', the neoliberal Conservative era of 1979–97, it is noted that *'the welfare retrenchment of the 1980s and 1990s contributed significantly to substantial increases in poverty, inequality and homelessness.'*
(Anderson, 2004:376).

This 'welfare retrenchment' included cutting down the level of social benefits that young people (aged under 25) could access, and effectively the end of any benefit eligibility for 16 and 17 year olds through the implementation of the 1988 Social Security Act. Welfare provision was radically altered throughout this period, leading to a clear widening of inequality. Housing policy, it is argued, 'spearheaded' this process (Smith, 2005a:3) – for example, there was a sharp reduction in social rented housing available due to Conservative housing policies such as the 'Right to Buy' scheme; and a reduction in payments provided for unemployed people to pay for their 'board and lodgings'. These policies were sometimes implemented as a response to what was perceived as prevailing public and political discourses about 'welfare reliance' among some people who could be in paid employment but 'chose' not to be (Hutson & Liddiard, 1994). Other complex processes underpinned a widening of housing inequality over this period – this was in a time of increasing unemployment however and growing economic crisis; there was a general lack of housing being built; the growing residualisation of social housing; the aging population and increase in one person households, all contribute to pressure on housing supply (Mullins & Murie, 2006). Socially these changes were underpinned with a growing ideology of liberal individualism (Dean, 1999).

In England and Wales the 1977 homeless legislation was modified by the 1985 Housing Act, and in Scotland by the Housing Act (Scotland) 1987, but the content and effect of this legislation remained essentially the same throughout this period (Anderson, 2004). In this period statutory homeless figures (Wilcox, 2002) and visible 'street homelessness' (rough sleeping) greatly increased (Jacobs et al, 1999; Pleace & Quilgars, 2003). Homelessness became high on the political agenda. The response developed to address this initially focussed on the highly visible, 'problem' group of rough sleepers. The Rough Sleepers Initiative (RSI) (a funding programme for services to target and address visible street homelessness) was launched in London in 1990 and then introduced throughout other areas of the UK, including Scotland in 1997. Homelessness has remained a sustained problem however and statutory homeless applications rose to a record high in 1997 (Randall & Brown, 1999a). This was the context in which the Labour government came to power that same year.

New Labour, homelessness, and the social welfare system

Homelessness was taken as a key target of New Labour's endeavours to address 'social exclusion' and homeless legislation and policy has gone through a period of intense change over the last ten years. The devolution that has developed in the UK (particularly in Scotland) since Labour came to power in 1997 also means that whilst broad frameworks of policy still exist across the UK, important regional variations have developed with regard to homeless policy. New legislation has been introduced through the Homelessness Act 2002, in England and Wales, and the Housing Act 2001 and Homelessness etc Act 2003, in Scotland. Localised strategic measures to provide accommodation, housing and support have been developed and put in place as part of the statutory obligations local authorities now have for people experiencing homelessness in their area.

In Scotland, in particular, a strategic approach to tackle homelessness has become evident and Scotland now has what is viewed as the '*most progressive homelessness legislation in western Europe'* (Homelessness Monitoring Group, 2004:6). A raft of new research into homelessness was commissioned and the results of this fed into the Housing (Scotland) Act 2001 and Homelessness etc (Scotland) Act 2003. In theory this meant that the distinction between those deemed 'in priority' need of housing due to their vulnerabilities or circumstances, and those who are not, *should* be abolished by 2012. However the implementation of such policy is complex and dependent on housing being available. Furthermore there is still much scope for someone to be deemed intentionally homeless and therefore as not statutorily homeless. Social housing is still intended to provide only for the most vulnerable in society, based on need, and some people experiencing homelessness may have little recourse to access social housing.

Through an increased policy drive to 'target' individualised problems (such as drug addiction, worklessness) with specialist support and services, 'the homeless' as a group have continued to be conceptualised as problem 'individuals'. The introduction of increased policy measures to tackle anti-social behaviour focussing on the homeless (Fitzpatrick & Jones, 2005), alongside homeless policy providing more 'support' to people, illustrates that different and contradictory discourses about the nature of homelessness and how to deal with it through policy measures, operate simultaneously and homelessness remains highly associated with deviant behaviour and lifestyles and a topic high on the political agenda.

Therefore homelessness must be understood as an outcome of the political and social structures that are in place (Pleace, 1998). These structures define who should be provided with which resources and why, and who can access welfare services, and which ones. Yet, as active agents consuming these services (if indeed as Le Grand, (2003) argues people are now perceived) and operating within this social and political context, the rationale behind the actions people take also has to be explored. Development in social policy and how it is implemented are operating within a broad macro societal level, and social changes will both affect and be affected by policy in an ongoing cycle. The development of more reflexive services, and view of service users as active consumers (Le Grand, 2003) could also be framed within debates about the changing ontological nature of society (Beck, 1992; Giddens, 1991) and the liberal individualisation is now claimed to characterise this (Furlong & Cartmel, 1997).

In this study the concept used to discuss the current system of social policy in place is that of 'reflexive governance', as defined in the work of Dean (1999) on neoliberal systems of governmentality. This system of governance is characterised by a 'politics of behaviour' (Furedi, 2006) where people are held responsible for their own actions, and coerced or assisted to act in certain ways, through a process of governance.

4. Reflexive governance, risk and regulation

Dean (1999) in his book, *Governmentality – power and rule in modern society*, genealogically charts the development of neoliberalism throughout history. His argument is that the current form of western democratic government can be characterised as a 'reflexive government'. Reflexive government is governance through processes. Individuals are increasingly given opportunities and education to govern themselves – to act in responsible ways, through their actions and lifestyles, to reduce collective social problems. So for example, healthy eating programmes have been introduced to address obesity and poor health associated with bad diets. Thus individual action and responsibility for it is both promoted, and in turn regulated, by this system, whilst broader structural issues (free markets and production that have led to an overabundance of rich food being available for example) that may explain such problems remain untouched. There is now a 'politics of behaviour' with policies increasingly focusing on individuals and how they live their lives. It is argued that this indicates a reorientation of the principles of the welfare state away from a focus on broad 'social' forces, and instead onto micro-level individual actions (Furedi, 2006).

Through this process of reflexive government: *'responsibilities for risk minimization become a feature of the choices that are made by individuals, households, and communities as consumers, clients and users of services'* (Dean, 1999:166). To assist these individuals, families, and communities, to exercise this responsibility there is a 'regime of the social'. This regime of the social is made up of government agencies, experts, social workers, voluntary sector agencies, who have become *'partners and tutors'*, assisting people avoid and manage the risks and resources they may have access to. Engaging in this partnership effectively should lead to a society of 'active citizens' who operate effectively (make the 'right' choices). There is a need therefore to continue providing this 'expert' advice in an ongoing cycle, so that each individual can continue to draw on these resources to manage their lives. This means this reflexive model of governance goes on generating itself. However, these agencies do not work as 'partners and tutors' with all sectors of society to the same degree. Some people will have relatively little, if any, explicit contact with these 'regimes of the social' although they may be influenced or educated by the policies and practices in place or make up the workforce whose role it is to activate this regime. However there are distinctly and actively targeted populations, whose lives become embedded in micro-level interactions with the services that make up this system.

Targeted populations

Targeted populations include the unemployed, the homeless, single parents, and those who live in 'socially deprived' areas, for example. These groups through their entrenchment in contact with welfare services have lives defined as those that require the explicit intervention of specialist agencies to assist them. There has been a proliferation of specialist agencies, often within the voluntary sector, but funded through central and local government, whose role it is to do this – *'agencies and specialists for dealing with targeted groups. They employ technologies of agency to transform 'at risk' and 'high risk' groups into active citizens'* (Dean, 1999:170).

In Chapter 5, it is shown that people accessing services for the homeless are often 'targeted' in such a way. Furthermore, the individual factors identified as prevalent in the lives of people experiencing homelessness means they are often experiencing a range of other problems, such as addiction, poverty and criminality that has led to them being intensely targeted by many regimes of the social. The key question may be in what circumstance, or for which groups, does this targeting represent a positive or negative influence or effect.

This model of reflexive government parallels the social welfare provision currently in place for people negotiating with homelessness in the UK. There is a raft of different support services and accommodation 'options' available to people experiencing homelessness, provided through both statutory and voluntary sector agencies, funded primarily by government bodies (Kennett, 1999). There has been an increased emphasis on the need to consult people actually experiencing the problems these policy and service developments aim to address, and to involve them in the organisation of the services they access in a reflexive process in recent years. However these 'choices' and consultative measures only exist due to the competitive tendering for funding to provide different services by agencies in a market driven format. This has been viewed as part of move towards 'entrepreneurial cities' and welfare systems. As Kennet argues, and much in line with the idea of targeted populations, within this entrepreneurial system *'the homeless population is thus reclassified as provision fragments and funding focuses on the pathological and individual characteristics of the homeless (that is, alcoholic, mentally ill) to which specialised professional skills are matched to specialised populations'* (Kennet, 1999:51).

These developments may be part of the 'utopianistic goal' that Dean (1999:35) identifies neoliberal governments are pursuing, to improve society through reform. However (as Dean also highlights) these 'utopian' goals are underpinned by the neoliberal ideology that human beings are active individuals that *can and should* be reformed. As Kennett (1999:51) also notes, with regard to how this system may affect people who access it, *'not only do these developments influence the labelling and stigma attached to being homeless, but also affect how the homeless person perceives themselves'*. The struggle has been the modernising of approaches alongside an awareness of the ongoing unintended (or otherwise) consequences that this can generate (Giddens, 1984).

What is also central to the theory of reflexive governance is the concept of 'risk' – of how the risks targeted populations may pose to themselves, and others, is managed through this system of governance. And this preoccupation with risk and risk management can in turn be cast within broader sociological theories on risk.

Risk society

Clearly, over the last 50 years, significant changes have taken place in the social and political context that people operate within. This is occurring on a global scale and often as (an unintended but inevitable) outcome of the process of industrialisation, capitalism, and the liberalisation of governance that has developed throughout modernity (Giddens, 1990; 2002; Beck, 1992; 1999). New cultural, economic, and social ways of living and being in late reflexive modernity have developed (Lash, 1994; Beck, 2000; Giddens, 1991).

The explicit term 'risk society' was identified and popularised by the work of Ulrich Beck (1992; 1999). Beck argues that the consequence of the ongoing development of modernisation through global capitalism, within a neoliberal political framework, has created a new 'phase' of modernity – a second modernity. The processes of globalisation, individualisation, the gender revolution, underemployment, and the increasing recognition of global, ecological risks that cannot be managed or insured against, has created, and characterise, the conditions of second modernity (Beck, 1999:2). And these processes are the consequence of the 'success' of first modernity, the 'success' of global capitalism, and the social and political systems that underpinned them, such as increased access to education, new technology, and new forms of communication, social relations, and an ensuing ageing population, gender revolution, and increase in one-person households for example.

Beck argues that in 'first' modernity, society was structured in such a way that the risks populations faced could be predicted, calculated, and insured against. As these insurances (such as the welfare state, full employment, the nuclear family) fragment and change, a new onto-logical and social reality emerges, where the outcomes of this ongoing modernisation, or indeed of each individual's life course, cannot be predicted as it once could have been. This has had a collective affect on how life in late modernity is ontologically experienced – all we can really know is that there is nothing we can be sure of knowing. 'Know-ledge' has become increasingly available to people, but paradoxically also increasingly undermined and questioned, through the continual develop-ment of 'new' (sometimes conflicting) information, technologies, and forms of communication. It is argued that individuals now live in a dis-tinct period of uncertainty and precariousness – assessing, avoiding, aware of risks, real or imagined, in every action and decision they make in a reflexive, individualised process. Structural changes also underpin this sense of insecurity, such as an increase in flexible or contractual employment, increasing family fragmentation, lifelong returns to edu-cation and constant retraining. Constant reinvention is not only possible, but encouraged over the life course. However as this accelerates, our sense of security – both material economic and social ontological security about 'who we are', has more risk of deteriorating. Through this process of accelerated modernisation 'all that is solid' melts into air and this may have profound effects on lives as they are lived in late modernity (Bauman, 2000).

Marsh & Kennett (1999) have argued that in this structural context of second or late modernity there is now a 'new landscape of precari-ousness'. With the advent of *'(f)lexible labour markets, greater job insecu-rity, the erosion of the Keynesian welfare state and a greater fragility in relationships (...) it is possible to fall further and faster and (...) risk and insecurity are now more pervasive* (Forrest, 1999:17). In this context, homelessness affects heterogeneous groups. They argue that the risk of homelessness may now become a reality for more people, and for more diverse reasons, than in previous eras – as lives and circumstances con-tinue to change at accelerated rates, more cracks appear that it may be possible to fall through.

People are embedded within the external structured material 'reality' of their lives; however there is also a need to recognise the 'emotional landscapes' they operate within (Smith, 2005a: 7). Whatever structural context they are operating within, even one of precariousness and risk, there will be an emotional dimension to the choices and actions taken. For those operating on the edges of society, and negotiating their risk of homelessness within this 'landscape of precariousness', the emotional landscape of their day-to-day interactions has to also be considered. Only then can their actions and the choices they made as they negotiate with these risks within a certain structured material reality, be better understood.

Management of risk

Dean (1999) engaging with Beck's thesis, argues that social and political change has led to a distinctly individualistic and reflexive ideology now underpinning the management of risks in society. Different forms of 'risk rationality', to manage the risks faced by populations within societies, are identified by Dean as: insurance (against losses of capital); epidemiological (against loss of health and well-being); and case management. The 'case management' of risk refers to the management of the targeted populations, discussed earlier. Here, groups or individuals having been identified as 'at risk' of certain outcomes, such as homelessness, or as being 'a risk' to the wider population, are defined as requiring the intervention and management of specialist agencies to minimise these risks. These targeted populations are both managed, and 'educated', through this case management system to become active citizens – active individuals, in control of their own life in responsible ways.

To understand why risk, or the management of risk, is now so important within late modern society, understanding the process of individualisation that has occurred, and how this may now affect life transitions, is crucial.

5. Individualisation and transitions in late modernity

It is argued that one of the key developments characterising contemporary social life, and how it is experienced in late modernity, has been the process of individualisation that has occurred (Giddens, 1991; Beck, 1992). As predictable trajectories of life, such as the transitions through education, into employment, and into family life, have diversified, individuals now have to reflexively 'negotiate' with the options that are available to them in a constant process over the life course. This appears to allow them the opportunity to develop lifestyles, and create their own socio-biography, from the options they have, through the actions they take (Giddens, 1990; 1991; 2002). Beck argues that '(t)he ethic of individual self-fulfilment and achievement is the most powerful current in modern western society. Choosing, deciding, shaping individuals who aspire to be the authors of their lives, the creators of their identities, are the central characters of our time' (1999:9) and this is backed up by prevailing neoliberal politics and cultural discourses. But how does this impact on the actual transitions people take over their life and how these are experienced?

Understanding transitions in late modernity

Whilst it may be argued that there has always been a *degree* of complexity to the transitions people made over their life course (Goodwin & O'Conner, 2005), it is now also recognised that there are more options, choices, and unpredictability (Furlong & Evans, 1997). So to what extent has individualisation really taken hold or changed the ontological experience of social life in late modernity? There may be more 'choice', fluidity, or options, however there are also still clear 'plots' or 'scripts' that are collectively recognised in different societies and cultures. Normative assumptions in the UK (and indeed in most cultures) about the transitions people should take over the life course to 'succeed' would define homelessness as the outcome of a transition that has 'gone wrong'. Ezzy (2001) argues that transitions over the life course should take an 'integrative' course – for example, someone moving from their parental home to their own, moving into a larger home to have children; or moving somewhere for new employment, are all transitional stages that maintain an individual's integration to society over their life course. They adhere to the norms of society. 'Divestment passages' occur when the transitional events in life lead to what is perceived to be a failure in this.

Rather than actually being 'free', it is asserted that due to the ontological effect of individualisation, people *perceive* their individual choices to be the central tenet to how secure, or insecure, they are (Furlong & Cartmel, 1997) – 'they see their decision-making as individual 'choice' rather than the product of structured constraints' (Ball, Maguire & Macrae; 2000:2). However, as Furlong & Evans note:

> The fact that people feel that they act autonomously and independently over their own biographies is not necessarily at odds with the view that much of their biography continues to be structured and determined by external factors. (..) The issue now is the relationship between structure

and agency arising from 'manufactured uncertainty' – uncertainty created
by acceleration of information and the 'knowledge society' and the increase
and diversity of individual risk situations.

(1997:37)

The chance people have of being able to negotiate with the risks they face is still grounded to some extent in the external structures and institutions of the society they operate in. For it is through these structures that people access the resources, with which they can 'negotiate' their 'own' life course. This process of individualisation has led to a paradigmatic shift, with the individual, rather than the society they operate within, increasingly viewed as the key mechanisms affecting their life chances. However Furlong & Cartmel (1997) (in their study of youth transitions) argue that this is an epistemological fallacy of liberal individualism. The course each life takes, and how this is conceptualised and managed, as being potentially 'risky' or not, is still underpinned by the structures these transitions are embedded within. There is a material and social world that people operate within and transitions over time will also include ontological processes of change (McNaughton & Sanders, 2007). How people act within this, and how they experience, this subjectively, will be affected by and go on to affect this material reality, in an ongoing cycle. This is the critical realist stance taken in this analysis – and a stance fitting with Gidden's theory of structuration, outlined in more detail in Chapter 2.

Structure, agency and outcomes

This acknowledgment of how structural factors may actually underpin what appear to be highly individual actions as been asserted in a number of empirical studies. For example, Buchanan (Buchanan & Young, 2000; Buchanan, 2004) argues that increased heroin use and addiction throughout the 1980s can be directly related to the structural conditions this occurred in. As traditional industries, class identities and the relative security they brought declined, a generation of working class school leavers found themselves 'surplus to requirements': *'With little to lose, and little to gain, many of these discarded young people turned to heroin. (…) A painkiller with euphoric properties heroin helped many young people block out the social economic realities of their lives'* (2000:411). In a later analysis he ties the drug use his participants engaged in to the individualised negotiation of risk they now face: *'uncertainty, choice, diversity and risk taking have become key themes of postmodern life. In this context it becomes much easier to view taking illicit drugs as just another of many life choice options, all involving inherent risks and benefits'* (2004:119). But it is also recognised that this drug use brings problems, and acts to further stigmatise and marginalise groups that are already structurally excluded.

So the actual motivation for and outcome of the acts people engage in, within these conditions of late modernity, are generated by the lived reality of late modern society. Even for those not at the edge, it has been argued that it may be becoming increasingly difficult to attain the living standards of previous generations. People may be becoming relatively richer, but feel a constant pressure to attain more, and therefore can never 'have enough' (Dorling, 2007). The 'emotional landscape' that people operate within, alongside the structural conditions, has to be penetrated and understood for broad social processes to be.

The modern discourse of risk relates to the desire people have to control and predict the future and this relates to the ability people have to assess which options carry more or less risk to them as they negotiate their life course (Mythen, 2005). How their life develops is supposed to fit with the 'lifestyle' that they associate, with the identity they feel they have (Giddens, 1991). However as studies such as Buchanan's outlined above have emphasised, this life is still grounded in the externally situated structured interactions people engage in as individuals. These interactions are embodied acts and grounded in normative assumptions about how gender, age, ethnicity and class, for example, should be and are acted out in certain contexts. Agency and structure must continue to interact in this continuing relationship, for society to exist, over time (Giddens, 1984).

In this study the concept of edgework is used to examine this interaction of agency and structure, and the dynamic, complex mix of emotional and rational actions that interacted and led to different outcomes for different people within the context of late modernity. This concept of edgework and the epistemological framework for the study are outlined in the next chapter, before introducing the people whose lives 'at the edge' are presented here.

2
Emotional and Material Landscapes of Life

1. Edgework

Risks are usually perceived as something to be avoided, however there can also be positive outcomes from risk – to gain the 'best' or most 'fulfilling' outcome can require taking risks. Lyng (1990; 2005a; 2005b) examines this other side of risk negotiation in his analysis of 'voluntary risk taking'. Voluntary risk taking, as Lyng defines it, encapsulates actions that people voluntarily engage in, that carry inherent 'risk' and, crucially, involve negotiating at the 'edge' of normative, 'responsible', behaviour. These actions include extreme sports, such as skydiving; sexual activities such as promiscuity or sado-masochism; or behaviour such as excessive drug or alcohol use. Lyng argues that engaging in such actions, that carry clear risk (the risk of death, pain, unconsciousness, insanity, for example) can be understood as ways to exercise individuality and freedom within an increasingly rationalised, disenchanted, modernised society. In a time of uncertainty, underpinned by a changing structural context (the landscape of precariousness outlined in the previous chapter) these actions are also a way of *facing up to* risk, of evidencing ontologically that the individual is indeed master of their own destiny, by facing up to and individually overcoming risk.

In Lyng's (1990) initial development of the concept it is used as a way to explore irrational actions, fusing together Meadian and Marxist theories, and later incorporates Weberian perspectives (Lyng, 2005a). The overregulation (the iron cage of rationality) and alienation (due to being divorced from the means of production) wrought by the process of modernity is something that it can be viewed as rational to attempt to escape, even if the means to do so involve facing extreme risks. This therefore renders irrational risky actions as the rational means to attempt to gain re-enchantment.

Edgework and experiential outcomes

Experiential 'satisfaction' or 'escape' are therefore the key motivations for edgework – negotiating at the liminal borders of 'normality' allows the repetitive, routine nature of normality to be challenged, and transcended (Jenks, 2003). People lose sense of time and space when they engage in these activities. They find self-actualisation, but risk losing themselves, by breaking free of the norms, structures, and the myriad of choices increasingly imposed on them as they negotiate within the social system of late modernity. These acts also only reinforce the celebration of the individual as sovereign and the rationalisation of modern life. To gain re-enchantment through rationalised, consumable means, is a paradoxical form of escape from the rationalised, consumerised and simulated society of today (Cohen & Taylor, 1992). Therefore edgework appears highly individual, but can be understood as actions that are embedded in, motivated by, and made possible, by the structural reality that people operate within. Edgework is the very outcome of the reality of modernity people are in.

As borders and boundaries increasingly breakdown in a globalised, accelerating time of knowledge and technology, edgework may also be required so that people can test out what the 'frontiers' of normative behaviour are. If they can go to edge, negotiate it, and come back, then they must have some awareness of where the edge is. There is often a need to transgress, to progress, but with this comes the risk of falling into the cracks that this transgression opens up.

This assertion of self, and transcendence of material 'humdrum' reality through engaging in edgework, is something that people strive to attain in a variety of settings and in a variety of ways, from art appreciation (Courtney, 2005) to commodity trading (Smith, 2005b). It is something that most (if not all) people can identify with at times, but the means with which they achieve it may differ enormously. However edges must also be maintained – to *go over and not come back* is to lose your self, and your place in society, through death, insanity, imprisonment, or ostracisation.

The paradox of edgework

So the paradox of edgework is that, by being a means of evidencing the ability someone has to engage with risk, these actions only actually draw them further into an individualised process of liberalised risk negotiation. At the same time as they attempt to transcend the conditions that have led to 'disenchantment', they also are reproducing their need to rationally negotiate their lives and actions as individuals. They are actually drawn further into what they are attempting to escape, there can be no real resistance.

In this way edgework closely parallels Cohen & Taylor's (1992) 'escape attempts' first outlined in 1976. They identify that, with the increasing promotion of the individual in society, people are reflexively aware of the 'horrendous repetition' of day-to-day life. Routine may be a necessary for society to function, however it is also now despised. Hence people feel trapped and construct escape attempts that include hobbies, holidays, constantly changing jobs, houses, or partners, for example. Acts of edgework – drug use, extreme sports, and so on, are also forms of escape. People can temporarily escape the 'horrendous repetition' of the 'paramount reality' of day-to-day modern life in this way. But only ever temporarily, because each escape becomes a new routine at some point and new frontiers appear that need to be overcome, and so the cycle goes on. The form these 'escapes' take can also be viewed as due to structural changes occurring over time – so for example, more capacity to travel and disposable income has led to a mass industry selling the 'escape' of exotic holidays, gap years and backpacking. However the paradox is that each location still represents someone's normality, and each 'unique' trip has still been planned and packaged, and often sold to more than one person. The search for a 'real' authentic escape goes on, and the only way to do so is through continuing to push boundaries, and through constant, but ultimately nihilistic, changes being made throughout the life course.

There is another factor to this, central to this study. For whilst the motivation to assert the self and escape this horrendous repetition may be felt, at times, by all, the means they have to do so differ. As Cohen and Taylor (1992:225) argue, '*the ethos of possessive individualism extols the value of individual identity but the market economy of advanced capitalism cannot deliver the goods to everyone*'.

Edgework and resources

Inequality, if not absolute poverty, is increasing in late modernity (Young, 1999; Hutton, 1995). Just as disposable incomes rise, so to apparently do the diseases of excess among the young – sexually transmitted diseases, addiction, depression, psychosis, obesity, to name but a few (Patton & Viner, 2007). Many of these are also afflictions of the risks of edgework.

An individual's motivation to engage in certain activities of consumption or of edgework, may be the same for all. The key difference is their *ability to do so* due to the resources they have. The forms of edge-work people can engage in, and how safely they can engage in it, are affected by the resources they have.

This aspect of edgework – how it can be applied to the actions of people in situations of relative material poverty when it was originally developed to understand 'middle class' actions such sky-diving – is recognised by Lyng (2005b:28). He cites the study by Katz (1988) into criminal behaviour and the experiential emotional outcomes of this. Lyng argues that for those with few economic resources, and little social status, criminal activity may be a way of not only accessing resources, but also of asserting *control* ontologically, and to experientially transcend or escape the reality they are in:

> *In connecting the experiential foreground and the structural background in criminal action, Katz sees the emotional experience of humiliation as the lynchpin. Humbled by the prospect of entering a bureaucratic, technological society with limited resources and the stigma of lower class and minority status, aspiring criminals rely on emotional transformation as a way to escape (...) this reality is directly tied to the broader sense of disenchantment engendered by the rational imperatives of the modern social order.*
>
> (Lyng, 2005b:28)

The use of illegal drugs encapsulates edgework. Taking drugs is an act that may provide the means to 'mindscape' (Cohen & Taylor, 1992), to transcend space, time, and temporarily to alter the reality someone is in, as a form of escape or transcendence from it. Taking drugs is also voluntarily engaging in an activity that can involve going 'over the edge', and losing control, through addiction or overdose, it is an act that can be conceptualised as criminal, deviant, and that can damage people's mental and physical health. In doing so they are negotiating many edges. In the 2005–2006 British Crime Survey 34.9 per cent of all adults surveyed confessed they had taken illicit drugs in their life time. 'Irrational' acts certainly appear widespread. They may therefore be both rational (as a (existential) form of escape) and irrational (bringing many inherent, known, risks). And when acts such as drug use involve going 'over the edge' they may lead to complete loss of control over self – through addiction, surrendering to being controlled by a need for external objects and actions (Reith, 2005; Giddens, 2002; 1992).

This leads to the final key point about edgework, as Lyng conceptualises it – it is about going close to the edge, but *coming back*, the *management* of risk. To go over is to have succumbed to the risks that edgework encapsulates, to have failed to gain the benefit, and return safely from this. But as some people have more resources to engage in edgework than others, it may be some have less chance of going over the edge than others. Once people do go over the edge however, what processes, if any, may bring them back? This is a key exploration in this study of transitions back from the edges of homelessness, of addiction and chaos.

2. Edgework and homelessness

So edgework is a key concept used in this study to understand transitions through homelessness. Four key reasons why this is so are explained below.

Firstly, many people experiencing homelessness engage in and experience extreme examples of edgework. They are often negotiating with the edges of normative behaviour in many ways, involving both voluntary and involuntary edgework. They have often had experiences of attempting suicide, mental illness, addiction, of extreme violence, of being in institutions such as prison due to criminal activities. They are often engaging in, or experiencing, highly risky situations. The concept of edgework can be used to bring these disparate individual factors that are often identified as 'problems' in the lives of people who are homeless together as a conceptual whole. The motivation for engaging in these acts, or the emotional effect of them, are what is key, however unrelated these acts may appear to be. People who are homeless are often negotiating with risks on the edge of normative social behaviour, and this will be experienced emotionally as well as materially, and will underpin their ongoing actions and circumstances, as part of their 'life story'.

Secondly, the ability to engage in edgework is constrained or enabled by the resources people have, tied to the structural context they operate within. For example, not everyone may have access to the resources required to go sky-diving. However they may still have the motivation to engage in some form of edgework or to escape or transcend the material reality they are in. And this motivation stems from the structural and social conditions of late modernity. These acts (drug use, criminality, sky-diving) may carry different risks but what is important about them conceptually is how they are experienced emotionally. This is the motivation for and outcome of these acts. Edgework in this way refers to acts that can lead to transcendence or rupturing of normal day-to-day life, and with it a crisis of ontological security – going over the edge.

Thirdly, edgework is here also applied to actions and events that are *not voluntarily* undertaken, but that still involve the transcendence or rupturing of 'normal' life, ontologically, *and* having to negotiate with some clear risk in the 'here and now' of the time-space reality someone is in. So as it is conceptualised here, edgework is about acts that involve some attempt to negotiate control of a situation, to manage a clear risk, that also involves potential escape, excitement or empowerment. When these acts are voluntarily undertaken empowerment and escape may be gained. However even if they are not voluntarily engaged in, these 'risky' situations are still highly charged, emotionally. Negotiating with voluntary or involuntary risks involve many of the same skills, actions and emotions. Therefore traumatic incidents such as being assaulted, or psychotic episodes, or overdosing, can be considered at the extreme end of edgework, whether actively, 'voluntarily' undertaken or not. These also require a negotiation of risk, are highly charged emotionally, and rupture someone's sense of ontological security and 'normal' day-to-day life.

Fourthly, and crucially, when forms of edgework occur amongst those with few resources, they are then often targeted by or have to access services of the social welfare system to end, resolve, or manage the risk these actions encapsulate – be it substance use, mental illness, or abusive relationships. These acts, when they occur in this context, also carry the risk of being stigmatised – as an 'addict', for example, and involve being controlled even more by a bureaucratic system.

People who continue to engage in such acts – to strive to transcend the 'humdrum' rationalised existence of life in late modernity – may be stigmatised for more than the 'threat' their actions appear to indicate. Young (2006) argues that they are also a source of resentment for the 'respectable' responsible citizens, whose individuality, actions and escape attempts, are constantly curtailed by their avoidance and management of risk:

> *It cannot be an accident that the stereotype of the underclass: with its idleness, dependency, hedonism, and institutionalised irresponsibility, with its drug use, teenage pregnancies and fecklessness, represents all the traits which the respectable citizen has to suppress in order to maintain his or her lifestyle.*
>
> (Young, 2006:23)

So another tension exists about the edgework people engage it: it may carry risk, it may be viewed as irresponsible by the 'respectable' majority;

and these risks may lead to negative outcomes for people if they 'go over the edge'. However there is also an appeal, and may be a resentment of the actions and freedom that some forms of edgework represent. And this may discursively underpin the *fear, resentment* or *pity* directed towards those who appear to have 'lost control' of themselves. These emotional responses underpin public discourse about visibly 'outsider' groups, such as the homeless, within the conditions of late modernity. This may generate conflicting or emotive discourses about these groups and affect how these problems are experienced or addressed. Homelessness may in some respects represent 'escape' and the ultimate freedom from the confines of a structurally bound, 'responsible' existence. Yet it is clearly an escape that has come at cost, and a life that is at odds with the routine, ordered existence that is expected.

So to summarise, people have multi-faceted motivations for the actions they take, including a 'thin rationality' (Somerville & Bengtsson, 2002) that must be uncovered through research. These actions may be enabled or constrained by the access to resources, and structured embodied interactions they have. By taking the 'wrong' action, and going over the edge, such as becoming an addict, attempting suicide, becoming homeless, for example, people's actions may construct them as those unable to exercise their agency responsibly. Within the neo-liberal ideology underpinning the conditions of late modernity, and the system of reflexive governance that exists, these people may then be perceived as requiring the intervention of the state, through a process of case management, to come back over the edge.

Using this as the theoretical starting point, this study outlines the transitions through homelessness a group of people took. It examines how they described and conceptualised these transitions. The role of the social welfare system, identity, and the interaction of agency and structure, are explored. And this exploration takes account of the structural landscape that they operated in, and how this also impacts on the internal emotional landscape of their lives as well.

3. Happenings and causations – realism and structuration

This study embeds the actual experiences of 28 people as they made a transition through homelessness over a year, within the autobiographical stories of their lives since birth. These biographies were collected with each at the first meeting with them. Then using a qualitative longitudinal research methodology a series of in-depth interviews were conducted with each over a year. This was supplemented by low level contact with them such as occasional phone calls, speaking to people who knew and worked with them, or unplanned meetings with them occurring at drop-in's, accommodation projects, or at events being held, such as open days at homeless services.

Data collected in this way (using this biographical qualitative longitudinal methodology) can illustrate both 'what happens' in material reality, and how this is understood, experienced, and described by those that it happens to and may be particularly useful in homelessness research (May, 2000; Pickering, Fitzpatrick, Hinds, Lynn & Tipping, 2003). So for example it was a 'fact' or not whether someone actually had a tenancy, had moved into it and were living there, or had accessed a training course, as they made these transitions through homelessness. How this was actually experienced, and their motivations and feelings about this, were also collected however, supplementing understanding on the real complexity of this. Furthermore, the analysis of these actions and the events that occurred could be embedded in their whole life history rather than within the limited snapshot of their lives as 'homeless people'. People are rarely born homeless, this is not a static state, but it may become their objective reality at some point in their lives. The process that leads to this, and experiences they have, will also be something they subjectively experience and understand.

This concern with objective empirical reality and with how it is experienced, subjectively, illustrates a critical realist approach to how we can come to know about social processes (Bhaskar, 1979; Sayer, 2000; Pawson & Tilley, 1997; Fitzpatrick, 2005). This approach acknowledges that actions and outcomes are grounded in an actual material and social world that exists. This reality exists independently of our knowledge of it, but can only be understood and explained by recognising and analysing the constructed and discursive nature of how we as social actors, understand and interact with each other. These interactions and actions then go on to recreate and affect what that actual material and social reality is in an ongoing cycle.

The aim of an intensive research approach underpinned by critical realism such as that used here is to produce causal explanations and theoretical perspectives on the production of certain outcomes and events (Sayer, 2000). Causation however is not viewed positivistically – as something that occurs in a linear relationship: that A causes B. Rather it is recognised that events occur due to a complex relationship of causation embedded in an entire interconnected social system. Many divergent factors interact that potentially can trigger and cause an outcome to occur, in some circumstances, for some people. Uncovering causation from a critical realist perspective is about uncovering the different mechanisms that can explain certain outcomes, without asserting that these same factors will necessarily *always* lead to that outcome, for *all* people (Fitzpatrick, 2005). Although complex and messy at times, this ontology allows for a *'complex view of causality that denies any simple symmetry between explanation and prediction'* (Bassett, 1999:36).

This critical realist approach requires not only events and social relations to be described but also an explanation of them, through 'theory-building' to abstract latent and hidden dimensions, embedded within and generated by many multiple structural forces. To do so particular regard for the qualitative, constructed nature of social life, is required (Fitzpatrick, 2005:10). This approach therefore acknowledges the crucial importance of social factors, ideologies, and discourses to the construction of the world and to how people know and can understand it. However, this does not mean that constructed social factors, or a material world people are embedded in, do not exist independently of these ideas, rather this realist approach is based on a *'recognition of the constant interplay between social factors and pre-existing structures of reality'* (Bassett, 1999:40) that generates these entire social systems and the forces affecting them.

This approach complements the theory of structuration – simply put, that people produce, and are the products of, the society they live in, in an ongoing hermeneutical relationship (Giddens, 1984). The approach taken in this study fuses critical realism and structuration. This begins by asserting that there is a structurally generated material reality that exists. This reality is both created by and influences the individuals that operate within it, through the embodied experiences, actions and interactions that they have. This external embodiment in social structures is influenced by how it is subjectively experienced – by the emotional landscape that these actual material events and emotional reactions and interactions are embedded within.

Sometimes the 'best' outcome for an individual relates to emotional rather than 'rational', material outcomes (Lyng, 2005a). Smith's (2005a) study of house buying showed this – choices that should be rational, such as how much to pay for a house, become imbued with emotion. The house becomes a manifestation of home, of future hopes and achievements, something that is desired. People make offers over the valuation, offer amounts they can barely afford, they are devastated at the thought of 'losing' what they do not own, the entire process can be highly emotional, and these emotions drive the actions and choices made within structural constraints (such as the house market, mortgage availability) that are also then affected by this process – as this emotional drive to buy a house goes on affecting these structural components of the housing market, such as prices. This illustrates the need for an approach using the concept of thin rationality in research such as this – agents have logic behind their actions, but what this logic is, or what they are actually pursuing, cannot be assumed by researchers, but is *open to empirical investigation, where the social and institutional context is of crucial importance'* (Somerville & Bengtsson, 2002:124). In this study the rationale that the people had for actions that often resulted in homelessness is explicitly explored, alongside other key factors outlined below.

In Fitzpatrick's (2005) robust outline for applying a critical realist approach to the study of homelessness, four particularly significant causal mechanisms are identified. These can be affiliated with the different resources of individual capital discussed in Chapter 1. These mechanisms are identified by Fitzpatrick (2005:13) as: *economic structures* (relating to economic resources, and the structures through which they may be generated, such as education, employment markets, class); *housing structures* (relating to material resources and how housing can be accessed, such as housing supply, cost, access to social housing); *interpersonal structures* (social networks, and how these may operate to trigger outcomes such as domestic violence, abuse, breakdown, as well as may generate social capital and support); and finally, *individual attributes* (which may relate to personal resilience, and actions such as drug misuse, mental illness, and the human capital people may have).

Each of these four mechanisms have been important framing factors for examining the transition through homelessness the people studied took in this analysis. As a study of individuals, the focus here has been on how these structural mechanisms may have been manifest through the resources of economic, social and material capital they had access to rather than an explicit analysis of these actual structural systems. It is also asserted that the three mechanisms of economic structures, housing structures, and interpersonal structures, may triangulate in forming the foundation of the fourth mechanism – the resilience people are likely to have, and individual attributes and actions that affect them, which is the key factor analysed here. To strengthen this analysis however individual agency and social structure must be clearly defined concepts and this is discussed in the next section.

Two key units of analysis have been focussed on in the development of this study of individuals' transitions through homelessness. One is the role the social welfare system had in affecting or changing the material context the people studied operated within. And another is an exploration of their social networks, interactions, and how being homeless affected this, and in turn affected their ontological security, tied as it is to the day-to-day life and interactions they experience. By examining these two factors, using this critical realist/structurated approach, a new perspective on the social processes operating, that can be used to explain transitions 'at the edge', can begin to develop.

4. Agency and structure

As already discussed in Chapter 1, research into the cause of homelessness, and the influence of agency and structure to this, has been criticised for lacking clear conceptualisation of what is actually being referred to as agency or structure (Fitzpatrick, 2005; Neale, 1997). To remedy this criticism, how these concepts are defined in this study, is outlined below.

Defining structure

This account starts with the realist proposition that there is an external world that exists, independently of our knowledge of it. The social 'structure' here refers to what is called 'the real':

> '[T]he real is whatever exists, be it natural or social, regardless of whether it is an empirical object for us, and whether we happen to have an adequate understanding of its nature' and 'the real is the realm of objects, their structures and powers. Whether they be physical, like minerals, or social, like bureaucracies, they have certain structures and causal powers'.
> (Sayer, 2000:11).

Therefore it is understood here that the social welfare system, for example, creates, and is part of the structural context (the 'reality') that people operate within. The social welfare system provides some of the actual options people may be provided with to access resources. This system may also constitute the actual environment and set of interactions they engage in to access these resources. The social welfare system is not an actual material object that can be measured or grasped however. It may be a construct of the modern social order but this does not mean that the social welfare system does not 'exist', or crucially that it does not profoundly affect the material and social environment and interactions that individuals' experience. A social welfare system is one structure among many, and all structures join up to constitute the external 'reality' of our social world. Many different external processes, institutions and environments intersect, interact and overlap to generate the entire structural 'reality' that people operate within. Structures are external to any one individual, and will exist regardless of any one individual. Yet this collection of structures and structural principles only constitutes 'society' due to individuals shared understanding of them and the discursive knowledge about them people collectively hold. This understanding of reality impacts on individual actions and interactions, and in this way goes on to reproduce this externally experienced structural context once more, in the ongoing structuration of society.

For example, someone's sex (whether male or female) will be a biological fact and the structural principles of gender that relate to this 'fact' will be embedded in any given society or culture. This will in turn affect how and who we are perceived to be. Gender exists, it is 'real', whether we like this or not, attempt to subvert these principles, or act them to the full. This may also be context bound or culturally specific and change in different circumstances, however it is still grounded in the structures of gender, and we are embodied physically in this, in each interaction and moment in time. Even someone who 'acts' in ways to conceal they are male or female, can only do so with an acknowledgment and subversion of the principles of gender in the context they are in. And this is true even if they were doing so in the virtual world of the internet for example – they are still male or female and are constrained to act in ways that acknowledge the structures of gender that exist, even if subverting them as active agents.

It may be that the social welfare system or gender are not static, solid, or something that can physically be grasped. This does not mean they do not exist, or will not go on existing, independently of any one individual or their understanding of them. Nor does this mean however that they are naturalistic and cannot change over time or will have different causal effects on different people or in different circumstances. What these terms refer to may change over time, may be context dependent, but structures do exist, and have causal powers affecting lives, in a complex multi-dimensional relationship (Fitzpatrick, 2005).

Structuration and ontological security

In structuration theory it is recognised that social 'structures' are both enabling and constraining. Structural principles must exist for people to have the capacity to act and make knowledgeable choices within the society they operate in, to know how to act to maintain their place in society. As these principles become increasingly embedded they become the structural properties that underpin the institutions of a society (Giddens, 1984). People are socialised and physically embodied in and by the society they live in. Situated structured principles prescribe how people should or can act and interact with others. These actions and interactions are then complicit in recreating these rules and circumstances. This embedding of structural properties has a temporal span that overlaps each generation, and outlives any one individual as the previous example of gender illustrates. However this does not mean people lack the capacity to act in ways that may transform or alter these principles over time either:

Human societies (...) would plainly not exist without human agency. But it is not the case that actors create social systems, they reproduce or transform them, remaking what is already made in the continuing praxis.

(Giddens, 1984:171)

This continuing recreation over time and space is necessary to maintain the boundaries of social life, and the 'ontological security' individuals require to operate within it. People must follow, and recreate to some degree, these structural principles, to maintain their ontological security, to maintain within themselves who 'they are' and what their role in terms of others in society, should be. Some routine and predictability of social actions and outcomes are required in the socially situated micro-level interactions of day-to-day life for people to communicate, interact and operate socially. The expectations of behaviour have to be met for some degree of social order to exist. However this ontological security can breakdown if this predictability is disrupted by what Giddens (1984) terms 'critical situations'. Therefore the actions people engage in can implicitly be understood as stemming from their desire to maintain ontological security, within the structural context they operate within. This is security maintained through the predictability of their routine, through the predictability of how interactions should play out within these routines, and from their understanding of their *role* within the structural reality they exist in. Each person adheres to the role they have, to some extent, to maintain the predictable order of society, and secure their place (their identity) within this. If this predicted role is ruptured, people may face ontological crisis. They then have to attempt to regain some sense of internal ontological security once more by adapting to the situation they are now in through a process of resocialisation (Giddens, 1984:63). Therefore, ontological security is an important concept through which transitions can be examined and understood – people strive to maintain this security as they make transitions through life, whatever circumstances or crisis they face.

There may also be a tension here however. The recreation of social structures may be required for the 'boundaries' of social life, and social order to remain intact, but these boundaries are porous, fluid, and can often be transgressed. For social change to occur edges often have to be negotiated, and new boundaries forged. However this may not occur without risk or conflict. Therefore edgework – acts that transgress, push, or go over these recognised boundaries of social life – are crucially important acts to analyse and understand. There may be a constant tension over the life course, that for progression to be made, edges have to be negotiated and overcome. This is both at individual and societal level, for if enough people adopt a behaviour publicly, then it is no longer a transgression, it becomes the norm (think for example of co-habiting before marriage, and how that is currently accepted, but not long ago was not, and still isn't in certain cultures, families, or places).Transgression also carries risk, the risk that the edge may not be negotiated with successfully, that the structures someone forging these new boundaries are embedded within will not be fluid enough to transgress and remain intact. There is a risk that someone may fall through the tear that this transgression pulls in the fabric of their life (again the 'shame' of living together before marriage that once existed, and still does in some cultures or places, is an example).

So to summarise, here structure refers to the institutions, social processes and principles that exist independently of any one individual, but that constitute the society, and external 'reality', they are embedded in, in day-to-day life. This reality is recreated by their actions and the extent to which these actions adhere to the norms of their society or not. And these actions will also be underpinned by the sense of individuality that they have, the sense of how they should or could act in a certain circumstance to retain their internal ontological security – their identity.

Defining agency

Agency can be understood as the sense of individuality, of being 'an individual' that someone has. This is their internal sense of unique existence recognised by themselves and others. Agency does not refer to actual actions or outcomes, but to the internal processes, independent of but embedded in structures, that individuals subjectively experience. This will have an impact on how they act, tied to their sense of identity and the need to maintain a sense of ontological security they have. *Acts* of agency are actions underpinned by this internal process. Therefore agency here does not refer to the actual 'doing', but the internal narratives that people have of their lives that affects how they act, and are embedded in the course their life has and will take. A degree of agency is always being exercised in the choices and actions people take. There is always some capacity for choice to be exercised as people negotiate the day-to-day activities and interactions they engage in (Giddens, 1984) – even choosing not to act, is a choice and an action. Being forced under duress to act some way, still carries choices, and actions – when and how to succumb to the threat at hand, for example. When someone says they had 'no choice' they chose to have no choice, even if the alternative is pain, others may choose the pain – therefore there is still always, some choice at play, however difficult the situation. However this agency, that all functioning individuals have, should not be mistaken for free will, we are embedded in a myriad of choices, constructed, and affected by the structured material and social reality we operate in.

Exercising 'agency' relates to each individual's ability to construct a narrative (and narratable) identity – a conceptualisation of who they are, over time. The work of Ricoeur (1991a; 1991b; 1992) on narrative identity is used here to illustrate this. Ricoeur (1991a; 1991b; 1992) argues that through a process of 'emplotment', actual 'events' that occur, and how people present them and make sense of them, as part of their 'story' of life, become interwoven subconsciously by them, over time. In this way they can maintain a sense of narrative identity over time – they are the 'same' person today as yesterday, the same person as ten years ago, however much their circumstances change. By constructing a cohesive internal narrative of the different events that have occurred in their life, they can maintain ontological security and a sense of identity, despite changes to the context this occurs in.

This sense of identity and ensuing social role is crucial to the ongoing structuration of social life. The need individuals have to maintain an internal narrative sense of identity will impact on, and be impacted upon, the actions they engage in, in day-to-day life. These narratives are taken from all the cultural 'texts' – discourses, ideology, experiences, interactions, and media, individuals are exposed to over time.

Through this process of emplotment people maintain a sense of identity over time that brings together disparate events that objectively happen in the material reality they operate within, from the textual and discursive representations and knowledge they have access to. It is through this process of emplotment that they can synthesise categorical identity markers with ontological self-identity (Taylor, 1998). This will also impact on how they act, or feel they should act, in the embodied material reality they are embedded within, to maintain this 'plot' over time, in an ongoing interconnected flow. Transitional events over the life course, where the 'plot' of someone's life is changing, are important to explore: in this way how people attempt to maintain their ontological security, their sense of identity, and how their actions may affect the transitions they make, can be better understood.

So agency provides the internal rationale for many actions – actions engaged in to represent and assert the sense of identity, and individuality, that someone has. This process may be crucial to maintain ontological security. However there is an ongoing tension inherent in this, as people strive to maintain their sense of identity, as they make transitions through many changing contexts and circumstances over their life. These contexts and circumstances may not always 'fit' with the planned cohesive plot of their lives, but they have to attempt to maintain a sense of ontological security still.

This brief discussion of the key epistemological approaches used in this study is intended to provide a foundation for the findings. The findings provide a new perspective on transitions through homelessness, and on how agency and structure affect these lives and transitions. In the final section of this chapter the people whose lives are presented here, are introduced, and the process used to explore these lives, discussed.

5.   Charting transitions through homelessness

This study was set in a large post-industrial UK city. This city has a particularly high concentration of deprivation and social problems, typical of such post-industrial areas. However the city has also recently undergone a period of regeneration and economic development.

Whilst acknowledging that certain locations bring with them a specific micro-context, the broad context of this research is urban life in late modernity. This conceptualisation is underpinned by the idea of 'global cities' (Sassen, 1991). It is asserted that through a process of globalisation, urban environments are increasingly assimilating. Social processes and problems occur and are played out over and above the local context they occur within. This local context is still important. The embodied experiences people have will be underpinned by the micro-level setting they occur within. However it is also asserted that urban post-industrial cities share similar features and problems, and that these features and problems have occurred as part of the process of modernisation and urbanisation, and so can be analysed broadly as phenomenon generated within this context.

Each of the 28 people whose lives were followed over the course of this research was contacted through an agency that supports people who are or have been homeless. To ensure that there was a spread of different people and circumstances covered, a questionnaire survey was initially conducted at each of the 13 different services that this agency operates. All of the different forms of support for homeless people outlined in Chapter 1 were represented by these services – from street outreach work, supported accommodation and housing support workers, to employment training. I worked closely with this agency for some time (it remains anonymous to protect confidentiality) and obviously the context that it provided for the research was of great value, both as a key source of support for some of the people studied and at times to facilitate my own understanding of homeless services and information on the people studied. However the in depth, biographical and longitudinal nature of the research meant that many of the experiences recounted by the people studied were about other services they accessed, or times in their transitions through homelessness when they were not in contact with the recruiting agency and this needs to be made clear. The data covered a wide range of different service and agency interactions and the analysis engages with broad theoretical imperatives rather than being concerned with an analysis of agencies or service provision. Saying that, the agency that the people studied were recruited through was instrumental to the completion of this study and thanks go to them for that.

From an initial number of 70 people who completed questionnaires, a cross-section of different ages, gender and circumstances were selected. Using the most recent contact details they provided at the same time as they agreed to complete the questionnaire (such as a room in a hostel, a relative they could be contacted through, or their own flat they had recently moved into) this cross-section of 30 were contacted and asked if they would agree to be re-interviewed repeatedly over the next year to find out how they circumstances changed, and the reasons for this. They were also asked if they would take part in an in-depth biographical life history interview at the beginning of the research.

In the end 24 of the original 30 took part in three in-depth interviews spread over the year. Some contact over the year and a second interview was conducted with a further four of the 30. Therefore in total 28 people had their transitions through homelessness explored over a year, and detailed biographical case studies on their lives collated to complement this data. Two of the original 30 had no further input into the study after the initial life history and interview stage – one because no contact could be made with them, and another who, due to an offending history that came to light had to be excluded – an illustration of just how far some lives over the edge go, that they even have to be excluded from studies on it.

This group of 28 consisted of 13 women and 15 men, with an age range of 25 to 60. The average age was 39. In keeping with the typical profile of people experiencing homelessness in this city at that time all were white, and had been born in the UK. Nevertheless, this still represents a very 'real' portrait of typical transitions through homelessness, and biographies of homeless people, in an urban western context, at the beginning of the 21st century. The sample (and some details about their homeless histories) is listed in Appendix 1. None of the names listed are real, they were selected randomly and in alphabetical order, to act as labels and add consistency to the narratives presented in the finding chapters.

The different forms of homelessness that the 28 people studied had experienced over their lives were diverse and intersected across the different constructions of homelessness outlined in Chapter 1. Some had slept rough on the streets for years; others had never slept rough, but lacked permanent accommodation for various reasons, and were moving between hostels and Bed & Breakfasts; some had their own tenancy at the time of the first interview, but were still receiving support to 'maintain' this housing, having previously been homeless; two were accessing homeless services after being served eviction notices for their housing but had never had to leave that housing. Therefore the sample covered a diverse range of different circumstances, and people experiencing different forms of 'homelessness'. This study engages with the fact that homelessness may encapsulate a diverse range of material, social, psychological, and ideological dimensions. However some measurement to objectively chart the individual transitions through homelessness studied here had to be used. So in this capacity, 'homelessness' was here defined as *being without permanent housing*. Permanent housing was defined as a legal tenancy or ownership of a house or flat, and the term housing and tenancy is used interchangeably to describe this. Being or remaining homeless therefore refers to situations where someone did not have their own permanent housing. This includes being accommodated in Bed & Breakfasts, supported temporary accommodation, staying with friends, being in prison with no other housing available, and sleeping rough. It is important to emphasise this clear definition is a tool for charting their transitions, and is not intended to convey or override the other dimensions of homelessness that these people experienced and that are also explored. Therefore the categorisation of homelessness used here included both literal forms and functional homelessness (such as being accommodated in an institution) as outlined in Tsemberis et al (2007) research discussed in Chapter 1. Some of the people whose lives are presented here had been homeless for long periods and represented highly marginalised individuals. They had mental and physical health problems, addictions, histories of trauma and abuse, poverty. Eighteen had been homeless repeatedly over their life. They represented those who are both experiencing maximalist homelessness, and manifest minimalist accounts and understandings of the problem (as discussed in Chapter 1, Jacobs et al, 1999). They also spanned a wide age range, gender divide, and could be considered at different 'stages' in their transitions through homelessness. This is all explored in detail in the following chapters.

The interview process

The interviews were conducted at a variety of locations, including offices, interview rooms on the premises of homeless services or accommodation projects, their own housing, rooms in supported accommodation projects, and cafes. The interviews were taped and then fully transcribed. In this study the eight points identified by Pickering et al (2003:13) in their feasibility study for tracking homelessness were explicitly incorporated into the research design (including obtaining as many stable points of contact as possible, the same researcher throughout, persistence, flexibility and frequent low level contacts). Techniques used in other studies such as Craig, Hodson, Woodward & Richardson (1996) and Haracopos & Dennis (2003) longitudinal qualitative study of crack users in London were adopted from the outset to maximise contact with the sample. Notes were kept of every contact made. I also attended many social events at different services and drop-ins to maintain a presence and contact with the people who I came to know during the research.

In keeping with this critically realist approach, it was important there were opportunities in the interview for the people studied to discuss and describe their experiences and feelings in their own words, whilst also ensuring baseline questions on what was 'actually happening' in their lives were adequately covered. Each interview included a discussion focussing on the services of the social welfare system that they were accessing, and how they felt about these services. In the final interview general questions on their views on homelessness, what causes problems such as homelessness to exist, how the social welfare system can be used to address it, and what actions or circumstances they attributed to causing homelessness, were also discussed.

Conducting longitudinal biographical research

This study adds to knowledge in an area of homelessness research where it is recognised that there are key gaps (Pickering et al, 2003). Studies of homelessness that have included a longitudinal component include those by Fitzpatrick (2000) and Craig et al (1996) and some developed studies in the US (for example, Tsemberis & Eisenberg, 2000; Yanos, Felton, Tsemberis & Frye, 2007).

These studies have continued to highlight the complexity of both making transitions out of homelessness and of researching these transitions, by maintaining contact over time. The US studies have been instrumental in challenging and developing existing provision in the US for seriously mental ill people experiencing homelessness into what is known as the housing first approach (Padgett, Gulcur & Tsemberis, 2006) which is discussed more in Chapter 5.

Long-term contact with the sample has to be maintained. This is highly time and labour intensive (and at times impossible). Another recent homelessness study that consisted of longitudinal qualitative research is Fitzpatrick's (2000) research on homeless young people. In this research 25 young people were 'followed-up' after taking part in an initial interview. The concept of 'maximum' information – actual responses from the young people, such as an interview or questionnaire being completed, and 'minimum' information – information on that individual being obtained from agencies or other contacts (Smith & Gilford, in Fitzpatrick, 2000) was used to define the results of this follow up. In Fitzpatrick's research, maximum information was obtained from 11 people who took part in a second interview or completed a questionnaire, and minimum information on another 11.

As was outlined earlier in this chapter, in the research presented in this study maximum information (information obtained in an actual interview) was obtained throughout with 24 people who took part in all three interview stages. A further four took part in two interview stages, but only minimum information could be obtained about them at one stage.

As has been found in other qualitative longitudinal studies, obtaining maximum information and conducting longitudinal research can be challenging, time consuming, and required a high level of perseverance as well as researcher involvement and commitment (Plumridge & Thomson, 2003; Thomson & Holland, 2003). However it should not be assumed that such as methodology will necessarily bring with it problems. As has also been found in other studies, despite the challenges, some of the people researched were contacted via mobile phone number, at their current accommodation, or by letter, throughout the research (Harocopos & Dennis, 2003). One called my office at the third interview stage asking if it was time for their next interview. In any research there will be challenges and limitations to the data collection. Longitudinal qualitative research is certainly a methodology that can be used successfully to develop detailed biographies of research participants and to chart transitional stages over the life course. This methodology also brought additional ethical issues however as contact details are required, and ongoing relationships with research participants cannot help but develop and affect how the narratives of their lives unfold (Thomson & Holland, 2003). The potential difficulty and the level of resources required to conduct such research is clear (Pickering et al, 2003; Holland, Thomson & Henderson, 2004) and it is for this reason that few longitudinal studies are conducted, and those that are often still span relatively short time scales. This was also the reason for the limited time scale of the study presented here and it does have to be flagged up that one year is not a long time in a lifetime to have explored. Having said that, a key value of the longitudinal methodology of this research is that people's situation, and the contact they had with the social welfare system, changed over time. Therefore the experiences of those who lost all contact with services, but were still negotiating their transition through homelessness, could be explored, alongside the experiences of those that remained within the system, or that made a transition out of homelessness and obtained their own housing. By embedding this in their entire biographies from birth, it could also be unravelled how they had come to these points, over a long term retrospective period.

There are also limitations inherent when only a small number such as this is explored. The homelessness studied here is not meant to be representative of anyone, and everyone that may experience homelessness. Some people may make transitions through homelessness in different ways than those represented here and longer term studies, with larger samples, are still required. However these detailed and rich biographical cases studies do provide valuable insight and do represent a systematic study of people 'on the edge' and negotiating transitions over time within the conditions of late modernity, cast within a new theoretical framework. It also adds to the developing number of qualitative longitudinal studies and begins to address often cited gaps in homelessness research in this way.

The research presented here was privy to stringent scrutiny by Ethics Committees and Advisory Boards throughout. The interactional nature of most social research means that it will *always* to some extent be embedded in the social situation being studied. This interaction will be socially situated, with age, gender and class all factors influencing it (Edwards, 1996). The research itself will be a part of the day-to-day activities and interactions that those studied are engaging in and may in turn feed into the future actions of those involved. If it is recognised that research is an interaction, and can affect those involved then it must also be recognised that research findings also go on to influence the social context that they were produced from, and the understanding that people have of these issues creating a double hermeneutic (Giddens, 1984).

With this point in mind, it is in the next chapter that this story of lives on the edge – this story of transitions through homelessness – really begins.

3
Becoming a Homeless Person

1. Transitions into homelessness

As would be expected, the people studied had experienced complex and diverse life histories that are difficult to generalise. What they did all share was that at some point in their lives they had become defined as homeless, and had accessed services for homeless people. In this section their route into homelessness is explored, before considering their lives prior to becoming homeless in Section 2.

In the introductory questionnaire that the people studied completed they were asked to identify the cause of their homelessness. Drug or alcohol use, and changes in relationships that were often experienced suddenly or traumatically, were the main factors cited. Specifically: alcohol use (5); drug use (4); domestic violence (4); breakdown of family or couple relationship (6); bereavement (3); mental illness (2); leaving care with no where else to go (2); debt (1), and leaving poor quality housing (1).

Clearly on one level these individual factors – addiction, relationship breakdown, poor health – are what 'cause' homelessness, as has been found in previous studies (Flemen, 1997; Bines, 1994) although as the new orthodoxy (Fitzpatrick, 2005) would assert, this is only within certain structural conditions and due to complexly interrelated trigger points and individual factors operating. What requires further consideration is what *causes these individual factors to have such a hold over some people's lives*, and why they only result in homelessness for some people, in some circumstances, when anyone may experience them.

It was also often highly traumatic incidents (for example, being assaulted by a partner; or attempting suicide) that were the crisis points that triggered their actual transitions into homelessness, and the psychological effect this is likely to have also needs to be considered. It was therefore traumatic events that formed the backdrop to these people accessing temporary accommodation or support services for homeless people. And this is when, overwhelmingly, they described that they began to identify themselves as 'homeless', as the following story of Tommy's transition into homelessness illustrates.

Tommy's story

Tommy had had a relatively settled life, getting married, running his own business and living in his own housing. However his business began to falter, he started to suffer from depression, and left his family. He spent some time staying with friends, and then on his own sleeping rough, before attempting suicide, and being admitted to a psychiatric hospital. Below, Tommy describes how accessing homeless services through the welfare state was a defining moment in his transition into homelessness. This was the moment he *felt* he became homeless, subjectively, although this occurred within a cycle of increasing insecurity encapsulated by mental illness, leaving his family, staying with friends, and then sleeping rough:

> *I had manic depression. I left my family, and I spent a couple of weeks with a mate, a week somewhere else, and they couldn't handle me either, so I spent some time in the hills, and then I spent a long time in hospital. I think there were other things for me to go through… my mental health. I'd attempted suicide. And when I left the hospital [the social workers took me to apply for housing at a centralised office for people who are homeless] there wasn't a bed for me anywhere, and so that office is a suitable address you can be discharged too. I had nowhere to go. So I didn't really consider myself as homeless until I ended up in hostels. It wasn't until going through the application form, and it kind of hit me that if I don't get Housing Benefit then obviously I couldn't get somewhere to stay. So that was kind of the first time I thought 'I'm homeless'. Felt in the system.*
> (Tommy, 33)

Using some definitions of homelessness, Tommy became homeless before he entered the welfare system in place to respond to homelessness. This was found to often be the case, with many people studied here spending time in insecure and peripheral housing circumstances, such as staying with friends, or temporary private accommodation, before they accessed services or accommodation as explicitly homeless people. In some cases these peripheral housing situations were maintained for long periods of time and were not equated with being homeless or as problematic and this mirrors findings from other studies (Fitzpatrick, 2000). It was as complex factors interacted and caused these peripheral housing circumstances to break down (alongside the erosion of other resources they had) that led to them accessing services or accommodation for 'homeless people', reflecting both maximilist and minimalist accounts of homelessness outlined in Chapter 1. They were actually and subjectively homeless, and they identified themselves in this way. Many discussed how they had 'made themselves' homeless as an escape route from a crisis point they had reached in their life. This was a way to make a 'break' from this situation, and begin again and could be seen as a clear act of agency, but one that occurred at the same time as their circumstances were highly chaotic and appeared 'out of their control'. Services or accommodation were therefore usually accessed alongside a traumatic trigger point that had led to them entering the homeless system – such as being admitted to hospital after an overdose, being assaulted, or attempting suicide. Sometimes however they had not been aware that there was any support available, as their lives slid into chaos, as Elizabeth describes:

> *All my adult life I've stayed in this city and I didn't know a thing about the homeless scene, I didn't know about the drug scene. I didn't know about a lot of things. Then all of a sudden I had been homeless, and now, I'm more likely to go to places, and you can get dinners and you can get clothed and you can get a bed, but then I didn't know about any of these places. I just went about and starved for weeks on end.*
>
> (Elizabeth, 41)

Elizabeth first became homeless when she was 35 years old. She had been employed, been married, had a family and had her own housing prior to this. However her partners had been very abusive and she had had a breakdown after leaving one. She began to use heroin, the first time she had ever used drugs, with a partner when she was in her thirties, and then became homeless after they spent some time staying with a friend of his, where she had to leave when he was arrested and admitted to prison.

So what was also clear in all the transitions into homelessness studied, such as Tommy's and Elizabeth's case, was the prevalence of edgework – the vulnerability, trauma and concentration of risk taking – that they had experienced as this process occurred. In Tommy's case for example, this was manifest in extreme psychological illness (the line between sanity and insanity) and attempted suicide, (the ultimate act of going over the edge perhaps, voluntarily attempting to destroy yourself). For the majority (26 of the 28) this edgework included an escalation of drug and alcohol use, and often violent events such as being raped or assaulted by people they knew. Often these incidents of edgework were compounded by their economic and material deprivation, leading to the point whereby they relied on the state not only for resources such as accommodation or income, but also to provide some form of social and emotional support. They had become materially, socially and emotionally drained of resources.

It was after accessing homeless services that they then perceived themselves to be a homeless person, and became focussed on by welfare agencies as homeless people. A divestment passage had occurred that had led to them having a negative social status. Even if people do not have their own legal housing this may not necessarily be problematic to them, or be viewed as such as was often the case here. What is crucial to highlight here is that if this does become problematic *within the structural context* that they have no other capital available to obtain housing without *reliance on the state*, then their situation, and how this should be responded to, became the responsibility of the state. They had no 'safety net' of their own due to the lack of resources they had, and therefore had to rely on the state. However as will also be shown this reliance sometimes operated to exacerbate their marginality rather than provide a route out of it. So this was how transitions into homelessness were explicitly made – often embedded in a cycle of increasing material and psychological insecurity. This erosion of security could occur over many years, and although some had experienced intense marginality throughout their lives (as is explored in the next section) most also had had 'normal' lives prior to becoming homeless – with housing, families, marriages, and some form of employment. Hidden within these 'normal' lives however, their narratives often recounted a history of trauma and abuse, and of accompanying factors such as addiction, mental illness, self harm and violence.

When they became homeless they then became focussed on by services of the state. They were visibly over the edge. This process of accessing the welfare system defined them as homeless people. The reason for this focus of the state was often perceived to be their individual problems such as mental illness or addiction. But what led to these individual problems occurring, and what structural factors and conditions may be identified to explain this? This is explored below, using the stories of Val and William.

Val's transition into homelessness

Val was 59 when she took part in the first interview. She was living in her own tenancy at this point, after recently being homeless. Val had lived a relatively settled life. She was a housewife, had brought up her children, and had sometimes worked informally. She had always lived in socially rented housing. She identified that her problems first started when she moved into a new 'scheme':

> *I was married for 36 years before I lost my husband four years ago, and we were up in the [previous] house for over 20 years. I think that was really the cause of my downhill slope, once we moved to a new scheme and that. It was just, there was nothing to do and the men's work just dried up and the men found it easier to go to the pub. We ended up taking a drink because of the boredom.*
>
> (Val, 59)

Val had been moved to the new scheme when her old house was demolished as part of housing policies to regenerate certain areas. Her quote succinctly illustrates how factors that may be considered structural, such as housing polices and changes in employment opportunities, can affect individuals, and their actions and material reality, profoundly. In this case the ensuing intense boredom, disaffection, and alcohol use stemmed from this structural reality. Val began to use alcohol heavily after her husband died. She blamed this on the boredom, isolation and grief she now felt. She said none of her family or friends were housed nearby or could afford to regularly travel to see each other. She became homeless after being admitted to hospital. This was after she was found collapsed in her flat by a housing officer. She had collapsed due to chronic alcohol use. From hospital she entered the statutory homeless system (and was provided with a room in supported accommodation) before obtaining her own tenancy once more, a year and a half later:

> *And eventually I ended up in hospital with drink problems. I wasn't caring, you know, I was just waking up in the morning, opening a bottle and just sitting there all day. I was myself then, once he [husband] went, that was me. (...) I was taken into hospital through my drinking, and gave up my house. From there I went into [temporary accommodation].*
>
> (Val, 59)

Structural and societal changes that were underpinned by social welfare policies could be identified as some of the mechanisms that caused Val's homelessness. These structural changes underpinned the individual factors that led to her homelessness – her isolation and alcoholism. The grief of bereavement, alcoholism, and feelings of acute isolation may be experienced by anyone. However a high level of resources may be used to assist them negate or avoid it, and develop more resilience to ongoing negative affects. For example if people have enough economic resources to pay for their own housing privately they may be able to live in an area close to people they know, or where social problems are not concentrated (as the residualisation of social housing acknowledges as a problem (Fitzpatrick & Stephens, 1999). They cannot necessarily do this when they rely on the state for housing as Val did. It may also be that people with a high level of resources can appear to be less affected by the negative outcome of these structural changes (unemployment, family fragmentation, for example) because they can use their resources to manage their own lives as individuals and buffer themselves from the emotional negatives that may accompany these structural factors. They may still experience grief or isolation, of course, but have more resources to negate or buffer the effect of this. That these factors are experienced as individual then obscures how profoundly important structural factors and inequality are in influencing people's lives – on both material and emotional levels.

In Val's case an interaction of the emotional trauma of bereavement, of becoming socially isolated, coupled with excessive alcohol use that almost led to her death, were the actual events causing her transition into homelessness. These appeared to be individual factors but can also be understood as being structurally bound, within the material reality of time-space she operated in. Her transition into homelessness occurred when she became explicitly reliant on the support services of the social welfare system, due to no other resources or support being available to her. She had housing, but left it when she entered hospital and was referred to supported accommodation after this. In some ways her chronic alcoholism that led to this could be encapsulated as an act of agency – an interactional symbolic act that illustrated her suffering and isolation generated in the material context she operated within to those around her and led to her moving on from this – but only at the risk of destroying herself through death. However as will also be illustrated later, her broad contextual circumstance did not fundamentally change after this critical moment in her transition into homelessness, and later in her life story this symbolic act continued.

Another example of how structural and individual factors interrelated to trigger homelessness, in complex ways, can be illustrated in the story of William.

William's transition into homelessness

William was 29 years old and living in supported accommodation when he was first interviewed. William had been in care as a child. He moved to stay with relatives when he was 16. He stayed with them until moving in with a girlfriend, first to her parents, and then a flat they rented together. During this time he was working casually in manual employment:

I started working not long after [moving back to family]. [I was] Working for a friend's firm [in manual labour]. Eventually I started selling drugs. (...) I had been using cannabis at the weekends. It wasn't until my late teens that I took anything, like hard drugs. Then I got introduced to cocaine but it's quite expensive [so I started selling it to make extra money].

After he split up with his girlfriend he moved in with a friend (living there unofficially) for three years. He became addicted to heroin, as he describes in the following quote:

I went to stay with a friend. I think the first time I ever took heroin was when I was 25 cause I was doing that much coke I needed something to 'come down'. I woke up one day a heroin addict. I gave up work. As soon as I started taking heroin, drugs were the be all and end all of me. They sort of took right over my life, you know, nothing else mattered.

(William, 29)

He stopped working once he was using heroin. After a year William went into rehab and then moved in with relatives. He began to use heroin again. He then moved into a hostel for homeless people and his transition into homelessness was complete. He discusses in the quote below the processes that led to this relapse and eventual homelessness:

Within a week [out of rehab], I was back using heroin [with friends]. It was just the scheme. Maybe it's just a bit about being insecure in yourself, not wanting to be different, wanting to be one of the boys and all that sort of thing. I went to stay with [a relative] for about a month, then they realised I was back using heroin and said, 'I can't have you staying here', you know. So I moved into the hostels and I just got completely worse. Started injecting heroin and in that clique. It was brutal.

(William, 29)

So again, in a complex relationship, certain individual mechanisms interacted, over time, to lead to William becoming homeless. For long periods he stayed with friends or relatives, and did not see this as problematic. However when his addiction became problematic he had to leave, and now lacked the resources (both emotionally and materially) to obtain housing without accessing accommodation for homeless people through the state. So it appeared to be individual factors, particularly his drug use that led to William's homelessness. However as the British Crime Survey 2005/06 illustrates (noted in the previous chapter), many people use illicit drugs. If this transition into homelessness is to be really understood, a key question remains – what led to these individual factors, such as his extreme drug use occurring and leading to homelessness, when it does not for everyone?

Buchanan (Buchanan & Young, 2000; Buchanan, 2004) has argued that increased drug use and addiction throughout the 1980s and 1990s can be understood as something that occurred due to structural changes, such as the decline in manual industries. He argues that for working class youth with few opportunities ahead of them, living in declining housing estates, and socially marginalised, drug use could be understood as a rational response, an alternative to 'boredom and monotony' (Buchanan, 2004: 127). This 'disaffection' caused by structural changes characterising late modernity may again be used to understand why these individual factors that cause homelessness (the edgework that they may have experienced) have come to underscore some people's lives:

> (W)hen the excluded and economically unwanted face the prospect of growing up in a hostile individualistic society that promotes free enterprise and innovation, the emergence of a drug sub-culture could be interpreted as an unconscious but direct alternative.
>
> (Buchanan & Young, 2000:419)

Is this process what underpinned William's heroin use and drug dealing? If so, once again, far reaching structural changes can be used to understand why the individual factors that led to homelessness occurred. Perhaps it is therefore more rational to understand William's drug dealing and drug use as a form or escape, and as a means to generate money and a high level of social status within the context of his social networks, when contrasted to the low paid, low status lifestyle that he may also have faced.

So William's example also highlights the oscillating effect that on a micro-level, social relationships and networks can have on the transitions people make. He was able to stay with friends and relatives, as a 'buffer' to his visible homelessness for some time until he had to apply for accommodation through the welfare system and entered a hostel. However it was also the influence of the situation he was in – and people he knew – that created the conditions whereby his drug use became a rational choice. He was engaging in activities to 'fit in', in this material situation. These relationships and the social networks someone has are recognised here as constituting an important part of the reality people are embedded in, and the interactions they engage in within this. Yet in cases such as William's, these actions also ultimately took them over the edge, into lives of chaos and increased suffering.

2. Contextualising transitions over the life course – Resources, relationships, and edgework

In each of the 28 lives explored here, the people had come to be defined as homeless or at serious risk of becoming a homeless person, at some point in their lives. This was what they all shared, despite the many differences they also had. Key factors that interacted to lead to this were their:

1. Relationships and social networks;
2. Level of resources (economic, social, human and material capital); and,
3. Experiences of edgework (both involuntarily due to extremely traumatic events occurring, or voluntarily, due to substance use or criminal acts).

As discussed in Chapter 1, the first two have long been documented as causes of homelessness (Anderson et al, 1993; Fitzpatrick et al, 2001) however this is the first time that the other individual factors have been conceptualised as a workable whole. These three are also all factors that interact to create the material and social reality we all operate within. How they explicitly affected the lives studied here – and may have acted to lead to them 'going over the edge' is discussed below.

Social networks and housing

Social networks and relationships play a key role to how people experience their lives on a day-to-day basis, and also to how housing pathways develop (Clapham, 2005; Jones, 1995). For example, as Jones (1995) study showed when and why someone leaves their parental homes, will usually be affected by both push and pull reasons, relating to the relationships they have. It may be that the parents break-up, a step-parent moves in and there is conflict. A new relationship may lead to a young person leaving home to live with their partner, or after an argument, leaving to stay with friends temporarily. They may make contact with parents again, over time, and when their relationships with their partner or friends break down, move back to parents' houses. This may all occur without them attempting to live alone, gain housing of their own (either socially rented or privately), or perceiving themselves to have housing problems in any way. It is not just young people whose housing pathways are profoundly affected by social networks, and the resources these networks allow access to however. Throughout our life course, where and with whom to live, due to relationships, contacts, jobs, and the resources available, is something profoundly affected by social networks – be it obtaining a room somewhere to rent through a work colleague, to moving to a new city to move in with a partner, or if that breaks down, staying in the spare room of a friends house, temporarily, until new accommodation has been found.

Social networks played an explicitly important role in influencing the housing transitions presented here too. The majority of the 28 (16) grew up living with their parents (and siblings if they had any); two were brought up by their grandparents; four had spent some time in borstals, care homes, or approved schools as they grew up, although they also spent periods living with their parents; and a further six had been taken into care permanently as children (two of these were then adopted by other families). Most had lived in socially rented housing as they grew up (or for those taken into care, in care homes).

Social networks were important for informally providing access to resources such as housing. However this was only possible (or at least unproblematic) if friends or family had housing of their own, and enough room for them to be able to stay there. Clearly some of the people studied here, who had been care for example, may have had sparse social networks from an early age. This illustrates that it is the *resources* social networks provide access to, rather that the *existence* of these networks, that generates positive outcomes from these networks. In the transitions studies here, the pressure or conflict that occurred when people were living in crowded or temporary situations (such as staying temporarily with a friend, sleeping on their sofa, and not legally meant to be there, something that would not be a problem in an owner occupied house) meant that this situation often broke down. This was anther key factor influencing their lives as they became homeless – their social networks depleted or ruptured over time. Often domestic violence, relationship breakdown, or bereavement were precursors to homelessness and the social networks that remained intact did not provide access to many resources, other than (sometimes conflictual) interactions.

There is one further key tenet to understanding the influence and effect that relationships had on their circumstances, and that is the physical or emotional trauma that could occur when they went wrong. Relationships affect, and in many ways constitute, the material and emotional landscape people operate within. They have a profound effect on how day-to-day life is experienced. It was often difficult situations that involved relationships, such as physical fights, the ending of a relationship, or bereavement, that triggered divestment passages in their lives that were pivotal moments that they traced to their homelessness in the narratives they gave (and have been found in other studies such as Crane & Warnes, 2006). Sometimes this was experienced as a highly traumatic incident, such being severely beaten by someone they knew, or witnessing someone's death.

Many had experienced intensely abusive relationships over their life course. Even experiences that may at times be inevitable for all over the life course, such as bereavement, or relationship breakdown, are still traumatic and can involve a degree of edgework, as people attempt to manage the emotional effect of this. Relationships and social networks have negative as well as positive effects, they may deplete, as well as increase the resources someone has access to (Portes, 1998). They can be a source of trauma and difficulty as well as support and well-being. What is unavoidable is that they are something that will affect everyone's life course significantly, and that certainly did so here.

What was also clear was that these people were all positioned socially in a socio-economic position whereby the resources they had were not enough to negate their need to rely on the state to access housing, when other sources of support provided through their social networks were depleted, or did not exist. Many people experience periods staying with friends or relatives over their life course, without this being defined as problematic by them or others. The difference is perhaps that some people have access to a high enough level or resources (or the people they know do) to maintain accommodation or gain their own in the future without this reliance on their social networks ever becoming problematic, or being something that they have 'no choice' but to do. When it does become problematic (they are asked to leave after an argument, for example) and *they have no other means to access housing themselves with the resources they have*, they have to access the state to gain accommodation, as a homeless person, or sleep rough. In this way they became defined as a homeless person. And almost all those studied here had experienced this process of decoupling from social support networks to welfare support networks, at some point. Some had relied on the state for such support all their lives – such as those who had been in care as children.

Resources and capital: Education and employment histories

Twenty seven had left mainstream education by the age of 16 (the legal age to do so in the UK). Some of the people interviewed described school as 'alright' or they 'got on fine', and some had obtained standard grade level qualifications. However the majority described their experiences of mainstream schooling negatively:

I had a hard time at school, just the reading and writing I can't do it. Never got any help with it.

(Brian, 35)

I used to work in packaging, it was a factory. I started work at 13. I didn't learn anything at school. Didn't go back.

(Helen, 35)

The majority had never returned to mainstream education after leaving school. Some had attended college at different points in their lives and some had accessed adult learning courses. Some of these courses were specifically for people who were experiencing homelessness. These courses assisted them with their 'life skills', computing, or literacy, for example. None had a degree level qualification, although some had other qualifications relating to the employment they had had, such as licenses to operate machinery from when they had worked in construction.

Four said that they had never been employed. The majority (24) had engaged in some form of (usually manual or service sector) employment over their lives. This included working in kitchens, bars, shops, factories, bakeries, as cleaners, as security guards, as builders, roofers, floorers, in construction, as panel beaters, mechanics, or dental nursing. While some were in stable (albeit sometimes relatively low-paid manual or service sector) employment for long periods over their life course, others had always had more peripheral employment experiences, engaging in the formal and informal economy, and long periods of unemployment.

None were working in formal employment at the time of the first interview, or since their most recent episode of homelessness had began. The reasons given was either that they were unable to work due to health or other problems (such as addiction or their homelessness) or that the cost of paying their own rent in whatever form of accommodation they currently had (such as being in a hostel, or a socially rented flat) was perceived to be higher than the income they could attain through paid employment, making this untenable. The following quote from Brian illustrates both his transition out of employment and a barrier to employment he then faced. Brian was a chef and had worked successfully for periods over his life. Brian started claiming Incapacity Benefit (welfare income for people who cannot work) whilst in a rehab due to his drug addiction. He was living in temporary supported accommodation when he discussed this:

> *I've always worked, up until about four years ago, I'm on the sick the now, I'd never thought about going on the sick in my life, but the rehab put me on it, and then I came out and stayed on it, but I still know people, there's a guy, I used to work with, he's asked me to go and work with him, but he thinks I'm still staying at my mum though, so, I don't think I can do that. Not until I've got a house.*

(Brian, 35)

So it was Brian's addiction that had led to him initially ceasing his work. Then he felt unable to work until he had his own house once more. Due to the perceived stigma of the situation he was in he told people he was staying with his family instead of in accommodation for homeless people. This case also illustrates how important social networks can also be in affecting other aspects of someone's life, such as their access to employment.

Resources and edgework: Illegitimate sources of incomes

Over their life course, many of the people studied had engaged in activities such as begging, prostitution and drug dealing to generate income. In this way they may have been individually attempting to negate the effect of their low socio-economic status and the relative poverty it brought (as theorised by Young, 2006) and therefore be rational as an alternative career (Craine, 1997). Despite this rationale, these are also acts deviating from what is considered normative social behaviour, and engaging in such acts usually involved a high degree of risk – more edgework – that could contribute to them going over the edge, despite the fact that there could be rationales for these acts, as Claire's story illustrates.

Claire's experience of edgework and income

After being in care as a child, and then becoming homeless when she left care, Claire obtained a flat and started a college course. However she said that she could not afford to be in full time education, and pay her rent, so she returned to working in prostitution (something she had done previously). This was often dangerous and emotionally distressing. She said to 'block' out this work, to escape the reality she was in, she started to use heroin (once more). She became addicted to heroin, left college, left her flat, and became homeless once more:

> *I was living in a flat and then I got into prostitution and then from getting into prostitution I started taking heroin again to forget the fact that I was working... and then I lost my place on my college course 'cause I was more interested in chasing my next hit, and then I lost my flat.*

(Claire, 26)

This was another episode of homelessness in a life course characterised by repeatedly gaining and losing tenancies. In Claire's case the very acts she engaged in to assist her integrate into society, (such as attending college) could also lead to the situation whereby she resorted to actions that led to further divestment in her life, such as working in prostitution. Due to the lack of economic resources she had, she had to try to generate income with the only human capital she had – selling herself, through her work in prostitution. In a spiralling effect the actions she engaged in as an individual to try to improve her situation were acts involving high degrees of risk and stigma, and so actually led to her material situation deteriorating once more. And in this way, this deterioration of her situation could also be individualised, although it stemmed from the low level of resources she had, which was structurally grounded. It may also be that working in prostitution had initially been an option to Claire due to the social network she had – she worked with women she knew, and had first started working in prostitution due to contact with other women who worked that she had.

Claire's story also illustrates (and as other studies into transitions have highlighted, such as Furlong & Cartmel, 1997) that transitions will not necessarily be experienced in a linear way – people may 'churn' at the edges of their past and future lives, in the time-space of the present. They may pull on resources and knowledge from their past to attempt to negotiation their transitions in the present, pulling from the 'plot' of their life that already exists to try to move on, but therefore ultimately only recreating it. How they construct narratives of these events may also be pivotal to what follows from it (Ezzy, 2001).

Trauma and edgework

Another crucial mechanism that affected all the lives studied here was that they had all experienced a high concentration of acts that encapsulate negotiating the edges of normative behaviour, such as drug use; experiencing or engaging in extreme violence; attempting suicide; criminal acts. This was clearly another important mechanism that interacted with certain factors in their lives, as they attempted to reconcile this trauma with their future lives, and deal with the emotional effect of this. The following quotes from Margaret and Rachel illustrate some of the intensely traumatic incidents referred to:

When I was 16 I was raped by three guys (...). I tried to kill myself twice, but that was about a year later, I took a nervous breakdown.

(Margaret, 43)

Margaret had been taken into care as a child, due to her mother's alcoholism. She was raped shortly after she returned to live with her mother, aged 16. She had been homeless, living in hostels, sleeping rough and staying with people she knew, ever since. She had chronic alcohol problems. Rachel had also been in a cycle of repeated homelessness and had experienced violent relationships all of her life, as she described for example:

Then I got married, when I was 17, I was getting battered about, but I didn't really drink then. I ended up stabbing him, my first man, and in prison for a time. (...) Then the next one he was worse, he did this to me [leans over and shows a large scar on her head] with a bottle.

(Rachel, 46)

Traumatic incidents were prevailing factors affecting almost all these lives. This indicates that these factors – actions and experiences that can be conceptualised as edgework – have to be recognised and understood to understand the lives and circumstances of the people studied, who had all at some point become homeless.

Furthermore these traumatic experiences often interacted with and exacerbated other forms of edgework they then engaged in – such as alcohol or drug use. The emotional effect of the victimisation some had experienced, or the physiological effect of their drug use, could also exacerbate or lead to a deterioration of their mental health. It may also be that the lack of resources they had, made them especially vulnerable to such incidents – they could not afford to live in 'safe' areas;

take taxis home at night; leave an abusive partner because they had no where else to go or other risk avoidance strategies. Their low socio-economic position and the lack of resources they had not only marginalised them, but may also have meant they were more likely to engage in or experience edgework, due to this marginalised position.

So they must be understood as a group of people who had faced both intensely traumatic incidents and risks in their lives (almost all of the women and some of the men discussed sexual and physical abuse they had repeatedly experienced, and many had attempted suicide) however different they also were. They had also often engaged in acts that may be considered deviant or dangerous (such as intravenous drug use, criminal acts such as assaulting and robbing others, working in prostitution). These experiences and actions have to be understood, explored, and recognised for their situation, and what may have led to them, to be understood. At some point in their lives they had gone 'over the edge', and become archetypal 'outsiders'. Complex, long processes interacted to lead to this, peppered with material marginalisation and intensely traumatic experiences. The crucial question to consider here is *why* this edgework came to be so prevalent in their lives, and how they experienced and dealt with this. They had gone over the edge – but how and why had this occurred? To understand this requires a consideration of both the material and emotional landscape that people operate within, and the many structural factors that intersect with this to constrain or enable individual resilience.

Emotional and material landscapes of poverty – The duality of edges

It was often recounted in interviews, that due to the stigma of their social circumstances and the status this brought (such as being home-less, or a drug addict) and the accommodation they were in (such as supported accommodation, a rehab), it felt uncomfortable 'fitting in', and integrating with mainstream society. This relates to a key point – that as they became homeless, and for many throughout their lives, these were people negotiating on the 'the edges' of society, on two levels. Objectively the actual socio-economic position they had was characterised by low levels of resources. They were also emotionally (and often physically) negotiating on the edge of what is normal or safe behaviour and circumstances, due to the edgework and trauma they had experienced. And these are also situations imbued with stigma that people have to reconcile with their day-to-day life. This effect is termed here as the 'duality of edges'.

This duality of edges is further illustrated through the work of both Young (2006) and Buchanan (2004). Young (2006) argues that a low socio-economic position leads to a 'double stigma' being experienced. Groups living in acutely deprived material situations (relative to the rest of society) not only suffer due to this poverty, but also feel subjectively an intense existential humiliation due to this – a sense of being 'nothing'. But they are still operating within society and have an ongoing need to assert themselves, and engage as individuals, with their society. They attempt to assimilate, or escape this, through the only actions they can – often actions that encapsulate forms of edgework. These actions may also be normalised within the material reality they operate within, and so be rational actions to assimilate to broad norms and ideals that people are culturally exposed to. Rather than being different, we are all the same – this is the problem. People want to assimilate with what they see, have high levels of consumption, and individual worth – but the means to do so are not equally accessible (Young, 2006). Therefore other means are adopted.

As noted earlier, Buchanan (Buchanan & Young, 2000; Buchanan, 2004) also identified a similar process in the lives of drug users. He argues that material deprivation and the psychological 'hopelessness' of being structurally marginalised in an increasingly individualised society may explain the prevalence of addiction in housing areas with a concentrated lack of resources. Drug use is a form of escape from this material situation. But it is also a stigmatising act, and once people have become stigmatised they face increased barriers to overcoming their marginalisation. Their initial drug use stemmed from being in a marginalised situation and the material and emotional affect of this. Their drug use then exacerbated this marginality. It was a process such as this – a duality of edges – that led to the homelessness studied here. Structures generated positions of relative insecurity, imbued with risk. As they attempted to cope with this situation on both material and emotional levels, the acts they engaged in to do so may have only acted to further marginalise them, in a vicious circle, until their security (whatever resources they had) eroded to the point they became explicitly homeless, and cast out – with nothing and no one to turn to.

So there is both a material and emotional dimension to understanding these transitions. The two key factors that have been identified that characterised the material and emotional landscape that they operated within were, firstly, their marginalised socio-economic position and low level of resources they had; and secondly, the concentration of extremely difficult and traumatic situations they had experienced, either voluntarily or involuntarily, such as domestic violence, rape, mental illness, and addiction. The process used to conceptualise why these individual factors that cause homelessness (and constitute voluntary risk taking) may occur, is here termed as the *rationale of irrational behaviour*.

3. The rationale of irrational behaviour

As already discussed, social networks can have negative as well as positive effects. For example, the day-to-day activities and interactions that William engaged in could involve both companionship and 'fitting in' but usually only alongside substance use, such as alcohol, or drugs.

Within a certain social context, the roles people adopt to fit in, to maintain the cohesion of the situation they are in, may involve engaging in activities that appear irrational as responses to the individual management of risk over their life course. For example: in William's case, his heroin use and drug dealing; Val's case, her alcohol use; and Claire's case, working in prostitution and heroin use. It has already been outlined that these may appear irrational but why they engaged in them could also clearly be understood and rationalised, on a human level (as previous studies of deviance have asserted, such as Craine, 1997 and Katz, 1988).

So there is a tension between being responsible and controlling actions, and in some contexts, those *same actions* that should be avoided being the *means* to fit in with the social role expected, or the means to *escape* or *resist* the material situation someone is in. If the micro-level context that someone is experiencing (their structural reality), is one whereby certain activities (such as drug use) may bring some relief from or resistance to that situation, as an 'escape route' (Cohen & Taylor, 1992) the irrationality of engaging in them can become increasingly understood as a rational response. It is also argued here that the structural conditions of late modernity may have led to these actions being likely to occur – people engage in edgework as a means to individually find some self-actualisation or control in the context of an increasingly disenchanted, liberal individualised modern society; or to escape the isolation or disaffection they feel by being marginalised and 'poor' within the structural conditions of inequality and poverty that exists. Some of these actions also provided them with the means to engage in activities that are promoted within late modernity – to consume, to have a sense of individuality, and in this way to have a role, and a value (Young, 2006).

It could also be argued that some forms of involuntary edgework, such as mental illness, may be underpinned by the social changes that have occurred due to the process of modernity (such as theories on addiction by both Giddens, 1991 and Reith, 2004 illustrate for example). In a recent medical review, Patton & Viner (2007:1130) identify that there has been a '*modern rise in psychosocial disorders*' such as depression, substance use, and antisocial behaviour in young people. This they attribute to the 'mismatch' that now exists in transitional phases over the life course, with people increasingly enmeshed in a state of suspended animation, pursuing youth 'lifestyles' and excitement in an ongoing state of individualistic consumption, characteristic of late modern secular societies – the anomie of the rationalised iron cage, identified in classic studies such as that by Weber (1930), and Durkheim (1952). And therefore the actions – such as being violent towards others – that occur when someone experiences involuntary edgework (such as being assaulted by someone they know), may also be underpinned by the pressures and reality of the cultural and social existence of life in late modernity as for example, Cohen & Taylor (1992) identified – or rather the constant need to escape it.

This '*rationale of irrational behaviour*' means many *individual* actions that appeared to cause the transitions into homelessness presented here, can be understood as simultaneously being *structurally* generated. These actions both stem from, and then have, structural implications – they feed back into the discursive knowledge that exists about the outcomes this leads to and how they are viewed and addressed socially, and also directly affect the material reality the person experiencing them is in. Therefore both minimalist and maximalist account of homelessness (Jacobs et al, 1999) are correct as the new orthodoxy asserts (Fitzpatrick, 2005) – it is individual actions, deviance often, that causes homelessness but both these actions and an actual loss of housing is still generated by broad structural forces that they are embedded within.

The universality of edgework

This process of negotiating with irrational actions is something that everyone may be experiencing in the increasingly individualised and liberalised conditions of late modernity. Everyone engages in some actions that may appear irrational if they are purely understood as a means to avoid risk. Actions can also have contradictory outcomes – an action that can lead to positive effects can also have negatives – for example exercise can lead to fitness or injury. People are increasingly being informed (through systems of governance, and the media) of risks they face, and of their responsibility to manage these risks. This includes, for example, the risk fatty food has to their health, the need to recycle due to environmental concerns, to avoid excessive alcohol use, that people should exercise certain amounts a week. Yet most people still eat fatty foods at times (with obesity at record levels), do not recycle everything they could, (environmental concerns continue to escalate), may drink excessive alcohol (as media stories of binge drinking illustrate). In the developed west health problems such as depression, drug use, and sexually transmitted diseases are on the rise among the young – a tipping point of 'diseases of excess', as opportunities for such actions, and lifestyles that promote actions that may lead to these health problems, increase due to structural social forces (Patton & Viner, 2007; Reith, 2004).

Therefore, within the conditions of late modernity, it is asserted here, everyone is increasingly becoming 'edgeworkers' to some extent. In a time of excess people have to constantly weigh the risk that each activity brings alongside the experiential pleasure or escape it also brings, with individualised responsibility to do so placed on them. And many people are going over the edge – as the obesity and alcohol related death figures are testament to. These actions may not appear to be as extreme cases of negotiating risk, of engaging in edgework, as those experienced here by those making a transition through homelessness, however the process that underpins them can be understood as the same. Therefore we are *not* fundamentally different, showing minimalist accounts to be wrong, although grounded in truth. The difference lies in the amount of resources that are available to buffer the risks and traumas that people face as they navigate their life course in the structural conditions of late modern society and therefore returns to maximalist structural accounts, incorporating the entire social system. Resources to buffer such risks are also structurally generated within power dynamics, but on individual micro-levels, has profound effect on the actions, choices, lifestyles and identities people then have.

The actions people take may not be entirely rational as a response to managing risk, yet they are often rational as an emotional response to the material situation they are in, and the interactions they have to engage in, within certain contexts. They are rational perhaps as a means to escape or resist the pressure of having to negotiate and manage the reflexive knowledge, choices, and risks people now perceive they have. These actions may also be understood as actions that have become possible or endemic due to the structural conditions of late modernity – the rampant consuming and excess of food that leads to obesity, for example. Yet for those whose edgework involves actions that are close to the edge of clearly defined societal norms of accepted behaviour, the similarity in the actions between them and others, and what motivates these actions, may not be recognised and may lead to stigma, and further exclusion for them. But increasingly many people are going over the edge in one way or another, negotiating with these proliferating 'edges' as they make individual choices in the management of the risks they face and lifestyle they have – and this myriad of options and choices are only possible due to the current structural reality they operate within, the reality of the risk society (Beck, 1992).

Edgework, risks and resources

This negotiation of risk and the forms of risk taking people may experience, are tied to the resources they have. Those who have a low level of resources and engage in edgework may be perceived to be different from and 'other' to the supposedly responsible mainstream, yet many people engage in what could be considered deviant acts at times, if their actions were entirely rationally played out as a means to avoid risk (such as drug use). The people 'over the edge' become the feared and imagined others (Young, 2006). However it is asserted here that their actions must also be understood as actions underpinned by the structural conditions people operate within. These actions are damaging, and can be 'anti-social' on an individual level. They cause real, individual suffering to many people – but this may stem from collectively experienced structurally generated conditions, and means with which to manage and control them may need to recognise this to succeed.

So to summarise, William, Tommy, Claire, Brian and Val's cases highlighted the process that can occur as people make transitions into homelessness. Their social, economic, and human capital became increasingly eroded as they become 'alcoholics', 'drug addicts', and had to rely on the social welfare system. Often this reliance was not only to address their lack of accommodation, but also the other problems in their life, such as addiction, that underpinned this situation. It was individual acts that may appear irrational – excessive alcohol or drug use for example – that they cited as the cause of their homelessness. However it is argued here that these acts can also be understood as part of a broader structural context, and also of the emotional landscape this context has created. These individual factors, often cited as the cause of homelessness, come to define how the people experiencing it are discursively understood and labelled in popular and political discourse (Liddiard, 1999).

This is the process that occurred in these transitions into homelessness. Whilst this reflects what is already known about routes into homelessness from previous studies the theoretical interpretation develops this further, and embeds this homelessness within broad structural contexts. Their material situation led to increased edgework, which eventually led to their resources being depleted to the point they had to rely on the state for accommodation. Their material situation then continued to deteriorate. This interaction of edgework and homelessness is discussed in Section 4, before going on to present the 'stressed' perspective on homelessness and causation, developed in this study.

4. Over the edge – Edgework and homelessness

'Trips to the edge', away from normal social interactions and actions, trips away from everyday life and routine, can bring relief, excitement, or escape. However they also bring risk, the risk of not returning to this ordered routine from which ontological security is generated, and of going over the edge (Cohen & Taylor, 1992). The extent to which people can safely engage in different forms of edgework and the actual risk this edgework entails is dependent on the resources they have. Forms of edgework that Lyng first identified, such as sky-diving, are likely to be out of reach of those with few resources of social or financial capital. Whatever socio-economic position an individual has however, their motivation for voluntary risk taking may be the same, whether they gain escape or transcendence through extreme sports, the use of substances, criminal acts or emotive relationships and interactions. Furthermore, involuntary forms of edgework people experience such as grief and bereavement, mental illness, and victimisation, may be harder to manage – to negotiate the edge – for those with low levels of resources, and low levels of resilience, even though they could occur in anyone's life.

If someone is materially 'outside' of normal society, they may then become further excluded, culturally (Young, 2006). It has been argued here that some of the edgework discussed by the people studied, could be understood as ways to escape the material reality they were in, and the low social status and lack of resources they had. It could also provide them with the means to escape from or control the trauma they had experienced. In this way it was triggered by the structured context, and in an ongoing cycle, these structures continued to exacerbate this situation by triggering individual actions that acted to embed these people within circumstances of marginality, poverty, and trauma. They had to attempt to manage or control the effect of their edgework individually – come back from the edge – and this could be intensely difficult, psychologically. The following cases of Francesca and Helen are used to illustrate this.

Francesca's edgework as control

Francesca was living in supported accommodation when she was first interviewed. She was 28 years old. Francesca cited drug use as the cause of her homelessness. She had become homeless after being evicted from a socially rented tenancy, due to drug use. She then slept rough, with her partner who was also abusive towards her. She left them when she was admitted to hospital due to illness, and then moved into a hostel There she began to work in prostitution with the other women. Eventually she attempted suicide and was moved to supported accommodation after this where she was first interviewed. She still found it intensely difficult to cease using drugs, however, as it was actually a way to take some control over her life, ontologically, and to escape the material and subjective 'reality' she was in:

> *Because of everything that's happened to me when I was younger [abuse, violence, rough sleeping, working in prostitution] it's about finding coping strategies because for so many years, it was just...taking drugs, get absolutely mad with it and then not have to think about it. And now that's not the case, I'm not taking drugs, so – I don't know how to cope and I freely admit I don't. So I'm either sobbing my heart out or I'm screaming like a maniac.*
>
> (Francesca, 28)

In this way, actions such as substance use could be understood as not only a form of escape, but as a way of taking some *control* over her situation. This could be a way to gain control through individual actions, over the emotional pain she was experiencing. The alternative for her was to go over the edge in another way – to psychologically break down. The paradox inherent in this is that these actions (the edgework engaged in) only ended up leading further over the edge in other ways. This triggered more problems, and created more trauma and vulnerability she then had to reconcile with. The edge, back over into 'normal society', receded further, with each difficult situation and divestment passage experienced. This spiralling effect is explored in more detail in the next chapter, and here Helen's case is used as another example of this.

Helen's cycle of edgework

Helen had experienced repeated homelessness over her life. Her home life as a child included many violent incidents between her parents. She had left home and school aged 14. She had then spent many years living and working in peripheral circumstances, such as staying with friends, and working in casual employment, such as factories, shops and cleaning. She had also been addicted to heroin and alcohol for most of her life, had experienced numerous abusive relationships, and had worked in prostitution. For most of the last decade she had lived between partner's houses, refuges for women, temporary accommodation, rehabs, and her own tenancies, which she had then moved from once more. Her children had been taken into care due to her chaotic lifestyle. Often it was distressing incidents (such as being assaulted, or finding out her children were to be taken into care permanently) that triggered actions such as her alcohol and drug use. This then led to her making a transition back into homelessness:

> *I know why I ended up put out of [my house], cause I got a social worker came up telling me my daughters weren't coming back, so I suppose that was my way of escaping. It was the wrong way but anyway, I ended up mad with drink, drugs. Seven days a week.*

(Helen, 35)

In this way many of the people studied here became trapped in a cycle of engaging in edgework, as the experiential ontological means they had to handle what actually happened to them in the structural reality they were in. This then further exacerbated the marginality they were experiencing within that structural reality. Through these acts they could assert some control as individuals, or attempt to escape and manage the effect of the traumatic incidents they had experienced. However this edgework was also what often appeared to be the cause of their homelessness. In 'going over the edge' – becoming addicts, mentally ill – they only became embedded further in a negative material situation, where they felt they lacked control. The few means they had to assert their individuality, or manage risk, within this reality, remained the same. So too did the *very need* to control and manage risk individually that they felt they had. Therefore they continued to fall back on the only means of escape they felt they had – back over the edge.

Understanding homelessness and causation

The homelessness studied here was 'caused' by an interrelation of individual factors and trigger points, occurring within a certain structural context whereby people lacked resources to negate it, as recognised in the 'new orthodoxy' to understanding homelessness (Fitzpatrick, 2005). However this analysis goes further, and asserts that this structural context also generated the *conditions that lead to the individual factors* seen as causing homelessness. There is an emotional and material context that means these actions became rational responses to the structural situation people were in, on a micro-level. The motivation for edgework may be generated by this reality of life in late modernity, as Lyng argues, and this is then exacerbated further by the pressures of being 'poor', stigmatised, of being surrounded by trauma, difficulty, and poor material conditions, in a world of increasing inequality. This is coupled with having few resources to negate the ongoing trauma and difficulty they faced.

The resources someone has will affect the capacity to negotiate with risk they have, when something goes wrong in their lives (Furlong & Cartmel, 1997). Individual factors that cause homelessness (addiction or bereavement for example) could occur in anyone's life. It is asserted here that the key difference in circumstance that means these events lead to homelessness, is when people lack the resources of human, social, material, or financial capital to *negate the effects* of these individually experienced negative events. The motivation for people to engage in edgework can be rationalised, but depending on the material situation someone is in, and the access to resources they have, the *outcome* of their edgework will be very different.

Ensuring that there is an adequate supply of affordable housing, of the right kind and in the right locations, will assist in reducing structural forces that may add to homelessness as maximalist accounts would assert. However the complexity of homelessness of the type studied here, means that housing alone is unlikely to solve the problem (Franklin, 1999). It is these interrelated factors of social network, resources, edgework, and trauma that also need to be considered and addressed. The role that the state has in both addressing and constructing the nature of the problems it is addressing is also important.

In the transitions studied here the people had all, at some point, come to rely on the state as a source of both social and financial support. They also became defined as 'homeless people', a term that can be stigmatising, and indicates being outside of mainstream society. The individual factors that cause homelessness may occur in anyone's lives.

The resources people have, will underpin the ability they have to manage these events, without going visibly over the edge. And these resources are distributed through the structures and institutions of society that exist. Anyone may go over the edge, most people negotiate with edges at points in their life, but the risk of going over increases if they lack resources to buffer the risks this edgework brings. The focus of the state goes onto them and then may render them as a visibly 'different' group, however this 'difference' may in some cases be imagined, and certainly is a construct of complex social forces.

5. Homelessness, causation and individual actions – 'Stressed'

The cause of homelessness is recognised as certain structural conditions, whereby individual factors and events interact to trigger homelessness (Fitzpatrick, 2005). This has been reaffirmed by this research. However to begin to go beyond this, what is called here the 'stressed' perspective on homelessness and causation is developed. This term is used as an amalgamation of the key concepts that underpin this perspective – structuration, realism and edgework. This is also a play on words, indicating how it is asserted here, that actions underpinned by the 'stress' of late modern life may play a significant role in the how transitional phases develop.

This stressed perspective on homelessness and causation has been developed by examining how certain events may have been triggered within the structured reality the people studied operated in and led to their homelessness. The role that individual actions (agency) and the society people operate within (structure) had in triggering these events is critically assessed. So this perspective represents the outcome of a fusion of structuration theory, realist ontology, and the concept of edgework being applied to this analysis.

Agency, structure and causation

Clearly the edgework (such as drug use or mental illness) that 'caused' the homelessness studied here, could occur in anyone's life and does not necessarily always lead to homelessness. It is argued here that it is the (structurally generated) resources people have access to that allows some people more protection and resilience from the risks traumatic incidents bring over the life course. If these events do occur in their life, some people have the resources to maintain a stable and positive social status, whilst they recover from this trauma. In this way they can avoid further divestment passages in their life course – they return from the edge and negotiate with it successfully. Even if they do go over, (become an addict for example), this may remain hidden, so long as they retain a predominantly integrative social position until they resolve this. In this way they retain the appearance of someone who can manage their own life course, as a liberal active citizen, even if they are engaged in some of the same activities (drug use, alcohol use, or are experiencing intense psychological distress) as those who do not retain this status.

For example, if someone with high levels of social, economic, and human capital, leaves a partner suddenly, they may immediately be able to move into housing of their own. They may move temporarily to live with friends or family who also have high levels of resources (and as such may have their own house with a spare room). In doing so they may also access a degree of emotional support that assists them manage excessive alcohol use or depression that may accompany the stress of their relationship breakdown and sudden divestment passage. Due to their own access to resources of human and financial capital (through their employment and income) they may have no concerns about obtaining their own housing again in the future (such as a private rented tenancy). They will be able to continue their integrative passages and maintain the positive social status, and ontological security this provides, over their life course, due to the high levels of social, economic and human capital they have. This capital acts as a buffer to the individual problems anyone may experience in their lives. This outcome may occur despite engaging in the same forms of edgework, such as excessive alcohol use or depression, as a response to the trauma of their relationship breakdown. Someone who lacked these resources may have to rely on the state at some point to access accommodation and social support. The paradox that has been found in this study is that then rather than this system acting to buffer them from further divestment, it was often at this point that their lives spiralled further away from secure and normative circumstances.

Those who have to rely on the state then become a 'homeless person' and they may also become physically segregated, by being housed in temporary accommodation, or institutions such as rehabs. The focus goes onto addressing the individual factors cited as the cause of their homelessness. The individual factors *seen as causing homelessness* can occur in anyone's life. Homelessness could happen, in principle, to anyone. Many of the people studied here had had relatively settled lives at some point in their histories. However complex processes led to them becoming people on the edge of society and marginalised socio-economically. That most of them had never experienced a particularly high level of resources was likely to have compounded this affect, but they had usually had their own housing prior to becoming homeless, and it was the trauma, edgework, and need to escape the situation they were in that actually led to them becoming homeless. This was often as act of agency, to try to take control, leaving a chaotic or traumatic phase in their life, such as leaving an abusive partner, or a mental breakdown.

Therefore structuralist maximalist accounts that focus on the housing supply that exists are on one hand correct, however minimalist accounts, focussing on individual actions are also evident but these individual acts can be linked back to broad structural forces of the risk society. It is the emotional landscape alongside the material context that generates it, that needs to be taken into account and the broader landscape of the community, social networks, and social forces that operate alongside, and attached to, the housing or accommodation circumstance someone is in. People may (and do) become homeless even when adequate housing is available for them. Val for example had housing and refused to return there once she was admitted to hospital, because she knew she could no longer live there alone. Elizabeth had given up her tenancy and moved into a friend's house before she had left this and become homeless. Tommy left his family and house, and could not be accommodated by friends, due to his manic depression. Acts of agency clearly play a role in these transitions, but these are acts embedded in the structural and social reality they occur in and the very real pressures, anguish and need to 'escape' that these people felt within this reality.

People may become homeless despite having enough financial capital or state support to have their own housing. This may occur due to their very need to assert their individuality, or to escape from the reality they are in, a structured reality that the housing they live in plays a large part in constituting (Easthope, 2004).

Stressed – A perspective on homelessness and causation

It is important to highlight that this perspective has been informed by the ontological and epistemological approach outlined in Chapter 2. Realist ontology, as it has been defined here, and structuration theory, have been fused to develop this framework. This perspective incorporates the following key tenets, as a means to understand how individual actions can appear to lead to homelessness, but are actually structurally grounded:

1. This perspective is concerned with material and social reality, a reality that is structurally generated and that all individuals operate

within and 'actual' events happen. It has been argued that this structural reality has generated conditions whereby actions that encapsulate edgework occur or are motivated, as a form of escape or resistance from it in an ongoing cycle. The resources people have within these conditions, that they can use to negotiate with or engage in edgework, are not equally distributed. Social problems do occur; they are real. People do actually lose their housing; experience traumatic incidents; use drugs, for example. However:

2. How these actions and outcomes are interpreted and understood, and the resources that people have to engage in or negate them, will lead to very different outcomes for some people than others, even though they may experience the same individual 'real' problems.

3. For those who go on to become visibly homeless, or need to rely on the state to access resources, their individual actions become the focus of why they are in that situation. The broad structural underpinning (which has led to increased alienation and isolation) to why people engaged in those acts in the first instance becomes obscured. This broad structural underpinning is the reality of life in late modernity.

4. And, a crucial point for the rest of this study, as this structural underpinning has not necessarily changed once people gain 'surface level' resources from the state to resolve their homelessness, it then once more generates the same need to engage in edgework that people initially had, and the same risk of homelessness occurring in their life goes on. The fundamental structural precursors and context that led to their homelessness (and edgework) remain the same.

Furthermore this material reality that someone is in is also particularly embodied in the condition and location of the housing they can access, which in turn does crucially return to housing policy. Economic, housing and interpersonal structures all intersect to influence the material reality an individual experiences, which will in turn affect their actions, resilience and circumstances over their life course.

This was illustrated in the cases of Val, William, and Connor. Individual problems may also occur among those with a high level of resources, but it is asserted here it is easier for them to be *hidden or negated* in their lives. People with resources can engage in or experience edgework and be more likely to return from this edge – some may not, addiction and mental illness for example, do affect people across the social spectrum. In some cases even people who once had a high level of resources may find them eroded to the point they too become homeless and rely on the state. But it is still those whose socio-economic position has always been one of having few resources that are more *at risk* of such an outcome, and have fewer means to assert themselves as individuals within these conditions. And the key point here is that the motivation or cause of such acts of edgework that can lead to homelessness can be understood as the actual conditions of life in late modernity, and the reality this brings. These conditions can be distinguished from economic and housing structures, such as markets, housing costs, welfare systems, and employment levels, as being socio-structural, relating to interpersonal relationships and also cultural and lifestyle factors that appear to be individual but are constrained and generated within the structures that make up the society people operate within. Together in a complex web they generate the reality people operate in, and underpin the actions they take as individuals.

A lack of resources cannot just be reduced to or explained by economic or housing structures alone. Demographic and cultural change and how it is to ontologically experience them, also play a part. Collectively these are the socio-structural forces that motivate and create more opportunities for the 'individual' problem factors that can lead to homelessness – addiction, relationship breakdown, depression, the breaking away from the unbearable 'stress' that people were experiencing. Structural conditions generate individualised problems, in a feedback loop involving complex, multiple casual mechanisms, that are experienced on different ontological and structural 'stratas'.

The specificity of homelessness

So ultimately the management of risks, such as homelessness, people face, is still underpinned by their access to resources within the structural conditions of the society they live in. This is not to say some people with a high level of resources will never become homeless, or that people at risk of homelessness will not sometimes be able to negate this risk. Some people do not have the social, economic, or human capital to negate the effects of these individually experienced problems themselves and have to rely on the state to provide them with this support. These groups may then be defined as also culturally distinct from the mainstream. In this way the differentiation between those who have to access or be targeted by the state explicitly, to negotiate with risk, and those who do not, may be becoming the key cleavage of stratification in society in the conditions of late modernity – a key form of differentiation between groups.

Indeed the people studied here did often engage in deviant or damaging acts, but a rationale for this, due to the emotional and material landscape they operated within, has been described. The actual difference is not that people engage in these acts of edgework, but the ability they have to hide or buffer the effects of this, and the risks they face, with the resources of human, social, or financial capital they have. Poverty may generate the conditions that lead to some forms of edgework becoming a rational choice, and also exacerbates the stigma that accompanies these actions. The liberal individualistic conditions of late modernity has generated the motivation to engage in acts of edgework that people have, but not the equal distribution of the resources required to come back from the edge when people do.

Policy measures and housing supply are important to address homelessness. The point is that they are not the *only* mechanisms that need to be understood to address it. In some cases this policy creates the material reality people operate within that may trigger these problematic individual actions. So for example as Fitzpatrick & Stephens (1999) argue, social housing allocation based on need rather than desert led to the residualisation and decline of certain areas. Those people who are not in greatest need (have family they can stay with for example) can wait longer to obtain adequate social housing. Those who cannot wait as they have no where else to live will be more likely to take the first tenancy offered. This may well be in an area with a high density of less popular social housing. Therefore there will also be a high concentration of the more 'needy' in society in that one location, with ensuing vulnerabilities, and low levels of social, human and economic capital being generated by the community there, and less opportunities for them to move on in the future. Dench, Gavron & Young (2006) have also criticised the unintended consequences of the welfare state and housing policies based on individual need. For example, it may be rational for people to live alone rather than with a partner, as they are provided with more benefits in this way. This can put pressure on their relationships and family life however. Dench and colleagues also (controversially) argue that this policy of allocation due to need, led to the dispersal of traditional working class communities, who had less 'need' than new migrant groups, in the East End of London, which in turn led to community resentment between these groups and fragmentation, despite the intention being (of the middle class liberals that introduced this policy) that this was that it was a more just distribution of scare resources to do so due to need rather than 'desert' or local connection.

The feminist theorist Selma Sevenhuijsen (2003:182) argues that in the face of structural change, '*society as a whole is faced with designing a new social infrastructure of care'*. As is further illustrated in the next chapter, it may indeed be that fundamental changes to the infrastructure of social life are needed to address the 'root' cause of the marginality studied here – the increasing inequality, individualisation and alienation apparent in these lives.

4
Being a Homeless Person

1. Transitions through homelessness

So how was 'being homeless' actually experienced by the people studied here? For the majority it involved a cycle of housing insecurity – staying with friends, relatives, and in hostels, and other forms of temporary accommodation paid for by Housing Benefit and arranged by workers in the homeless system. For some this was a short term experience, lasting a year or so before they gained their own tenancy once more. For others, this could span ten or 20 years, as part of a life interspersed with spells in hospital, prison, and residential drug or alcohol rehabilitation centres. For many (17) it also involved periods sleeping rough, sometimes alone, and out of sight, up alleyways and in stairwells, or with others in the same situation, under bridges and in parks.

These different phases and circumstances bled into each other, mirroring other studies that have highlighted the fluidity and complexity of homeless pathways (Fitzpatrick, 2000; Rosengard et al, 2002) with some people sleeping rough for a few nights, then obtaining a place in a hostel or Bed & Breakfast, and perhaps then being moved to more 'appropriate' accommodation such as a rehab or supported accommodation when they became available. In this intervening time they may have stayed with friends for a couple of nights and perhaps back to sleeping on the street or a hostel again. Eighteen of the 28 had experienced repeated episodes of homelessness throughout their lives – obtaining and moving into a tenancy and then becoming homeless once more, through another distinct divestment stage. Many survived each day as it came, and over the years, homelessness and peripheral housing circumstances had become deeply imbued in their lives.

Living in homeless hostels

Almost all (25) had spent some time living in large hostels and temporary accommodation, such as Bed & Breakfasts. Two had not actually lost their tenancies, but were referred to services for homeless people after being served eviction notices. Overwhelmingly, and as found in previous studies (Rosengard, 2001; Franklin, 1999) living in hostels was described negatively. The rooms and the conditions were often cramped, dirty, and insecure. Even when the conditions were good people often felt threatened, depressed, and 'out of' society for actually being accommodated there. The quote from Frank illustrates the conditions he described:

You just had a wee room, with your bed, and your wardrobe. People were throwing urine out the windows, and God, it was smelling. It was really dirty.

(Frank, 39)

Some has spent ten or more years of their lives moving between such accommodation. Programmes to improve and upgrade hostels are being introduced, and are clearly important – however it must be remembered that stretched over time as these lives and transitions were, legacies of past mistakes or problems cannot easily be erased simply through new rooms and conditions being provided. There was also an ontological and emotional affect generated through these conditions, which Francesca here describes.

Francesca's experience of living in a hostel

Francesca had started sleeping rough after her, and her partner, (who were both addicted to heroin) were evicted from their flat. After her health failed she was admitted to hospital. This was also an opportunity for her to leave her partner, who was abusive towards her. Once she was ready to leave hospital a room in a hostel was found for her. In the quote below she describes her experience of living in a hostel:

That homeless hostel broke me. Emotionally and physically. I believe that they break so many people. They are hell on earth, just the whole environment in general, the whole ramming, like chicken farms, ramming all of the chickens all into one building as many as you can, these are people, these are people with feelings and emotions, and a lot of them might not act like it, but, at the end of the day they are.

(Francesca, 28)

The negativity of living in hostels related not only to the material conditions there, but also the effect that this environment had ontologically – the hostel 'broke her, emotionally and physically'. Living in hostels is often felt by people to expose them to greater risk than staying with friends, or even than sleeping rough. These risks included being exposed to increased drug or alcohol use, being assaulted or victimised, and their mental and physical health deteriorating. This was attributed by them in the interviews to the concentration of people with many vulnerabilities and problems living in the one place, and the sense of having no 'control' over their life they felt they had there. For example, rather than improve, Francesca's situation continued to deteriorate once she was housed in a hostel. Her drug use increased, and she started working in prostitution with the other women she had met there. She then attempted suicide. She was admitted to hospital once more and then moved into a rehab. From there she moved into supported accommodation. She was living in this supported accommodation when she took part in the first interview and felt that her life and health was improving. By the final interview she was living in her own flat once more.

So a central consideration in this study is this continued identification of the potentially 'dehumanising' effect that living in temporary accommodation and being homeless can have, particularly when this accommodation is in poor condition (which has been flagged up in previous studies also (Neale, 1997; Rosengard, 2001; Hutson, 1999). The stigma and difficulty of the material reality they were in, once they became homeless could also affect people ontologically in profound ways. After Francesca moved into a small supported accommodation project, she began to feel more positive about her life:

About a fortnight after I moved in here, after that I'd say I started feeling more positive. I could start getting into, that there is life, and there is light at the end of that tunnel.

Transitions through homelessness

What is distinct about this study is that it tracked what actually happened to people, over time, as they attempted to resolve homelessness, rather than presenting a 'snap shot' of homelessness at a single point in someone's lives as previous studies have often been (Pickering et al,

2003). As noted in Chapter 2, one year is not a long time in a life time, however this is still one of the first studies to follow people over (an albeit short) time in their life, qualitatively exploring the process of resettlement and continuing homelessness that ensued.

At the point of the first interview ten of the 28 had their own housing (all Housing Association tenancies). All were in close contact with support workers whose role it was to assist them resolve homelessness long term. Two of these ten had managed to avoid eviction and becoming homeless, due to this support, and the remaining eight had recently moved into their own housing after a period of being homeless. For some their homelessness had lasted more than ten years before they had regained this housing.

Over the year of the study, nine of the 18 who were actually homeless (in temporary accommodation, for example) at the first interview had moved into their own flats. Their experiences of making this acute move, alongside the longer-term experiences of the first cohort, were explored.

Finally, nine were homeless at the end of the research (eight remained so throughout the study and one became homeless again). Over the course of the research those who remained homeless at the end had all moved between different forms of accommodation, such as staying in supported accommodation, hostels, Bed & Breakfasts, sleeping rough, staying with friends or relatives, being in rehabs, prison, or hospital. By the final interview three of the nine who remained homeless were living in supported accommodation, three were staying with friends or relatives, one was living in a hostel, one was in prison, and one was in rehab.

These figures are not intended to provide a quantifiable analysis of the number of people who may or may not make a transition through homelessness. However the three distinct circumstances – of remaining homeless, moving out of homelessness, and of resettling over time, after being homeless, are analysed here to paint a picture of the human complexity and reality of such transitions.

Transitional phases

To develop this 'picture' three transitional routes, that appeared to represent the transitions taken, are used to explore them. These transitional routes have been developed using the concept of integrative and divestment passages (Ezzy, 2001). These routes are:

1. Spirals of divestment passages
2. Developing integrative passages
3. Flip-flopping effect of integration diverging

2. Spirals of divestment passages

Different 'passages' lead people throughout their live from their past to their future, in an ongoing, interconnected web. Divestment passages occur when transitional change leads to a social status that separates someone from what would normally be the expected, or 'positive' outcome (Ezzy, 2001). Divestment passages are what happen when things 'go wrong'. These passages lead to a negative social status, relative to the position someone was in before. The paradox of divestment passages is that once they occur, they may then spiral into more and more divestment – feeding into and exacerbating each other.

As was highlighted in the previous section, accessing accommodation for people who were homeless did not necessarily trigger a more integrative phase in the transitions through homelessness studied here (and the potentially damaging effect of some accommodation (Hutson, 1999) and long term entrenchment into homelessness (Fitzpatrick, 2000) has been identified previously). The same mechanisms that influenced the transitions *into* homelessness – social networks and interactions; edgework and trauma; a low level of resources – continued to affect people's lives when they were homeless. In Francesca's case for example, she moved into a hostel, the conditions there and interactions she engaged in led to opportunities for increasing her drug use, and working in prostitution. Both could be rationalised as ways to cope with the situation she was in on a micro-level – to earn money and to 'block' out her circumstances. However as her social status and material reality continued to spiral downwards, the emotional and physical effect of this led to more divestment. Eventually she had reached the 'bottom', ontologically separated from status – she had attempted suicide.

For the majority, their situation continued to spiral downwards in this way after they became homeless. Many felt that the conditions they experienced once they became homeless acted to continue triggering more problems and divestment in their life, as Brian described. Brian had been employed, had his own flat, and then lost this due to debt and alcohol use. He slept in his car for a while, and began using drugs heavily once he was in a hostel. By now he had also left his employment. He then entered a rehab some time later and was interviewed for the first time in a supported accommodation:

You're standing there and there is no where you can go, no way back, you get stuck in the hostels and you can either go down as far as you can go and then you die, or you can get back up. I had to go away down to the

> *bottom before anybody would do anything for me, I had to go away down*
> *before anyone would help.*
>
> (Brian, 35)

Their social status continued to be separated from normative, integrating routes. Their material situation often deteriorated, and they were living in poor quality temporary accommodation with little income, resources, or possessions. Often the edgework, such as drug use they engaged in, increased. They were existing, day-to-day.

Although all of the people studied here had experienced these spiralling divestment passages at some point, the transitions of the nine who remained homeless at the end of the research were particularly illustrative of this ongoing spiralling effect.

Remaining homeless – Over the edge

Nine people were homeless at the end of the research. This group consisted of two women and seven men, with an age range of 35 to 60. Those who remained homeless throughout the research did represent people particularly experiencing spirals of divestment, and often that had done so for many years. They had few, if any, resources of human, social, or economic capital, and were in a long-term cycle of homelessness. They had all spent periods of their lives in prison and hospital, they were barred for local shops and welfare services, some had visible scars, they had chronic health and behavioural problems, they often described feeling acutely stigmatised and 'outside' of mainstream society. They also engaged in extreme edgework, alcohol and drug use, suicide attempts, risky behaviour such as criminal acts or violence towards others. So in the structural context they operated within these were people who were acutely over the edge, both materially, and also negotiating at the extreme edge of normative social behaviour.

Frank's story

Frank was 39 and living in supported accommodation at the first interview. He had spent most of his life in and out of prison and staying with relatives or partners. He had been in borstals and care home's as a child. He was addicted to heroin. Over the course of the study Frank was evicted from the supported accommodation where he had been living at the first interview. He was evicted due to ongoing drug use, staying overnight with a partner, and threatening behaviour:

> *It ended up they took me to the door [he was asked to leave supported*
> *accommodation]. I was using drugs again. My relationship [with my*

partner] went wrong, see when you've been on drugs for years and you've not had a relationship, you're not prepared – relationships are hard. I found the emotional side of that hard. They [support workers] tell you not to get involved in relationships for at least a couple of years after you're clean, but I'm a man. It's difficult.

(Frank, 39)

He then moved to a large hostel. His drug use continued to increase and he began shoplifting every day to fund his habit. By the third interview he was in prison for shoplifting:

I feel I came so far and now I've come so far backwards. I know, I need to get into a rehab. This is the third time I've tried to get myself sorted though. I prefer myself clean. The pressures though, relationships, just, it's hard.

Frank's situation illustrates this ongoing spiral of divestment that some experienced. They adopted individual survival techniques in the day-to-day actions and interactions they engaged in, such as shoplifting and using substances. Often these survival techniques were the 'norm' for them. In doing so however they only continued to be further separated from integration to mainstream society. The emotional complexity of each day that passed also had to be taken into account. In Hutson's (1999) review of homeless accommodation and support she highlighted that there can be a lack of fit between the lives of people accessing these services and the rules and regulations imposed upon them there. This not only highlights the need for flexibility but also the importance of informal networks and support to make a transition out of homelessness (explored in more detail in Chapter 6). People will enter into relationships, will be grappling with the past they have had, and with many emotions as they make their transitions. Living in homelessness accommodation, they had little to do to occupy their time. The intensity of this, within the structural reality they operate within, could lead to actions, such as ongoing drug use, as a means of escape.

The edgework engaged in was not always voluntary risk taking either. These were people on the edge of society in many ways and were also victimised by others. This victimisation occurred both symbolically and literally. For example they were banned from or moved on from public places due to their appearance, and often had been assaulted by others (such as one interviewee who was badly beaten by a group of young people just prior to the first interview). They personified the image of the homeless person as 'outsider', as both vulnerable and threatening. They did have temporary periods where things improved, and some people who had experienced long term homelessness such as this, did make a transition out of homelessness. Therefore once someone is 'over the edge' it is not inevitable that they stay there. What did emerge however was the immense complexity and effort required to even begin to come back over. And the difficulty in then moving far from it.

The actual provision made for people once they are homeless and reliant on the services and institutions of the social welfare system may create the conditions whereby these spirals of divestment continue. For example, the pressure and tension of living in hostels, coupled with the drug and alcohol use that was endemic there, could lead to violence between the residents. This could lead to them being evicted from this accommodation, with nowhere else to go, and lead to them sleeping rough. In this way they became further marginalised and alienated. Or, as other studies have highlighted (Hutson, 1999) they could experience intense vulnerability and victimisation in temporary accommodation, such as being attacked or sexually assaulted by other residents, as the next story outlines.

This situation was created by the very condition of being homeless, which further exacerbated their vulnerability. Both the material conditions they experienced, and how these conditions and the events that occurred there, affected them, has to be considered, to understand the actions that they engaged in when they were homeless – a rationale for irrational behaviour. Franklin (1999) notes that need to support people to 'reintegrate' as they make transitions out of homelessness – that obtaining housing is not enough to make this transition alone. As has been highlighted here, it can be the damage inflicted by the very experience of homelessness that people need support to move on from.

Once they were homeless many went completely 'over the edge' leading to a 'crisis point' in their lives – this included increasing their substance use to overdose levels, having mental breakdowns, attempting suicide, and engaging in, or being victims of life threatening violence. Bess for example, was one of many that described highly traumatic incidents occurring once they were in accommodation for homeless people:

I took an OD, it was like a proper cry for help, do you know what I mean? And after that I thought, you can get help now, and you'll be alright. I was in a hostel, and they [staff] found me because they did a room check. A guy tried to rape me as I was blanking out, and there was like a com-

*motion going on in the hostel, and then the staff came round, and found
me, and called an ambulance.*

(Bess, 25)

This situation was often exacerbated within the material reality that the
accommodation they had been provided with as homeless people constituted. Their situation then continued in this spiral of divestment, often
until they reached a point of complete destitution, or a life-threatening
situation, such as attempting suicide, occurred. They reached a 'breaking'
point. This was when their situation then changed once more. Sometimes
they move into a rehab, were admitted to hospital, and moved into
another supported accommodation, for example. For some it was at one
of these points their lives began to take what appeared to be more integrative passages – or at least this was the point that they described retrospectively as when their lives began to improve. This only occurred after
they felt they had reached the 'bottom' however. How many other
people may have reached this 'bottom' but in their case it did lead to
death, and their stories cannot be told?

3. Developing integrative passages

Integrative transitions occur when transitional phases lead to a clearly
delineated new social status that adheres to 'taken for granted' normative assumptions about the social status someone should have. In this
way transitions occur that continue integrating someone to the society
they operate within. For the people here, gaining their own housing
was clearly a key outcome required for them to adhere to normative
ideas about how integrative passages should develop. Normative
assumptions are that homeless people will want to obtain their own
housing and that once someone moves into their own housing they
are no longer homeless, and have 'reintegrated' to society. Transitions
are rarely so one dimensional however, and instead incorporate structural, material, social, psychological and in some cases (such as those
that ceased drug use) physiological change occurring as they develop.
Nineteen of the people studied were living in their own housing (all
rented and paid for through Housing Benefit, and Housing Association
tenancies) at the end of the research, and so objectively *appeared* to
have made successful transitions out of homelessness.

Obtaining their own tenancies was part of a long process, occurring
after they made many 'micro' integrative transitions. These 'micro'
transitions included moving to semi-supported accommodation from

one that was staffed 24 hours a day, reducing alcohol or drug use, making contact with relatives; and, accessing training courses for people who were homeless. These were all actions that seemed to adhere to the norms of expected 'responsible' behaviour, to assist them to reintegrate into society. However each of these 'micro' transitions brought new challenges and risks. For example, contacting family once more brought the potential to develop social capital but also ran the risk of being rejected or of old conflicts emerging. Ceasing to use drugs brought the pain of withdrawal, and brought the risk of relapse. *Many* changes, not just those relating to housing, had to occur as they made their transitions through homelessness, and each change potentially brought new risks and challenges.

Obtaining a tenancy – Integrative transitions?

Some did *appear* to make fairly linear integrative transitions through homelessness. After moving into a rehab, and then supported accommodation for example, they moved into their own tenancies and continued to live there throughout the research.

Usually obtaining their own tenancy was something that was planned and prepared for with the assistance of various agencies and professionals of the social welfare system. These interventions of the social welfare system are analysed in more detail in the next chapter. The significance of informal networks of support when making a transition out of homelessness continues to be downplayed (Hutson, 1999:219), and is recognised and discussed here in Chapter 6. However, despite many of the people researched here spending periods living in accommodation provided outside of the 'system', such as staying with friends, only one person obtained their own tenancy privately, without the advice of housing support workers (and this tenancy was paid for by Housing Benefit). This may reflect the extent to which the people studied (all being recruited initially through a support agency) were in contact with services that could provide the advice and assistance they needed to access housing and in other studies more 'independent' routes out of homelessness have also been identified (Rosengard et al, 2002). Then again, some of those who remained homeless at the end had negotiated some form of accommodation independently, such as staying with friends. The lack of legal formality to this may be an indication of how the most marginalised have limited options – rely on the state or take informal routes to 'construct' their integration to mainstream norms such as housing. They may not have been able to access private tenancies for example, due to having few economic resources or references. It may never have been a housing option that they considered open to them.

The one person that did obtain her own tenancy privately in this study was Francesca, whose initial transition into homelessness was outlined in the previous chapter. Her experience illustrates how important charting transitions *objectively* (housing circumstance) alongside how they are *subjectively* experienced is, to really understand these transitions. This also illustrates they rarely actually took clearly integrative routes, and just has been found in other studies, such as those on youth transitions (Furlong & Evans, 1997) or pathways out of street sex work (McNaughton & Sanders, 2007) life pathways often churn and fragment, as different aspects of that life develop and change, interacting with each other, and external factors.

Francesca's transition out of homelessness

Francesca's experiences of living in temporary accommodation were described in previous sections. Francesca's life appeared to take an integrative transition out of homelessness after she entered supported accommodation. She left the supported accommodation to move into private rented housing with a new partner, in a tenancy in both their names. By the third interview she had moved out of this flat, and was living in her own privately rented tenancy, paid for by Housing Benefit.

However when the qualitative account of this transition is analysed it is one that involved less clear integration. She still had a life imbued with risk and insecurity. She said she felt 'forced' to leave the supported accommodation she was in to move in with her partner. They were abusive and threatened her. While she was staying with them she experienced extreme physical violence, including being stabbed. She left and moved into her own private tenancy, but this was close to where her (now ex) partner lived and was managed by the same landlord as the flat she had previously lived in. She continued to see her ex-partner, and sometimes was threatened and assaulted by them. She continued to use drugs heavily, and was also on methadone.

Charting her transition objectively, it appeared to end with an integrative outcome. She had made the transition out of homelessness and was living in her own tenancy obtained through a private landlord. She had a degree of integration (she did like the flat she lived in and felt relatively settled there, she also had started to spend time with her family, who had helped her move there) but she also faced continued divestment. She was still close to the edge – relying on Housing (and other) Benefits financially, engaging in drug use, experiencing traumatic incidents and vulnerability through the threats and assaults made to her by those she knew. Her situation may have improved in that she had her own housing, but she was still fundamentally in the same risky situation as before, marginalised, close to, if not over the edge. This was the case for many of those whose lives had *appeared* to take integrative passages. Val's experience for example, can be used to further illustrate this point and also to illustrate that the key mechanisms already identified here (social networks, edgework, and resources) continue to interact to affect lives, as they make ongoing transitions.

Val's transition out of homelessness

Val's transition into homelessness was outlined in Chapter 3. Val had then obtained her own housing once more and was living there at the first and second interview. However in the six months between the second and third interview she began using alcohol heavily once more, and was admitted to hospital. She attributed this relapse to the isolation and loneliness she felt, after a relative she had been spending time with had moved away. This was a similar process of loneliness, isolation and alcoholism that had led to her homelessness initially. In the following quote, she describes the process that led to this relapse:

I've been OK but I relapsed over a month ago and I went into hospital. Since she [relative] moved I just felt lonely. I was hitting the drink and I just happened to collapse and I was taken to the hospital. The thing is I was seeing her almost every day. Of course she's got her own life, but I just felt down and numb and alone. I did it gradually, I didn't just go on a binge. When you're on your own it's terrible, you go to the pub to get a wee bit of company and of course that sets you off with the drinking. During the night you've got the telly, whatever, but during the day, there is nothing....

After this relapse she had moved back into her flat, but continued to experience problems with isolation, loneliness, and alcohol use. Val may not have been homeless, but her life was 'flip-flopping' back and forward between potentially integrating and potentially divesting passages, in an ongoing cycle. In this way she was trapped in limbo in the space at the 'edge'. And this was something she experienced on both material, interpersonal and subjective, individual levels. The same fundamental factors that had led to her homelessness – low level of resources, reliance on the state for material and social support, poor health, social isolation, emotional distress, and her alcohol use – remained key mechanisms affecting her life. She remained caught up in the duality of edges identified earlier – that material marginality, impacts subjectively, leading to edgework, and the negotiation of the boundaries of normative behaviour as a form of escape. This duality could lead to further spirals of divestment in the materiality she operated within. And as was argued in the stressed perspective on homelessness and causation, this outcome only occurred in the first instance due to the structured reality of life in late modernity Val was in. Without this structured social reality altering, her risk of homelessness remained, despite certain mechanisms (her access to support and housing through the welfare state) having operated to resolve this problem on the surface level.

The space by the edge – The space between

Val's example illustrates the complexity of the different factors that converge and interact over people's life course. Their transitions through homelessness may take what appear to be integrative passages, as they are no longer 'homeless'. However other areas of their life may continue along divestment passages that could spiral once more. Their social status was caught, flip-flopping in the space on the edge of society. Many – both those who remained homeless over the course of the study and those that obtained tenancies – were experiencing this flip-flop effect. They were making transitions, but could not move far from the marginal 'edges' of society. And this also impacted on their lives subjectively and emotionally. In this way their risk of going over the edge, of experiencing homelessness once more, and their reliance on the state remained integral to their life, despite their housing status changing.

In this study, these qualitative aspects of their transitions could be explored alongside the actual objective housing transitions made. Some *appeared* to make integrative transitions out of homelessness by obtaining their own tenancies. However their transitions were actually characterised by a flip-flopping of integrative and divestment passages, interacting with, and triggering each other. This flip-flop effect is discussed in more detail below.

4. Flip-flopping effect – The 'Dance on the Periphery'

So rather than their transitions out of homelessness taking integrative routes, they were actually characterised by a flip-flopping effect. Sometimes there would be periods of what appeared to be integration, but the fundamental structural situation they were in remained the same. Furthermore as these transitions developed and circumstances changed, they were faced with new risks and challenges they had not faced before, such as living on their own, or managing their own tenancy. The pressure or difficulty of this could act to trigger further divestment passages. Claire's experience illustrates this.

Claire's transition out of homelessness

Claire was first interviewed when she lived in a supported accommodation. She had been in care as a child, and had been sexually abused there. She had then spent time in her own tenancies, hospitals, and temporary homeless accommodation throughout her adult life. She had been addicted to heroin and worked in prostitution, but had also had periods of more security, in employment, going to college and having her own housing. This had broken down once more due to drug use, and after being raped whilst working on the streets in prostitution one night, she had entered rehab and then the supported accommodation she was living in at the first interview. By the second interview she had moved into her own tenancy, and was still living there at the third, six months later. However between moving from supported accommodation to her own tenancy she relapsed with her drug use. She was evicted from the supported accommodation and moved into an emergency crisis rehab. This move was organised by the staff at both projects working together. She had to be evicted from one agency for her funding to be transferred to the other. In the following quote she describes the process that led to her relapse:

> *I relapsed, I ended up in a rehab for three weeks. I felt like I banging my head off a brick wall in there [supported accommodation]. I did feel pressured to just take [my new tenancy] by that time, I really wanted to get away from [the supported accommodation]. I couldn't handle that life anymore, the 'them and us', you feel pressurised to hang about with the other women, because there's nobody else to talk to. In that building you just feel isolated. I can't really remember much about being in rehab to tell you the truth. I had drug psychosis from the amount I'd taken.*
>
> (Claire, 26)

Again, Claire's experience highlights an earlier point – that the actual material conditions people find themselves in when they are homeless can also be the trigger for ongoing divestment passages, and for engaging in edgework as a means to cope with or escape this, emotionally. This has been noted and critiqued, particularly in recent US research into pathways through homelessness (such as Padgett, 2007; Tsemberis & Eisenberg, 2000) and is explored in more detail in Chapter 5.

As Maslow's (1987) theory on a hierarchy of needs famously fore grounded as people make transitions, even in ways that appear integrative, changes and circumstances will affect them on all levels – socially, psychologically, materially – and these intense changes could trigger actions that could potentially lead to further divestment passages. In Claire's case she felt she was 'banging her head against a brick wall', she felt pressurised to move into the first tenancy she was offered. She risked losing this tenancy after she relapsed. In this case, with the support of staff, she moved from the rehab to her own tenancy a few weeks later. She managed to maintain a degree of integration, and continue making her transition out of homelessness. However as the following quote highlights, moving into a tenancy was also intensely difficult. This new situation brought with it new problems (and risks) to manage and negotiate with:

> *I mean things are still really hard. Like just learning all the simple things in life again, things people like you take for granted, learning what's right, learning what's wrong, after six years on drugs. I mean how long does a loaf of bread last for? Now you have everything to learn. [Moving in it was] Like the silence, was going to cave in on me.*

> (Claire, 26)

Remaining homeless and flip-flopping effects

Those that remained homeless did continue to access different forms of accommodation, such as rehabs or supported accommodation, over the course of the study. They appeared caught up in a cycle of transitional phases. They were constantly attempting to make what were perceived to be integrative 'micro' passages out of homelessness, such as going from sleeping rough to being accommodated in a rehab, but these moves only occurred for short-periods, before spiralling back. A crucial aspect of this flip-flopping was that it was often events that occurred *due to them trying to make integrative passages* that actually *created the conditions that caused this ongoing divestment*. Therefore they were trapped in this space by the edge. For example, once they moved into temporary accommodation they could no longer use drugs, and may have been evicted if they were caught doing so. The physical and psychological effect of ceasing their drug use could lead to difficulty and conflict with other residents however. This conflict could then lead to them being evicted.

The actions that caused this divestment may have been individual – such as continuing to use alcohol, or conflict with other residents but were also embedded in and triggered by the material circumstances they were in. And these were circumstances that people with high level of resources were unlikely to find themselves in.

So those that remained homeless appeared to be caught in a spiral of divestment passages that also interacted with this flip-flopping effect. They experienced short-term integrative moves (such as moving into supported accommodation) that ended with another divestment passage, spiralling them into increasingly vulnerable and difficult situations. Each time this occurred any form of capital or access to resources they had was eroded once more, they 'failed' once more to make a transition back over the edge, and this reinforced and rationalised their 'plot' of their life as a homeless person.

The 'reality' of transitional stages

Obviously transitions over the life course are not experienced in simplistic ways, particularly when they involve breaking disordered pathways. Even when they take what appear to be positive integrative passages that assimilate to the 'taken for granted' norms of society, such as a homeless person wanting to move into their own housing, the qualitative experience of this can be intensely difficult, complex and multi-faceted. Different narratives of what is occurring can illustrate that this is multi-faceted with no one 'truth' about how it is being experience, whatever 'objective' outcomes occur (Plumridge & Thomson, 2003). During transitional phases such as these, different aspects of someone's life may be changing, simultaneously (McNaughton & Sanders, 2007). These different aspects flip-flop back and forth, some diverging, some integrating, each time creating a new material reality that can hold new risks and require more transitions to be made to negate these risks. Furthermore there was always also a subjective, emotional aspect to these transitions. As the material situation each person was in changed they had to subjectively reconcile this new 'reality' with their lives, and with the abilities they had, and the new social role and interactions they were engaging in. For many, transitions through homelessness were experienced as intensely difficult, despite an apparently positive outcome having occurred, such as gaining their own tenancy. Furthermore, the structural conditions they operated within had not fundamentally altered, just the surface. The same circumstances and triggers that had caused their homelessness in the first place often remained. This is a pivotal factor.

Transitions over the life course occur objectively, and can be defined by certain outcomes, but how they are subjectively, emotionally, experienced will also always interact with and affect this (Plumridge & Thomson, 2003). Due to this duality, barriers to making integrative transitions out of homelessness could be identified here that are structural (the actual material reality they were in, the actual resources they had, the housing supply generated in this structured reality) and agent-led (the actions that stemmed from the desire to assert their individuality, to escape, to exist as an individual). These are explored in more detail in the next two chapters. In Chapter 3 the stressed perspective on homelessness and causation, underpinned by structuration theory and realist ontology, was first outlined. Now this perspective is contrasted with the *transitions through* homelessness the people studied here made to develop it further.

5. Stressed: Life on the edge in late modernity

In this chapter the key assertion is that, even for those who made a transition out of homelessness, obviously the broader structural context that they operated within had not fundamentally changed. As has been argued here, it was these conditions that generated the motivation and circumstances underpinning the individual factors that caused their homelessness, their risk of homelessness remained. The same lack of resources and concentration of edgework that led to their homelessness often continued (to lesser and greater extents) in their lives. Furthermore, their lives continued to be embedded in the support they received from services of the welfare system and the resources that they could access from this. Their status as individuals who had to rely on the state to assist them (or target them) to negate risk also remained, even though they were in a different position on this continuum, now that they were not homeless.

Helen was homeless at the end of the research, but had been living in her own tenancy at the first interview, after a previous episode of homelessness. Her story is examined to assess how the stressed perspective on homelessness and causation articulated in Chapter 3 fits with making transitions through, and sometimes out of, homelessness.

Helen's story

Helen had experienced repeated homelessness since she left home aged 14. Over the years she had lived in hostels, refuges for women fleeing domestic violence, supported accommodation and rehabs. She had often stayed with friends and partners, although these relationships were usually violent. She had had her own tenancy, and each time had become homeless once more. Sometimes this was due to leaving abusive partners. Sometimes this was due to being evicted or abandoning it. She had been addicted to heroin, used drugs regularly, was on methadone and had chronic alcohol problems. At the first interview she was living in her own tenancy. She had recently moved there from a supported accommodation project:

> *I've been there two months, my house. And I've not lost that, and I'm like – I couldn't believe it. I've not got an inckling to go back and take a bit of smack, and that's the first step, do you know what I mean? It's the first step right back.*

Over the course of the research she began spending more time at her partner's flat. She gave up her tenancy to move into her partner's, with the intention being that this would be changed to be legally in both their names. However, due to domestic violence she left suddenly, with nowhere else to go, and became homeless again:

> *I hadn't done nothing, and next he grabbed me by my hair, and I ran down the stairs, out like that...he kicked me out. I feel so frustrated, so angry. I've had to leave everything.*

> (Helen, 35)

This divestment passage in her life could not be planned for. With the lack of resources Helen had, and at that moment, in the street, in just the clothes she was wearing, she called her housing support worker. She was admitted to a hostel. She was homeless once more. She had no possessions. She began to use alcohol and drugs heavily. She was living in a hostel at the third interview.

Just as relationship breakdown often triggered an initial transition into homelessness it can go on doing so over the life course – obviously this will not *necessarily* be a 'one off' – particularly if people remain in the situation whereby they have to rely on the state for accommodation. They still have less capacity to leave partners and move to another house they privately pay for, or social capital that can provide access to adequate accommodation with friends or family, if this relationship goes wrong.

As was highlighted in the previous chapter, social networks, resources and forms of edgework particularly influenced these transitions through homelessness – at times leading to spirals of divestment. For example, in Helen's case, after leaving an abusive partner, and entering a hostel, she had found herself in an intensely difficult situation. She had no clothes, and was back in a hostel. She had no other social networks and was attempting to manage the emotional effect and trauma of violence; of relationships breakdown; and of leaving her home. She started using drugs and alcohol heavily, the 'step backwards' she had been worried about. And if, due to her substance use, she had to leave the accommodation she was in, her life would keep spiralling once more. This had occurred after she had spent years 'rebuilding' her life, going through rehab, developing a new relationship, obtaining and moving into her tenancy, and starting to attend training and life skills courses. Taken within the context of Helen's life – where she had experienced repeated homelessness, addiction, mental illness, repeated abusive relationships – this passage was just yet another trauma for her. On a micro-level, her escape or resistance to this material reality was through substances. Although in some ways her relationship and moving into her partner's flat was the 'cause' of this episode of homelessness, what had been her alternative? A life where she had never entered a new relationship? Never taken the risk of moving in with a partner? Her motivations for doing so may be the same as anyone else, but she lacked the resources to avoid homelessness when the risk that this relationship went wrong became reality. Each time she became homeless, her resources became further eroded, as she spiralled back into the divestment passages of homelessness and addiction, and had more traumatic incidents to reconcile with in her life.

Helen had been in close contact with services of the social welfare system most of her life. When her social and material security broke down due to domestic violence she had no one else to call that could assist her other than her support worker. She lacked the human, social, or financial capital to be able to obtain accommodation herself 'privately'. She could not afford a private rented flat, and did not feel she could emotionally cope with having her own tenancy, she had no other friends or family that she could stay with or obtain support from. So she remained reliant on the welfare system. She became defined as homeless once more due to this reliance on the state for both material and emotional resources. These factors (domestic violence, drug use) did interact with this situation and did cause 'real' damage. They could also occur in anyone's life, but are likely to lead to different outcomes if they have the human, social, and financial capital to negate the spirals of divestment that may then occur. At times we may all come close to some 'edge' in life, are tempted by trauma or difficulty to let ourselves go over. But most have too much to lose, and have resources to negotiate with this and return from it unscathed. These resources however are obviously more than financial, they may also be found through social, human, and cultural capital. A lack of any of these may lead to a greater risk of divestment occurring when people make transitional stages in their life. A lack of them all multiplies this risk. These resources collectively make up the capacity for resilience that people have, to manage their lives, relationships, and traumatic incidents. High levels of resilience – the ability people have to emotionally as well as materially survive – assist in increasing their capacity to continue developing integrative transitions over the life course, wherever they started from.

The stressed perspective on transitions through homelessness

Just as was the case with Claire and Val, whose stories were outlined earlier, Helen made a transition out of homelessness at points in here life, but the structural conditions and the resources she had access to within these conditions, did not fundamentally change due to this. The risk she had of repeated homelessness remained. She had been, and continued to be, supported and assisted by professionals within the social welfare system. Without this when her relationship went wrong, she would have become destitute. However this reliance also highlighted once more a key cleavage of stratification in society between those who have to rely on the state and those who do not, to negotiate with risk. And that whilst the outcome of this negotiation of risk is still structurally grounded, this may be becoming obscured by individualistic accounts (Furlong & Cartmel, 1997). For example, if Helen could have paid for her own accommodation, or had friends with a high level of resources that she could have moved in with, then she would not have relied on the welfare state and would not have had to move into a hostel. For some the 'stigma' of this reliance may mean they will exhaust all other resources before doing so – as to do so would be a massive divestment passage in their lives. For those who have had nothing but the state to care for them for many years, it is unsurprising that this is what they continue to rely on, as they have no 'status' to become separated from due to this, it is a much smaller level of divestment to access these support services. This is their 'role' as a targeted, marginalised population and therefore a 'responsible' response. When they do not, they appeared to reject the welfare provision provided by the state, but also had few resources with which to support themselves in the material structured reality they operated within.

Anyone may experience domestic violence but the outcome is likely to be different depending on the resources they have. Over the years, all forms of social, human, cultural and financial capital Helen had, had become tied to the social welfare system – a system she was embedded in – therefore when something went wrong in her life, this was the only resource she had to assist her with this problem. Her motivation to engage in relationships may have been no different from those who have a high level of resources, but the outcome of this, if it goes wrong, was likely to be. Anyone's resources may become depleted at points in their life, but if they have less to begin with, the likelihood they will become homeless and then enter a socially alienating spiral of divestment is greater. And this desire to continue to negotiate new outcomes, and new micro-transitions means that people have to keep negotiating with risks over their life, whatever resources they have to begin with.

Of course what happened to Helen will not happen in every case. She and her partner could have stayed together, and had a supportive relationship. People with high levels or resources may leave their home due to domestic violence and have abusive, damaging relationships also. The point from this stressed perspective is that is it much *less likely* to lead to homelessness, or perhaps even to occur in the first instance when they have resources and resilience to avoid this extreme divestment. It does not mean they are fundamentally different in any way.

6. Understanding transitions through homelessness

In the final section of this chapter the findings of this, and the previous chapter, are brought together and summarised to set the scene for the next two chapters. Four key assertions can be identified that can be used to understand these transitions through homelessness – why they occurred, to whom, and when.

Firstly, from the life histories it was ascertained that whilst some had more than others, all the people studied had relatively low levels of human, social and economic capital, due to the socio-economic position of their birth, and institutional resources of educational and employment experiences they had. Another key similarity in all their lives was that at some point these lives had become imbued with experiences of highly traumatic incidents, and involuntarily experienced risks, such as abuse, mental illness, and attempting suicide. Many had also engaged in extreme forms of voluntary risk taking such as intravenous drug use. Due to this they faced a 'duality of edges', materially lacking resources, and also facing stigma and intense emotional trauma. These were people negotiating at the edges of normative behaviour, within a precarious and difficult material reality.

So the transitions that they did make over their life course were particularly influenced by: their social networks and relationships; the edgework they engaged in or experienced, such as drug use or abusive relationships; and the lack of resources they had. Their homelessness occurred due to an interrelation of these factors – their social, economic and human capital became increasingly depleted due to their edge-work, coupled with the low level of resources they already had. Due to this they came to the point that they had to rely on the state to access accommodation, and had to access services or apply for housing as a homeless person.

The second key point is that these people's homelessness was indeed caused by individual factors and trigger points, occurring within a certain structural context whereby they had a lack of resources. This is why there is high prevalence of such problems amongst people experiencing homelessness. This is recognised in the 'new orthodoxy' to understanding homelessness in contemporary western societies (Fitzpatrick, 2005). Here, this orthodoxy is reasserted – this is how homelessness and causation can be understood – this is how structure and agency interacts. However a perspective that develops this further has also been developed. This structural context and the interactions people engage in within it, may also generate the *conditions that lead to the individual factors seen as causing homelessness* and provide a rationale for actions that may appear irrational as a means to avoid risk – the rationale of irrational behaviour. Furthermore these individual factors (drug use, alcohol use, mental illness) may technically occur in anyone's life, the key difference leading to homelessness is when people lack resources of human, social, or financial capital to avoid them, or negate the effects of these individual factors – to negate the risk of going 'over the edge' their edgework may bring. If they cannot negate this risk, they then have to access the homeless system to obtain accommodation. In this way they became defined as a 'homeless person'. This is the stressed perspective on homelessness and causation developed here. Anyone *may* become homeless, but they are more likely to when they have a low level of resources. Anyone may engage in or experience extreme forms of edgework, but they are far more likely to be able to do so 'safely', be able to 'buffer' the effects of this, or engage in acts not deemed 'deviant' when they have a high level of resources to do so. The social context of the late modern risk society underpins both the resources people have access to, and the motivation or conditions that generate this edgework – or the need to escape. Both structural and individual (maximalist and minimalist) accounts of homelessness converge here. It is individual actions that caused this homelessness – but actions embedded and motivated by broad socio-structural mechanisms (as discussed in the previous chapter).

Thirdly, by the end of the research, 19 of the 28 people studied had their own housing and so appeared to have made a transition out of homelessness. Three routes were identified to analyse the transitions through homelessness they took. These are: spirals of divestment passages, developing integration, and a flip-flopping effect of integration diverging.

Spirals of divestment passages occurred for all as they became homeless, and the transitions of those who remained homeless over the course of the research particularly characterised these spirals. Those who made a transition out of homelessness may have appeared to have made integrative passages. However by analysing both the actual outcomes that occurred as they made these transitions, and how this was qualitatively experienced, it was clear that these transitions were actually characterised by a flip-flopping effect of integration and divestment. New challenges and risks occurred as transitions were made. Making a transition out of homelessness can be intensely difficult on both material and emotional levels. The fundamental structural context they operated in had not changed just because they had obtained housing. The same pressures, risks, and trigger points that led to homelessness in the first place remained.

A fourth, key issue identified is that the outcomes of these transitions were particularly embedded in the social welfare system. The experiences analysed here particularly illustrate the lives of people that had at some point actually gone 'over the edge' in late modern society – objectively due to lack of resources, subjectively, negotiating the edges of normative behaviour. In this context, their edgework could be seen as a form of potential resistance or escape from the material reality they were in, and also as being generated by this material reality. However this edgework then often only led to more traumatic incidents and more separation from status, to be reconciled over their life course. They became explicitly targeted by the services of the homeless welfare system when they attempted to resolve their homelessness. The distinction between those who have become explicitly targeted in this way to manage the risks they pose or face in their lives, and those who are not, may be becoming a key cleavage of stratification in late modernity. Their actions may not initially be so different, but how they are interpreted and responded to, is. And this may go on to further alienate and isolate people, so that their actions and lives become increasingly problematic. These points are developed in the next two chapters.

5
Homelessness, Social Welfare and 'Targeted Populations'

In this chapter the micro-level interactions with services of the social welfare system that the people studied here had to assist them resolve their homelessness are analysed. To begin to unravel this, two specific services (supported accommodation, and housing and resettlement support workers) are first singled out for explicit examination. These two forms of support represent explicit targeting and case management of people due to the level of vulnerability, need and risk they represent.

There has been increased demand for more direct access to accommodation that by-passes the need to work through levels of intermediate accommodation, in recent year (Fitzpatrick et al, 2000:41). 'Floating support' provided by specialist support workers is one way that this may be done, and this provision has increased in recent years (Quilgars & Pleace, 1999). Some elements of the tension between these models and how they integrate are explored here. In Section 4 of Chapter 1 the system of 'reflexive governance' used to conceptualise the homeless system of care, and in particular 'targeted populations' was discussed. It may be useful to revisit this section as the argument in this chapter develops.

1. Living in supported accommodation

Supported accommodation projects may differ enormously but are usually small-scale shared accommodation units with communal facilities (Fitzpatrick et al, 2000). At the time of the first interview, examples of the type of supported accommodation that the people interviewed were living in included:

• Converted Victorian houses, or traditional terraced housing from the 1960's, with a number of bedrooms for residents, and a shared lounge, meeting rooms, kitchen and laundry facilities, often set in their own grounds. Sometimes the bedrooms had been converted to be self contained bedsits, with cooking and bathroom facilities. All had communal areas, and an office room where support staff were based.

- Modern purpose built blocks, again with a number of bedrooms and shared communal areas and facilities, and office areas for staff.
- A collection of self contained flats, in one block or close to each other, with an office and communal facilities acting as a 'satellite' facility. Sometimes this 'satellite' is also part of a larger supported accommodation project, with staff also on-call for the nearby self-contained housing. This begins to merge into the style of 'floating' support offered by housing or resettlement workers and explored in the next section.

Supported accommodation projects vary in size and each type of project is distinct. So for example, they may be mixed or single gender. Some will be staffed 24 hours a day with support staff sleeping over in a special designated room. Others will only have support staff visiting for part of the day, or present in 'working hours' with an emergency number that can be called to contact staff if advice or support is required at other times.

The rules at each project differ too. For example some may have strict curfews, and residents are locked out if they miss this. Others, particularly when they are self-contained flats or only staffed for a short period each day, will be more like independent housing, although staff may review what is happening there regularly. Some projects do not allow visitors to stay over, or to be in the bedrooms, and residents have to seek permission to stay away overnight or for longer periods. The rules governing behaviour may also differ – some, unusually, allow alcohol to be consumed on the premises, in a controlled environment. These are known as 'wet projects'. On the other end of the continuum some may require that the residents are teetotal whilst they reside there and do not consume any alcohol, even when they are 'off site'. Different accommodation projects differ enormously and the exact nature of this will influence the experience of living there and ensuing transitions people take, and as Hutson (1999) notes, may not always fit with life 'as lived'. The intention in this study is not to assess different forms of supported accommodation, but rather to broadly analyse how living in them was experienced by the people studied here.

Once people move in, each resident is allocated a room and a key worker. The role of the key worker is to assist them maintain stability in their lives, access other services, such as drugs counselling, manage their appointments and time, and discuss problems they are having and how to respond to them. Some supported accommodation projects also provide courses or activities for residents to participate in, encourage them to attend such courses, or provide transport to them. Staff review residents' progress and situation, manage the general running of the unit, and liaise with other support workers that the residents have. There are usually cleaners or a cleaning rota for the house. The rooms are furnished and people may sometimes put their own possessions, such as pictures, in their room. Often people who have been homeless have very few possessions however and some additional facilities such as bedding may be provided. In some projects the residents may take turns at making dinner each evening, or meals such as breakfast are provided. At others people provide all their own food, and may eat in their room. Projects differ depending on the building, staffing, ideology of the organisation that manages it, and size and the people whose experiences are researched had often stayed in a wide range of accommodation projects throughout their lives, such as rehabs, hostels, and large- and small-scale temporary accommodation projects.

People usually move into supported accommodation with the assistance of a social (or other support) worker. These workers are provided with a list of vacancies available in their area each week, or may actively seek out a room for someone who is moving on. In a self-referral project people may call up and seek out a room themselves, but this will usually still have to be funded by social services therefore they have to usually be eligible for Housing Benefit. In most cases potential residents will visit the accommodation and have an assessment with the staff, before a decision is made as to whether it is appropriate for them to move in. Some supported accommodation is intended as short term – less than six months, for example, and others much longer periods, two years or more. After this time residents may have to move on, either to their own housing or somewhere offering different levels of support if they are still perceived to require it. People move to supported accommodation from rehabs, other temporary accommodation they have already been provided with, or sometimes from friends or relatives, where they have been staying temporarily whilst they wait for a room to become available. Sometimes people may wait long periods for a room to be available, or may first be housed in one supported accommodation before moving into another. Therefore people may not always have much choice as to where they are accommodated.

Almost all of those whose transitions are studied here had spent time in supported accommodation, and 15 were in this form of accommodation at the point of the first interview. For many this was felt to be the first step in making a clear transition out of homelessness, however as will also be shown, for others this was another phase in their ongoing cycle of homelessness. Many had moved between a range of different supported accommodation units over years of homelessness.

All the experiences of living in supported accommodation, and how this may have impacted on these transitions through homelessness, are explored in this section. Two key arguments are presented: firstly, supported accommodation units were like 'training', representing an intense level of targeting on a micro-level, to become active citizens. However this was also seen as a positive input. Secondly, not abiding by the rules and ideology of this targeting could trigger ongoing divestment passages.

Supported accommodation as 'training'

Comments made on supported accommodation highlighted that living there felt like training: training to 'take responsibility', to behave in the 'right' way, to make the right choices and to be able to reintegrate into society. The following quote from William illustrates how this was typically described, retrospectively, once he had moved into their own tenancy:

> *[Supported accommodation] was a good time you know, it took a lot of responsibility off me, like that I have now. Bills: I didn't have to worry about all that, so it was a good experience. Then again a lot of that is false in that you don't deal with stuff, it is not real life, but it is good in that it gives you that taste of freedom, to make mistakes, to learn by them. Everyone has choices in life, but it is how you do it.*
>
> (William, 29)

So living in supported accommodation was a positive experience, but one that he also saw as not being 'real' life. He did not really have control over his choices, but was being taught to make the right choices, to manage his 'freedom' and the pressure this 'freedom' brought, before moving into his own tenancy once more. Similar themes were highlighted by others, such as Brian, who is also here commenting on supported accommodation retrospectively, after obtaining a tenancy:

> *It's like a boot camp! It's like training, it trains you for going back out into your own place, it calms you down, it takes all the bitterness away, it*

helps you. In the hostels you get away with everything, but [in supported accommodation] they get you back on track, like how to behave, but you need to want it yourself as well.

(Brian, 36)

So living in supported accommodation was a time when people had the opportunity to 'relearn' the ability to act responsibly. This was respite from the spiral of divestment and intense separation from status they had experienced. The comments above clearly highlight that although the experience of being in supported accommodation could be positive, the discourse of how it is to be an 'active citizen' – to utilise the opportunities that they have, as liberal, responsible, free agents – was imbued with living there. This discourse may also have fed into the comments made – that is has to be 'up to them'. Perhaps the fundamental question should be, why did they feel they had 'lost' this ability in the first place? Why had they become so 'bitter', this is not inevitable surely, therefore, what processes lead to this? Furthermore this further asserts the neoliberal ideology of reflexive governance – that people can and should be 'reformed' through such training. Both Brian and William were living in their own housing at the end of the study, and were fairly settled there so in some cases this targeting did appear to 'work', but a tension also exists – explored below.

Supported accommodation as control

At the same time as being trained to be responsible agents, many also felt that through being housed in supported accommodation, they lost their agency, and their capacity to act as individuals. Their behaviour was highly constrained, as were their choices over where they were accommodated and how they should act. This was ultimately decided by others, such as their social workers, working within the confines of supply and resources they had. The following case of Connor is used to illustrate this and his awareness of it – as a reflexive, active individual.

Connor's 'choices'

Connor was living in supported accommodation for the first two interviews. For over ten years prior to this he had moved between different hostels and rehabs, sometimes sleeping rough and sometimes moving into a tenancy, before leaving it once more. Prior to this he had lived with his parents, worked in construction, and then obtained a tenancy of his own when his parents died. He was a chronic alcoholic and suffered from poor physical and mental health. By the third interview he had moved to a residential rehab with the advice and planning of professionals. At the second interview he said that he did not want to move to the rehab, but that it was the only 'option' decided to be appropriate for him. In the quote below he sums up the tension outlined above – whilst being 'trained' to take control of his life by this system, he also had control taken away:

The system can work for some people, but this pressure on you to stop drinking, to stop taking drugs, it's too great, the pressure is overwhelming in you. They're saying, you're either in this [supported accommodation], or it's rehab, or it's the street. That's my options; options? Choice? That's no choice at all, that's staying within the system, they've got choice for you, they're choosing for you, they're saying you're going to the street if you stay on drink or drugs, or we can give you a nice rehab. No rehab is nice!

(Connor, 47)

So at the same time as promoting their capacity to make the right 'choices', their actions and choices were highly constrained by being within this system – as the previous description illustrates. Residents have to 'choose' to act in certain ways. The rules that exist in supported accommodation may be necessary to objectively manage them, however the form these rules take (such as not allowing alcohol, not having guests, not being allowed to stay away overnight and having to be in at a certain curfew time) also illustrate that the people accommodated there are currently not viewed as able to make 'responsible choices' or manage the 'risks' they face themselves risks they will face in 'normal' society. Therefore they have their actions highly constrained whilst being targeted to manage the potential risk their 'freedom' posed to them. This was not 'normal' life however, they were not able to engage in normal relationships or interactions whilst accommodated there. This was due to the risk that they may continue to engage in individual actions perceived to have caused their homelessness, such as drug or alcohol use, or spend time with people who may provide them with the opportunity for these actions. They had to pull apart their past, and reject it, to rebuild their future – clearly a sometimes difficult and complex task, embedded as we are in the (hi)story of our lives.

Being accommodated in supported accommodation was something that occurred due to their reliance on the social welfare system to access resources, and being deemed those in need of additional support and targeting due to the vulnerability and risks they represented. So their circumstances and the way they could act within this situation was still ultimately tied to the social structure (and the marginal position of power or access to resources they had within this structure). Other people who can afford their own housing due to the access to resources they have may not be targeted in this way, however they act. They may stay out for days at a time, drink too much (as long as no crime is committed whilst they do), and have anyone they wish as guests. The welfare system provides for those in the most 'need', and it is necessary to have rules and regulations operating to filter access to these resources. The point however, is that this still acts to create a cleavage of stratification, that also underpins how actions, circumstances and people are judged, managed, and perceived. And may also create the conditions that generate such actions and outcomes in an ongoing structurated process.

This is not the first time that this process has been recognised, although here it is framed within clear theoretical foundations. Recent research into transitions through homelessness made by those also affected by mental illness, addiction and lacking resources has identified similar processes whereby the 'cure' – in this case, supported accommodation, sobriety, treatment – can also be the 'cause' of ongoing problems, as the stress of these interrelated effects and the need to adhere to many rules can lead to people remaining in this system, in a cycle of relapse and eviction (Tsemberis & Eisenberg, 2000). Therefore access to housing and into the system of support services is contingent on complying with rules and restrictions (Padgett, 2007; Padgett, Gulcur & Tsemberis, 2006) that as Hutson (1999) noted about UK models also, may not fit with lives as lived by real people and illustrates that these people are not perceived as 'capable' of making the right choices and living independently – they are in effect not seen as 'real' with the same needs or wants as others (as Frank's comments on the difficulty of avoiding relationships when in supported accommodation although this was expected as part of his rehabilitation).

In the US a model (known as housing first) whereby housing is seen as a human right, regardless of whether people are accessing treatment for their related problems or not, and that avoids the need to spend periods in institutional settings such as supported accommodation by providing permanent private rented accommodation and support is being increasingly implemented after positive and robust evaluations of this (see for example, Padgett et al, 2006; Gulcur, Stefancic, Shinn, Tsemberis & Fischer, 2003). Whilst this may appear as a 'floating support' model the key difference is that it separates the pressures of treatment (such as detox, counselling, adhering to strict curfews in supported accommodation) from access to housing, an access that at the moment is still often tied to the perceived 'capability' to manage a tenancy that someone has. As is explored in this study it can often be a complex intersection of pressures wrought from making multiple transitions and accessing treatment for deep-rooted problems such as addiction and mental illness that can act as ongoing triggers for this behaviour, recreating a cycle. This is explored in the next section.

Supported accommodation and divestment passages

For those who remained homeless over the course of the research, a key trigger for their ongoing homelessness was being evicted from a supported accommodation unit. Often over the course of the research they had to leave supported accommodation due to their continued alcohol or drug use, lack of 'engagement' with their support workers, or not abiding by the rules, such as curfew times. Eddie's case illustrates this and the inherent 'vicious circle' that often underpinned it – as people tried to come back from their edge of chaos.

Eddie's story

Eddie, a 42 year old man, was living in supported accommodation at the first interview. He had been homeless and addicted to heroin for over 20 years. Over the course of the research he moved multiple times, due to being evicted from different temporary accommodation. At the point of the third interview he was living with a friend, temporarily. Here, Eddie describes how this happened:

> *They [the staff at supported accommodation] just said 'well there's nothing more we can do for you' you know...I'd stopped, like I wasn't playing their game sort of thing, I wasn't going to sessions, I wasn't going to key working, I wasn't going to [day courses] and all that. So they passed me onto a hostel, the rooms the same but there is about fifty guys there. Then [the hostel staff] said 'you need to move out' and my social worker told me they're the kind of place where they want you clean [not using drugs or alcohol] so I moved to my pals, they said I could stay a wee while.*

(Eddie, 42)

Because Eddie wasn't 'playing the game' he had no 'options' left within the system. He moved in with a friend, and his marginality and insecurity continued. It may appear that irrational individual actions such as his drug use caused this, however the motivation for the edgework Eddie engaged in (his ongoing drug use that appeared to lead to this divestment passage) can be understood as rational when cast within his life course. It was a form of escape from the current reality he was in, the life he had had, and how he subjectively, emotionally, experienced this. Eddie for example had recently started counselling for sexual abuse he had experienced in childhood. Below he describes how his drug use acted as a 'shield' to these experiences and how losing this 'shield' through the process of being in supported accommodation and abiding by the rules there, such as 'staying clean', was intensely difficult:

See when I get off all the drugs, I'm just naked, I'm going to break right down, (...) because the drugs are like a shield, a wall,...there was a period there where I went four or five months, when I got a right buzz out of being there [in supported accommodation], not using nothing. I was getting there...I was progressing, maybe that frightened me, I don't know.

(Eddie, 42)

The rationale of irrational behaviour, first outlined in Chapter 3, can be used here as way of understanding the rationale behind the actions that led to some of these ongoing divestment passages and to remaining homeless. These passages occurred when people were evicted from accommodation, or barred from accommodation, due to actions such as drug or alcohol use or conflict with other residents. However moving into new accommodation often brought intense difficulty, and new risks and challenges to negotiate with. These were people over the edge, and their ongoing acts of edgeworking may be understood as one of their only escape routes (albeit a destructive one) from the confines and regulation of their situation. These actions were also something motivated and generated within the structural conditions they operated within, the intense trauma, marginality, low social status, and lack of resources to remedy this they faced. At the same time as being trained to make responsible choices, they had responsibility, choice, and agency on an individual level taken away from them. Their only form of either escape from this, or of reasserting their agency in the face of this, may have been to go back 'over the edge' again, through the use of substances, or surrendering emotionally to hysteria or temper, for example.

So the subjective emotional experience of being targeted to address the problems they had, and assist them integrate could itself be the trigger for some ongoing divestment passages and trauma. For those who remained homeless over the course of the study, their individual actions were often what *appeared* to have led to their exclusion from the very institutional structures that may have provided them with the material resources to resolve their homelessness. However if the edgework thesis is used as a rationale for what may appear irrational behaviour on a micro-level, then these actions can be understood differently. They were perhaps the only means they had to escape from the intensely traumatic circumstances they had experienced, the highly regulated situation they were currently experiencing, and the low social status and lack of resources they had. In this way they went over the edge again into a continuing spiral of divestment passages. And in doing so a vicious circle was created whereby the actions they engaged in to ontologically 'cope' with their existence within the structures of late modern society, further excluded them from the institutions that could provide access to resources to resolve these problems and their problematic behaviour. They remained over the edge of society. But each time they attempted to resolve this, the conditions they entered could be what created the context that triggered this ongoing divestment – so how could they escape from this?

Supported accommodation and transitions through homelessness

So to summarise, many spoke of living in supported accommodation as part of an integrative process they went through, where they were trained to become active citizens and live independently after 'losing' this ability. Their homelessness could be taken as evidence that they had lost the ability to manage the risks they faced – the risk of homelessness, had become reality, the risk of becoming an addict through drug use, had become a reality. They had had to access accommodation through the social welfare system as a 'homeless person'. As they made more integrative passages through their homelessness and accessed supported accommodation they were being trained to be responsible agents again, in adherence to this neoliberal ideology. However at the same time, their actions, choices, and circumstances were controlled by the institutions, rules and staff at these supported accommodation units. Meanwhile their structural socio-economic position, their low social status, and the history of trauma they had experienced in their life, remained.

It must also be emphasised that the experience of being in supported accommodation often led to positive outcomes. These supported accommodation units could provide people with comfortable accommodation, and advice and support, whilst they obtained, and prepared to move into their own housing. However as was also highlighted in Chapter 3, the actual material environment and interactions that people engage in, in these settings can then have a crucial affect to how life is experienced, and their ensuing actions. It appears that supported accommodation has a contradictory role to play in assisting people make a transition out of homelessness. On the one hand it is important for respite from going over the edge, and from the chaos of homelessness, and often provided a positive, comfortable environment to live in and recover. However it was also not 'real' life, and the actions of people living there highly constrained and controlled, which may be counterproductive to producing 'active citizens' that are expected to act as such, as 'free' agents. This is increasingly recognised in the development of systems such as housing first in the US (explored earlier in this chapter) and of the increasing flexibility of floating support provision and reduced use of group living projects in the UK (Fitzpatrick et al, 2000). However there is also no panacea. Whatever stage in their transition through housing people were in, or ethos of housing as something everyone can and should have a right too, there remains many challenges when people do attempt to make a transition out of homelessness and into their own home (Franklin, 1999). The nature of this is explored in detail later in this chapter and in Chapter 6. Therefore supported accommodation may still have a role to play in assisting people make a transition out of homelessness.

Policy interventions have been criticised for the increasing reflexivity and governance of behaviour that is occurring (Furedi, 2006), however the problem with this criticism is that for some people this system can lead to positive outcomes, at least relative to the alternative they face and on a micro-level. For some this system does work on a micro-level, even if it is a system becoming increasingly embedded in their life, as the next section on housing support workers illustrates.

2.   Specialist housing, resettlement and tenancy sustainment workers

A popular form of support and targeting currently used to address homelessness, is the intervention of housing support workers (sometimes known as resettlement, or tenancy sustainment workers) (Fitzpatrick et al, 2000). They work with people who are homeless, or 'at risk' of homelessness, on a one-to-basis, often continuing to do so wherever that person is accommodated rather than being attached to a particular accommodation project. Tenancy sustainment workers support people living in their own housing, who may suffer from vulnerabilities and problems, to maintain this housing. Resettlement workers work with people to find housing, and to move in, and then to settle there in the long term. They do this by, for example, assisting them to fill in forms, visiting tenancies with them, ensuring they pay their bills on time, that repairs they require are completed, and that disputes with neighbours are resolved. The length of time that someone may work with a housing support worker is often limited, spanning perhaps six months to two years.

The majority of the people studied here had extensive contact with specialist housing workers as they made their transition through homelessness, and three specific phases could be identified that interacted with this. These are:

1. Avoiding homelessness
2. Resolving homelessness – obtaining housing
3. Managing housing

Avoiding homelessness

Jane and Allan were the only two people studied who had never lost their housing. Both had poor physical health, suffered from alcoholism, and were reliant on the state to access resources and social support. They had faced the risk of becoming homeless after being served eviction notices. They had then been referred to housing support workers by the officer that managed their rented housing for the local authority. Clearly that they had not lost their tenancies and become homeless was a 'positive' outcome, and this was something they attributed to the advice and assistance they gained from these housing support workers. On an objective level this intervention 'worked' for them. The following quote from Jane highlights the sort of support received:

Well, [Tenancy Sustainment Worker] first of all came to the housing [office] with me and made an arrangement for me to pay so much, and went to the Gas and Electricity [company] and cut that down on to what I could afford, you know. I've been trying to get on Incapacity [Benefit] and they've been quite good to come and represent me at appeals and all that. I think what they gave was a bit of clarity, when I met them it was sort of like 'are you dealing with this?' they gave me a kick up the arse to get things sorted, to go and deal with it, instead of putting things like gas bills to the side, they would be straight up 'have you done your phone bill, have you done this?'

(Jane, 29)

Jane had been served an eviction notice for non-payment of rent prior to being allocated a housing support worker. She had stopped paying her bills after her alcohol use increased. This happened shortly after her abusive partner left. She had had a nervous breakdown and given up her employment.

The same individual mechanisms identified as the 'cause' of homelessness among those who had previously lost their tenancies, were operating in Jane and Allan's life and could have led to them becoming homeless. This could have triggered ongoing divestment passages in the spiralling effect identified in Chapter 4. In their cases, becoming homeless was avoided. However, what was also clear was that their fundamental situation had still not actually changed. They were being case managed to avoid the risk of homelessness, but were still experiencing the same fundamental problems at the end of the research – alcoholism, depression and dependency on Benefits. Their circumstances also again illustrate, that even if people have avoided the risk of *homelessness* many are still close to 'the edge' of society, flip-flopping.

What requires more theoretical consideration in the future is what social forces underpin and lead to problems such as alcoholism, domestic violence, isolation? What caused the individual problems they experienced to lead to the risk of homelessness? Are they inevitable? Or can they be prevented?

Obtaining housing

Over the course of the research nine of the 28 obtained their own housing and moved in. Eight of these (all apart from Francesca who had obtained her own privately rented flat by the third interview) had housing support workers that assisted them with this. Perhaps a key outcome of this contact with specialist housing workers was the 'expert' advice provided on how to obtain a tenancy. Another key outcome was finding out how to access practical, material, resources once they moved in, such as furniture, or setting up utility bill payments.

Resettlement workers advise people about areas to apply for housing in, how to complete the housing application forms, contact Housing Associations to find out about applications, attend interviews, and visit potential tenancies and advise on their 'suitability'. They then also assist people obtain furniture, set up regular bill payments, visit them in their tenancy once they move in, and are a source of ongoing advice and assistance. The following quote from Ian, illustrates how people described this process. Ian was living in supported accommodation at this point, and had just been offered a tenancy:

> *My [resettlement worker], he deals with a lot of stuff as well, like he gets you starter packs, pots and pans. Kind of wee bits of furniture. He knows where he can dig you up furniture, so basically I'm moving into an empty flat. He's going to actually see what he can help me with. He's coming to pick me up on Tuesday at nine o'clock to view the flat. He'll be able to give me a bit more advice on that kind of thing then.*
>
> (Ian, 33)

These practical material resources are clearly important, to be able to move into, and settle in new housing. Most new tenancies are unfurnished and people have lost most of their possessions whilst being homeless, unless they can store them with friends or relatives.

Resettlement workers assisted them to *navigate* access to their own tenancy, in a reflexive process. This process developed in partnership with other professionals, and illustrated this case management system at work. These other professionals included drugs workers, social workers, and agencies that oversee the housing supply that is available, such as Housing Associations. In this way they collectively 'filtered' the distribution of the finite resource of socially rented housing that was available and shaped where and how people should live.

Where they could access housing related to the supply of social housing available. This meant they usually moved into housing stock in locations and areas where those most in need – such as the people who are homeless – are housed. These are often areas with concentrated material and social deprivation (Gibb & Maclennan, 2006) and become residualised due to the high concentration of the most vulnerable here (Fitzpatrick & Stephens, 1999). In this way the line of stratification between those who have to rely on the state to access resources and those who do not (identified earlier as a potentially widening cleavage of stratification in late modernity) was maintained, geographically.

As was also discussed earlier, people have to engage in interactions with others. People often described the social problems in the areas they obtained housing. The following quote from David, illustrates this. The potential effect this environment may have on the embodied, lived reality they experienced is clearly an important consideration in the findings presented here. If there is a high concentration of certain problems or actions occurring in one area or amongst one group of people, a rationale for edgework may develop or be exacerbated:

Well in [my area] there is a stabbing every Friday, Saturday, Sunday night and there are more CCTV cameras there than anywhere, so they don't work for starters. It's just constant hassle. Drugs have torn apart all the communities, definitely, I wouldn't bring a child up here, if I had any kids, I would try and get away into whatever area I could, but I suppose every area I could go to is the same and all, most places.

(David, 38)

David had been homeless and addicted to heroin for over ten years before moving into his tenancy. He was settled there but did say he felt very isolated, and repeatedly relapsed. His situation appeared to have improved, relative to being homeless, but he still faced many risks and problems, including his own ongoing drug use and mental health problems.

Being able to obtain housing and access the material resources required to move in and live in this housing was clearly important to facilitate transitions through homelessness. Ultimately, obtaining a tenancy was a positive outcome and the support received from housing support workers often assisted in facilitating this. However what is clear is that the ability they then had to move far from 'the edge' when they still had few resources of social, economic, human, or physical capital, was limited. Many who had lived in their own housing for long periods after being homeless were still in close contact with support services (such as drugs workers, counsellors, housing support workers) throughout the study and they had few other sources of support. This long-term contact with housing workers is explored in more detail below.

Managing housing

Some people felt that once they were living in their own tenancy they actually required more intensive support and ongoing targeting from support workers if they were to be able to continue to live 'independently'. The following quote from Tommy, illustrates this. Tommy had become homeless due to mental illness. He had attempted suicide and was admitted to hospital. He then moved into a hostel, before obtaining his own tenancy, with the assistance of specialist housing support workers. Below he describes how he experienced moving into his own housing:

When I moved into my house, for a while I used to say to people, I was homeless, probably for about a year. So that was quite a long time before feeling settled. The best help was I think, the support of workers. People need support to stay in their tenancy, for me anyway, for a long time after I went into my house, I needed support to sort things out. I think that's more the problem, people in their tenancy, and getting help there, getting used to being part of the community again.

(Tommy, 33)

This ongoing support and assistance was therefore crucial for people who had often lost many other sources of social support to begin to resettle once more. Services for people experiencing homelessness have shifted to respond to this in recent years, with more emphasis on support needs being given (Hutson, 1999). In this study, many spoke of being scared that their support workers would cease contact with them, and that they would not be able to cope when they did. They felt that they required long-term 'support' to manage their tenancy, and life, as 'responsible' active individuals.

Once again there is a tension inherent in this point. The intervention of housing support workers was an important source of support that facilitated making a transition out of homelessness. However further resources were then required to enable people to develop more social, human and related capital for themselves, to move on from this point. And this was rarely available. Many spoke of being dependent on the support of their support workers and the welfare system and of seeing no way to change this. It could be that there are people who require long term support, but there may also be some who do just need housing. The danger is that homeless services may become too caught in a (well-meaning) maximalist shift in seeing homelessness as solved when the individual problems some people experiencing it are managed through support. This may actually act to pathologies people who could otherwise avoid this. The balance however, is in ensuring that support needs are not underplayed either. Perhaps, as is explored more in the next chapter it is more fundamental changes that are required, that do then relate back to the structural reality of late modernity.

On a more micro-level once more, a key problem that may also arise when people were supported to make a transition out of homelessness, is that of 'dependency' on this support, or the perceived inability to manage their lives they then had. This could be conceptualised as actually the real 'transition out of homelessness' that they had to make – believing that they could manage their own lives, and feeling of belonged in their 'space'. This potential benefit of home (Kearns, Hiscock, Ellaway & Macintyre, 2000) and the need to have a sense of ontological security tied to 'ownership' of space (Padgett, 2007; Somerville, 1997) is well documented and remains a key challenge to be met as people make transitions, particularly those relating to housing, over their life course. This 'dependency' on the welfare system that some of the people studied here noted, may also be a key problem (or perhaps unintended outcome) of this reflexive system of governance and the case management of risky populations, and indeed an outcome of the entire welfare system as it currently exists (Dean, 1999). It is needed for those 'in need' but also may play a part in generating this need on both individual and structural levels over time, as was argued in the previous chapter. It is also only those that do not have the resources to negotiate with risk when something 'goes wrong' in their life that are targeted in such as way, separating them from those that may experience the same individual problems, but never have them publicly defined.

Some people spoke of feeling 'abandoned' when they ceased to have contact with the professionals they were in contact with – they could manage to live in their tenancies, but had few other opportunities to develop further integration passages beyond this situation, and few social networks outside of this welfare system. The only contacts they had were with professionals or people they met through the different support services they accessed such as training courses for people who had been homeless. Recent US research by Yanos, Felton, Tsemberis & Fry (2007) highlighted the problem with this. They investigated factors that assisted with integration of formerly homeless mentally ill people. Having a locus of meaningful activity that linked them into a wider community, out side of treatment or their own home, was found to be a key variable in how settled and integrated their sample felt, and how much they could move on in their lives.

In this study some of the people researched felt that they required *more support* from welfare services once they were housed, to continue avoiding the risks they faced, and the risk of repeated homelessness these may bring. A few did cease all contact with housing support workers and were settled in their own housing at the end of the study – however they still did not necessarily move far from the 'edges' of material insecurity. They often remained reliant on this system to provide them with housing and social support, and often continued to engage in extreme edgework. This edgework may have provided them with emotional escape or resistance from their marginal position. However it also brought the risk of them going over once more. They too often continued to flip-flop, caught at the edge, in this way, with few opportunities to move on from this. This edgework, or rather the motivation for it, needed to be addressed. On a more substantive level, this may also provide some evidence that long term support is indeed needed, and that rather than expect people to 'graduate' through treatment (learn to manage to live independently) some may need low level support throughout as part of their day to day life, indeterminately.

Many had long-term contact with housing support workers that was ongoing at the end of the study. The positive outcome of this was that that they continued to be supported, to live in their tenancies, and avoid the trauma and marginality of repeated homelessness. So at the end of the study the majority continued to rely on the social welfare system to access material resources and sometimes for social and emotional support. Some attended training courses, or 'life skills' classes for people who had been homeless. Some were involved as service users in forums, consultations, and peer education, feeding back into the services that had assisted them, in a reflexive process. None were in the situation of having no contact with some specialist services of the social welfare system by the end of the research. In many ways this was positive – they were obtaining the support they were entitled too, to assist them (and as they should be entitled to (Franklin, 1999). Yet an ongoing dependency was also being generated in this way, and the fundamental issues that had led to their marginalisation remained obscured (the outcome of the epistemological fallacy of liberal individualism that Furlong & Cartmel (1997) identified in their study of young people's transitions). In this way they could also remain pathologised with a focus on them, as people with something amiss in their lives (Hutson, 1999:218).

These key issues that have been identified from an analysis of the role the specific services of the social welfare system had on these transitions through homeless are discussed in the next three sections.

3. After homelessness – Trapped in dependency

Even once the majority of the people studied here obtained their own housing, most also continued accessing training courses and day centres for people who had experienced homelessness or addiction. They felt this was very important for them, however this was not often due to the actual outcome of the courses (such as any new skills they learnt) but because it was the only way to occupy their time, or only source of companionship, they now had. They often described the reason they attended these courses as a way to 'fill in their time' as 'something to do' in the face of few other options. This lack of future options was a crucial problem. In this way many remained 'flip-flopping', their lives, even once they were no longer homeless still fully embedded in services provided to support populations such as drug user, homeless people and the long term unemployed. And this was something that many wanted to change, but could see no way to. The cases of David and Keith are used to illustrate this.

David's story

David, was 38 and living in his own tenancy throughout the research. He had moved there after spending 20 years in a cycle of homelessness, moving between prison, hostels, staying with friends, and sleeping rough. He had been addicted to heroin and moved into his housing from a hostel, with the assistance of his housing support worker. He attended training courses and drop-ins and also had to go to the chemist every day to pick up his methadone prescription to manage his heroin addiction. In the quote below, he describes his life:

> *I know that without [going to life skills and employment courses] I'd just be sitting about [the house] demented, probably getting depressed. Probably end up back into drugs again. My day is just waking up in the morning, going to a class, whatever, and going back up the road again. And everything revolves around a chemist [to get methadone]. I've actually done all the courses and that now, you know.*
>
> (David, 38)

David had come far in his transition through homelessness. This may perhaps not have been possible years before, when different support to resolve homelessness was available (for example, in some cities there have been large scale hostel reprovisioning, with large accommodation units closed and funding provided for more floating support). But now what future did he face for this development? He went to the chemist to obtain methadone to manage his drug addiction every day; he went on courses he had already completed – he had few other sources of social contact or support, and could see few opportunities to have in the future. David felt if he did not continue to go on these courses, he would probably spiral back over the edge, and use drugs once more. But he also couldn't develop further integration. This sentiment, of being in limbo, was repeated many times by those who moved into their own housing. Keith's case, also illustrates this.

Keith's story

Keith, a 34 year old man, also had his own tenancy throughout the study. Prior to this, he had spent over ten years in a cycle of homeless, moving between rehabs, hostels, sleeping rough, and his own tenancies. He became homeless initially due to drug addiction, and mental illness, which had caused him to separated from his partner, and leave his employer. As his quote illustrates, homelessness, the edgework, and the trauma some of the people whose lives are studied here had experienced, may create in people an identity that they find difficult to consolidate within themselves once they have been assisted to resolve the problems that led to them being targeted in the first place:

It is a very traumatising thing to do, to be homeless, to be rough sleeping, to go through all the violence, the begging. There's a lot to think about and once you get your house and look back on it, it can be frightening. You do have a lot of guilt and a lot of remorse for what you've done.

(Keith, 34)

Keith identified a way of 'coping' with his life, and the material and emotional reality he was in, as being involved in different day courses, and going to drop ins. He also discussed how he felt that if he did not access these resources his own actions may lead to his homelessness recurring once more:

I couldn't see myself being in my house 24 hours a day, I have to get out of the house [and go to drop ins and training courses for ex-drug users and people who have been homeless] for my own good really, because my mental health, my state of mind, I would go crazy really if I was stuck in the house constantly. I might risk losing it again. I would probably turn back to drugs again, if I was stuck in the house constantly, just with my own thoughts, my own memories, regrets, guilt and stuff like that.

(Keith, 34)

The only other alternative he could see, the only escape from this current day-to-day existence, was actions that sent him over the edge again, such as drug use. The only future that Keith saw was as an ex-homeless person, and as an ex-addict, and he therefore felt he had to keep accessing support services for people who had been homeless and addicts, to cope with this. He was caught in this system, despite the advancement he had appeared to have made in obtaining his own tenancy. Again, just as in the case of being case managed due to living in supported accommodation, neoliberal discourses were also apparent in the narrative that Keith presented. He remained in the system for 'his own good', as a responsible 'choice', to avoid engaging in other activities that may have led to him risking becoming homeless again, due to his own actions. He had in many ways broken a cycle of institutionalisation he had been in, but now faced an empty future for all that.

And they did both risk losing their tenancies once more. Although they continued living in their tenancies through the research, and discussed the ways of coping they had, both Keith and David also did repeatedly relapse over the course of the research. Both spoke of how their mental health was continuing to deteriorate over the course of the research. Both had been admitted to psychiatric hospitals for a period, by their specialist housing workers, due to this. Their situation remained one of marginality, with few other means to experientially escape this, to gain more 'meaning', status, or identity, than through their edgework. Once again their fundamental situation had not changed. In fact now they were 'settled', back in to mainstream society, they spoke of their addiction and mental and physical health getting worse. Whatever generated these problems had not changed and continued to affect their lives in profound ways despite the fact that they were obtaining all the support and advice from medical and social work staff were entitled to.

There is a tension inherent in this. On the one hand the positive outcome of this targeting was that they did maintain their housing, access material resources and support through the social welfare system, and avoid the risk of homelessness. But on the other hand this meant that they continued to require more, rather than less, targeting. The system had to keep extending out, and developing more services, long-term support workers, courses, forums, that they could be involved in, as people who were, 'at risk' of problems such as addiction, homelessness, mental illness, criminality. Yet, the structural underpinning to, or root cause of these problems, appeared to remain. The focus of how to control and manage these problems went onto the individual. What had led to these individual problems and how they could be prevented or alleviated, structurally, remained underemphasised.

The role of the social welfare system to these transitions through homelessness was to case manage them. For many this did assist them to resolve their homelessness and access resources. However this management also created a population that required ongoing targeting (Dean, 1999). In doing so it continued, in a loop, to feed them back into this same system, in ever increasing reflexive cycles. Their structural situation had not fundamentally changed, so the mechanisms that triggered the actions and problems that led to their homelessness were unlikely to have either. They remained 'trapped', flip-flopping in this space between integration and divestment. And the focus of their problems remains them, as individuals.

4. Ever increasing circles – Constructing the system

In this reflexive system it was clear that the people targeted also played a role in the construction of the services they accessed, and the identification of what their needs were. Often this was through the myriad of monitoring, research, consultation and service user involvement that is now integral to this reflexive system (Dean, 1999). The following case of Tommy is used to illustrate this – and that, whilst also bringing positive developments it can lead to a vicious circle for those involved.

Tommy's case – Continues

Tommy had become homeless due to mental illness, and attempting suicide. He had lived in hostels, and then moved into his own tenancy. He had accessed many different services to assist him as he made his transition through homelessness and was now relatively settled and secure in his own housing. He was acutely aware however of a vicious circle that could be created by the very 'success' of this system to involve and support people:

> *I think what [policy makers] maybe really need to look at is the whole process of people going from one project onto another, from one course, onto another. They then get maybe caught up in something that's not helpful. Overdependent. So that when a course comes to an end for example or support comes to an end they're right back where they started.*
> (Tommy, 33)

Tommy was involved in volunteering as a service user and he often was consulted with about how best to develop and manage new services. He had lived in his tenancy for almost two years by the end of the research (the longest period of any of those who had moved into housing after being homeless), and below he describes his apprehension about moving outside of this system – the material reality he was involved in:

> *I'm looking at moving on [from volunteering] so there's a bit of apprehension at the future. Cause if I move on I know I'll have to leave a lot behind, and*

there will be a lot of changes. You've been through a horrible experience like homelessness, and you're involved in volunteering in the homelessness scene, and everything is geared towards it. But there is a time when you're not homeless anymore, you need to leave that behind and move on.

(Tommy, 33)

In this way he succinctly summed up the challenge integral to making transitions. That it involves rupturing the 'past', a change in the plot of life, and this rupturing may allow new risks to flood in. Furthermore, and with particular resonance to transitions through homelessness, Tommy found the role he had began to have in his life was of an 'ex-homeless' person. He was consulted on, and implicit in, the recreation of the system to assist people who are homeless. This may assist in developing services for the future, however it also illustrates the lack of other 'roles' that were available to people once they had made this transition out of homelessness. Tommy could no longer identify himself as a homeless person, but, what, or who could he now be? This is explored further in the next chapter, on homelessness and identity.

The long term targeting, support, involvement and consultation of service users, both continued to involve them in the system, and made them implicit in generating the ongoing construction of this system. As 'ex-service users' and therefore 'ex-homeless', they remained separate from those who were not, or had not, ever been explicitly reliant on support services as a targeted category. As these specialist services continue to develop to target certain groups, alongside a 'pulling back' of mainstream welfare services (Dean, 1999), this distinction may increase. Those who can afford it for example, may increasingly be accessing resources privately, such as health care, once provided for all, through the post-war welfare state, creating further polarisation and segregation.

The homeless services provided to the people studied here were important for many of them to make positive transitions and stabilise their life. They also, on an individual level, often provided positive social interactions, spaces to attend, and accommodation to live in. However on a critical macro-level this entire system represents an increasingly rationalised way to manage social problems (Kennett, 1999). Many services are under pressure from funding sources to work only with certain groups and meet targets of successful outcomes (Kennett, 1999) such as the number of people they move into housing, that does not necessarily reflect the complexity of the micro-level interactions and actions that are involved in this, and the work of the agencies illustrated here.

How this rationalised system operates can also create negative out-comes on micro-levels. For example, some, such as William, cited the pressures and difficulty the sheer number of options and choices they now had within this system could bring:

There are so many people involved with it [solving homelessness], so many agencies, you have to go and see this worker, and then you have to go and see that worker, it is just a load of nonsense (..) that's when they start to get annoyed, that's when they want to get full of it, drink away their days. It just depends how proactive the person [professional contact you have] you are dealing with is.

(William, 29)

William's quote illustrates once more a rationale for what may appear irrational actions. 'Getting full of it' was the only way to 'take control' of their situation, or deal with the pressure of so many options and choices some people have – but what was this 'it'? – escape? – and what did they use 'it' to 'opt out' of, to reject altogether? – this increasingly rationalised, reflexive, and individualised, alienating system? In acting in this way however they were recreating their own problematic situa-tion, and also the need for these regimes of the social to continue to develop, and increasingly more illiberal policies to 'control' those that continue to resist the targeting of this system, to exist. Even trying to reject this targeting by the welfare system, only drew people further into it, without actually improving their situation, as the following section describes.

5.   Recreation through rejection

A key trigger for those that remained homeless spiralling back into divestment passages was being evicted from temporary accommoda-tion. Often this appeared to occur due to their own actions, such as continuing to use alcohol, or not accessing the services they were pro-vided with. Once they were evicted from supported accommodation they often continued their ongoing cycle of homelessness staying with friends, sleeping rough, and sometimes in hostels or Bed & Breakfasts. In this way they remained in particularly vulnerable, marginal social situations, lacking the resources to access their own accommodation through any other means than the social welfare system, but rejected by this system also. They appeared also to reject it, by refusing to adhere to the constraints that it placed upon their behaviour. Therefore a 'deadlock' existed in their transitions – despite their repeated attempts to stabilise and improve their circumstances. It is also asserted here that these actions (such as ongoing substance use, violence) could be understood as one of the only ways to assert some agency or resist the reality they had experienced within the system they were in, especially given the level of poverty, trauma and marginalisation that their lives were imbued with. Lorna's case is used to illustrate this.

Lorna's story

Lorna, a 34 year old woman, remained homeless throughout the research. She had been homeless at this point for over ten years and had chronic alcohol, health, and behaviour. She moved between sleeping rough, staying with friends, and being in institutions, such as prison and hospital, during the research.

Lorna was in contact with street outreach workers and was first interviewed in prison. She had just lost a tenancy when she was in prison and had no-where to go when she was released. She was barred from most homeless accommodation due to her behavioural problems. By the third interview she was sleeping rough and sometimes staying with people she knew. In the following quote, taken from this third interview, she described being both embedded in a case management system but also 'outside' of it. She was unable to access the actual resources that could assist her due to the very problems she required support to address. Her actions meant she was rejected by the system in place to support people, but she also continued to be controlled by it. She had few other opportunities to provide herself with any more security or resources, from the intensely marginalised situation she was in:

> I can't go to the housing office myself, I could go and they turn around and say you're still on the waiting list, there is no houses. I mean I've been everywhere, [rehabs], hostels, B & B's and they all just say, 'there is no beds, we've got a ban on you, we're not putting you there', they just think if they give me a decent B & B I'll get drunk and cause trouble. I had a caseworker, and they said 'we're not taking you on' at the [centralised office to apply for housing] and I have a social worker but they are off ill. The [street outreach team] are trying to get me an appointment with a duty social worker.
>
> (Lorna, 42)

Street outreach workers had contact with Lorna to try to advocate for her, to obtain some form of accommodation, in negotiation with the other services that exist. The outcome of this advocacy could be positive – allowing particularly destitute people such as Lorna to access some form of accommodation, food, and emergency health care, when they may otherwise have faced illness or even death. However people like Lorna appeared trapped over the edge of society. It may be that she would have 'got drunk and caused trouble', but these issues still needed to be managed and addressed in some way. The services of this reflexive system required them to act in certain ways to access them. However in Lorna's case she was unable to act in this way, she was someone over the edge of society, with a history of intense marginality, abuse, behavioural problems and trauma in her life. The last time she had moved out of her housing was due to conflict with people she had asked to stay with her:

> *Well there this couple I knew, I took them in, they didn't have anywhere else to go, and I felt sorry for them, so I says come and stay here, and I went away for a couple of days and came back, and they had left it in a mess, and the guy, he was just sitting there, so I tried to throw him out, and he just set about me, kicking into me, broke my nose. I just run out the house, in must my t-shirt and trouser, no shoes – nothing. And then: I struggle when I'm homeless, I was taking a lot of OD's, just drinking for days in a row, into oblivion, and no caring.*
>
> (Lorna, 42)

What options did she have from this position and how should and can social services respond to such difficult circumstances and individuals? Highly entrenched groups of homeless people continue to exist, and their situation continues to be a difficult issue to address and resolve despite continued and often innovative development in doing so. They cannot be abandoned, but the complexity of their lives and the problems they have (and at times create for others) as they make transitions 'back' into society, given the level of marginality they have experienced, has to be acknowledged. The level of problems they can represent to others have to be tackled somehow also – they can themselves be violent, and create problems. In an ongoing praxis of structuration, these problems create, and are then created by individuals, within certain structural contexts. These actions can be symbolic manifestations of, as well as causing, real suffering.

Despite a welfare system being in place to resolve homelessness and vulnerability of a few of the people who took part in this study remained both materially and emotionally over the edge of society, sleeping rough, with many physical and mental health problems, at the end. And in the context of how far over the edge of normative behaviour some had gone over their life course – the intense trauma and marginality they experienced – their 'going over the edge' in the edgework they engaged in, was all they could do to escape this on a micro-level. These were real lives and real experiences of people operating in 21st-century Britain. Despite developments in homeless policy and services that have been introduced recently, and the improvements they have brought to how some people who are homeless may be assisted to resolve it, there remains people in situations like Lorna. There are people at the edge of society that this reflexive system has not 'worked' for, and their experiences, and changing circumstances have to continue to be explored. For these are the archetypal reviled 'outsiders' of late modern society, who may go on adding to those who sleep rough in the future. They still require understanding and perhaps radical new approaches to continue to try to address and alleviate the suffering their situation can bring and create. For many of the people whose lives are followed here this suffering included attempts to destroy themselves, through suicide. There are high rates of suicide among the homeless population (Baker, 1997).

Rejection of society – Rejection of self?: Suicide and homelessness

For some people, exercising their agency, as liberal individuals, to reject the options provided for them through the social welfare system, only acted to reduce the options they had to escape from the situation they were in, and exacerbated the marginality, and trauma they experienced. Suicide was sometimes felt by them to be one of the only remaining options they had, as the following quote from Connor about his experience of sleeping rough, illustrates:

> *I preferred it out on the street [rather than in supported accommodation], in the cold. It was safer for me. But I was getting dirty and you know, people look at you, I lay behind a building with an old carpet. I got mugged once. It's horrible. You go like that 'Do you want to kill yourself, do you want to live?' There's no easy way out. How do you do it without all the pain?*

> (Connor, 47)

Is suicide in this context the ultimate act of agency – of escape and resistance to the conditions of late modernity? Or the ultimate act of losing control over the self, leading to its destruction? During the interviews, 11 of the 28 discussed how they had recently attempted suicide. This theoretical aspect of suicide as edgework – suicide as the ultimate act of both losing and taking control over their individuality – may be something for further research and analysis in the future.

Clearly for those who remained homeless throughout the research and rejected, or were rejected by, the services currently available to them, the reflexive model of governance did not 'work' to resolve their homelessness. Yet they had few other resources they could use to resolve their homelessness or gain any more social security outside this system, in the reality they operated in. It may be that the only form of escape from this, underpinned by their lack of status, and lack of resources within this social structure, was to go entirely over the edge of normative behaviour. In the most extreme cases this meant attempting suicide, mental breakdown – although these may have medical and physiological roots, they could also be recognised as a response to the alienation of an increasingly individualised risk society (Lyng, 2005a), especially when people have very few resources to negate, buffer or escape this, through legitimate means of consumption and thrill seeking.

6. Transitions through homelessness and the reflexive system of governance

So all the people whose lives were studied here had contact with a range of different services that could be seen as making up a regime of the social (Dean, 1999), as they made their transitions through homelessness. Some of those who had moved into their own housing with the support of different agencies did describe how they had 'left homelessness behind'. For them the social welfare system had assisted them to access resources that had improved their material housing situation, and resolve their homelessness, within this reflexive model.

These services have been developed within a reflexive process through research, consultation and partnership with people who are experiencing these problems, and other agencies. This indicates that through this reflexive process a 'fit' may be being found between the macro-level policy developments and micro-level situation of individual homelessness, and policy responses to it. Certainly improvements are being made. For example, the number of rough sleepers in the UK significantly dropped after the introduction of the RSI (Randall & Brown, 1999a). In this way the reflexive model of governance may be going some way to provide a framework of social policy and a distribution of resources that does provide positive options and outcomes for people experiencing problematic situations such as homelessness. There may be positive outcomes from the process of reflexive governance for those who *actively engage in the options and possibility* for self-governance it provides. But it has also been identified that this system can go on recreating the reliance on it that some people have. Without addressing the fundamental structural and social problems that led to this need in the first place, this reliance will continue to go on. Furthermore, the very existence of this welfare system contributes to the fundamental structural context that also generates this dependency.

Reliance on the services of the social welfare system to access housing, social support, and crucially and perhaps unintentionally, for companionship and occupation, is due to a lack of resources. This lack is due to how these resources are distributed within the current social structure. This structural underpinning *may* be becoming increasingly obscured through the reflexive process of liberal individualisation that promotes the role of the individual and their choices and actions as key to how they negotiate the risks they face over their life course (Furlong & Cartmel, 1997).

So policy and welfare provision can create a system that does assist some people to gain positive outcomes, make transitions through homelessness, and access the resources they require to obtain their own tenancies – usually from the stock of social housing available. In this way the explicitly 'intended' outcome of this targeting (as part of a 'utopianistic goal' to improve society through reform and to resolve problems such as homelessness) may be achieved – but there is much to do to really solve the problems that underpinned this need for support. Some of the people whose lives are studied here may be manifestations of what can happen to people when they do not, or cannot, manage the risks and resources they face within the conditions of late modernity. They had had very real experiences of intense social, material, and physical deprivation, of inequality, marginality, poverty, vulnerability, and intensely traumatic incidents in their lives, and had to consolidate this within their life story, and their identity, on a micro-level. Their lives and actions do represent 'real' social problems. But they are also people with identities and emotions, and this also had to be taken into account if their actions are to be fully understood.

6
Homelessness, Identity and Social Networks

1. Identity and ontological security

The internal sense of identity that people have, stretched over time as they negotiate their life course, is obviously profoundly affected by external factors, such as their gender, age, ethnicity and the actual material circumstances they experience (Taylor, 1998). These circumstances include their (often changing) employment, housing and relationship status. These external 'real' factors are in turn affected by different and sometimes conflicting discourses that exist about how these categorical 'markers' of identity (Taylor, 1998) should be acted out or what they 'say' about that person (Goffman, 1969) and the extent to which it adheres to integrative, normative passages (Ezzy, 2001). Referring to the work of Ricoeur (1991a/b) it has been asserted here that these external factors are also woven subjectively by individuals into an internalised, narrative plot, creating a cohesive life story, and with it a consistent sense of ontological identity. It is through the use of discourses that individuals make sense of their own and others, identity, as it is manifest through these external factors and ontological security is maintained over time. However this requires a constant negotiation as external factors and events outside of the control of any one individual continue to affect their lives in ways that they may not predict, and because others may hold different discursive knowledge about.

Clearly the people studied here were profoundly affected by being homeless – this became an external identity factor that they had to reconcile with the internal narrative of their life. As theorists have asserted, housing (or rather having a 'home') is a crucial source of ontological security (Somerville, 1992; Kearns et al, 2000). By being homeless they not only lacked this, but had an external identity tied to discourses of

homeless people that exist – discourses that they were acutely aware
of. As has already been noted in Chapter 1, these discourses often
relate to the minimal conception of homelessness as rooflessness, and
as individual failing and deviance being the cause (Jacobs et al, 1999)
with victimhood or deviance a dominant motif (Fooks & Pantazis, 1999).
It is these discourses that people who are homeless are reflexively negotiating with as a marker of their identity.

Homelessness, stigma, and discourse

It has been identified (in Chapter 3) that entering the 'homeless system'
– the services, support and temporary accommodation that exists for
people who are homeless – was a pivotal point in the transitions
into homelessness studied here. At this point they had to explicitly
identify themselves as a 'homeless person'. This identity of 'being
homeless', and the social role that it brought, was then associated
with the discourses about homelessness that exist. Of course discourses on homelessness have historically been negative – an archetypal figure of someone 'over the edge' and outside of society (Kennett
& Marsh, 1999). As the following quote from Tommy highlights,
people who are homeless are also acutely aware of these discourses
of homeless people that exist. Why wouldn't they be? Most had
been on the 'other side' at some point, and may also have held these
views:

> *I think people still see homeless people as just addicts, or people with bits
> of string round their middle. And other people see it as you don't need
> to be on the street, there's places you can go, you don't need to be there
> because you can get benefits.*

> (Tommy, 33)

Some of the people studied here were addicts, some had slept rough,
some had begged. Many complex factors led to and exacerbated this, and
how it was responded to. What is important to highlight is that people
who are homeless are reflexively aware of the stigma attached to discourses of homeless people. They often feel an acute sense of stigma for
being homeless. Many indicated that they felt this stigma was not only
tied to perceptions about homeless people as deviant or 'other' to mainstream society, but also to a resentment of access to welfare entitlement
that exist for vulnerable people, who may be deemed 'undeserving' of
this entitlement due to the actions or behaviour – such as addiction
(Fooks & Pantazis, 1999). Keith's quote further illustrates this reflexive

awareness and also shows how they felt this stigma intensely when they engaged in interactions where their 'role' was that of a homeless person, such as with institutions of the welfare system:

I think, you still feel that stigma really when you're homeless. It's very hard when you go to the DHSS to get money, and stuff like that, you are stigmatised and really you are a second-class citizen. You are labelled.

(Keith, 34)

It is argued here that this stigmatised identity, and their awareness of it, had a profound effect on their sense of identity and social role in the interactions they engaged in. They felt internally that they were 'normal' people. But they also felt that other people would stigmatise them, and were aware of how marginalised they were. This sentiment mirrors the classic work of Goffman on stigmatised identities:

[the stigmatised individual's] deepest feelings about what [they are] may be [their] sense of being a normal person, a human being like anyone else (...) yet [they] may perceive, (..) that whatever others profess, they do not really 'accept' [them] and are not ready to make contact with [them] on 'equal grounds.'

(1963:19).

In this way, the homeless person they were, was someone who had been 'cast out' of the 'paradise' of belonging (Somerville, 1992) – both materially they were without housing, cast out ontologically, and out of the ability to interact with others on equal terms. In the context of the increasingly individualised and liberal social and political discourses of late modernity, they often had come to encapsulate a 'failed individual' (Bauman, 1998). The following quote from Brian succinctly highlights how they felt this. Brian was living in supported accommodation when he discussed how homelessness feels:

It's normal to go to work, and it's normal to go to the bank and get your wage, buy yourself a pair a denims, go out for a pint, go up the dancing. And that's why homelessness is so depressing, you can't do that, be normal. It's really bad, seeing everybody out enjoying their selves and you're stuck in a wee box. It's hard, I'm not a bad person, doesn't make you a bad person just cause you're homeless, but they [other people] treat you like a bad person.

(Brian, 35)

So Brian's felt he could no longer be 'normal' now that he was homeless. He equated the ability to be 'normal' and integrated, with the ability to consume and interact with other people. Bauman (1998:37) argues *'in a consumer society, a 'normal life' is the life of consumers'* and paid work is the means to have the economic resources to consume and have a normal social status. However the majority of those studied here had only ever experienced insecure or informal employment. None felt that they were able to work whilst they were homeless. Often this was because they would lose the funding for the services they were accessing, or perceived the rent where they were living was more than they could afford to pay if they were employed. Without a role – without the ability to produce or consume – they *felt* increasingly isolated and stigmatised, unable to interact with others as 'normal' members of society, although they of course perceived themselves to be normal people. And this, coupled with their lack of housing and with it a sense of 'place' would have affected their ontological security, acutely (Padgett, 2007; Kearns et al, 2000).

Now that they had made this divestment passage into homelessness, both the material reality they were in, and how they emotionally experienced this, only acted to reinforce their alienation and isolation from mainstream society. They felt they were conceived as 'bad' as individuals.

Furthermore, once they were accommodated in temporary accommodation they were not only isolated subjectively, but often actually physically separated from society by the very location and nature of this accommodation. This duality could act to further alienate people as they disengaged from other interactions they could have out side of this environment. The following quote from David illustrates this. David was homeless for over ten years, living in hostels, rehabs and sleeping rough:

When I was in hostels I kind of lost my family, I cut myself off from them. I don't know if it's embarrassment, because you're in a hostel, I think people see beggars on the street and just tar everyone with the one brush sort of thing, I didn't even feel part of my family, never mind part of society.

(David, 38)

As they became homeless they became increasingly isolated, cutting themselves off from, and being cut off from, the 'normal' activities of day-to-day life. What is suggested in this chapter is that this alienation underpinned the actions that they engaged in that could then further stigmatise and marginalise them. As Bauman (1998:93) has noted, underpinned by the process of increased individualisation, the 'poor', have become increasingly isolated: *'flawed consumers are lonely, and when they are left lonely for a long time they tend to become loners; they do not see how society can help'.*

So as these people went over the edge they were not only marginalised from mainstream society due to their actual homelessness, they also sometimes isolated themselves (Bauman, 1998). Homelessness is not a static state or identity however. All these people had complex life stories, stretching from before they were homeless, into their future. In the next section, this time before, and the sense of ontological security they may have had before their homelessness, is explored.

Another key point to illustrate from this study is the discriminatory nature of being part of an 'outsider' group, such being homeless. In a time when cohesion and equalities are high on the political and social agenda (Zetter et al, 2006), there are still groups that are discriminated against, due to the external characteristics and circumstances they are experiencing. Being homeless, or being an addict, for example, are just such discriminating markers – and as equalities continue to be debated (Vizard & Burchardt, 2007) this discrimination is surely a problematic and underemphasised issue, yet to be addressed.

2. Lives before homelessness

As was discussed in Chapter 3, some of the lives studied here had been entirely imbued with trauma, marginalisation, and institutionalisation. Others however had had more 'settled' integrated lives prior to becoming homeless. At the first interview, after discussing their life histories in detail, they were all asked when they had been 'most settled' in their lives. This question is here used as a marker to identify periods of relative ontological security (Giddens, 1984) in their lives – times they recalled as 'settled' and belonging in their place in the world.

Fifteen described being most settled in the past as when they were living with partners, and children if they had any. Three said it was in their childhood, when they were living with their parents and family. Eight said 'now', the situation they were in at the point of the first interview, was their most settled time. Five of these were living in temporary accommodation at that point. So 26 of the 28 fell into one of two categories: being most settled 'now', in their current situation; or their 'settledness' being related to domestic circumstances, when they were living with family or partners.

Identifying and analysing ontological security and the sense of identity that someone has can not be done in a prescriptive way. However three clear themes could be identified from examining how they described their lives prior to becoming homeless, and from how settled they were or had been, that related to the sense of ontological security and social integration they had.

Markers of ontological security

Firstly, the importance of social networks was once again highlighted. These were the markers that defined times when they had been settled (or not) in their lives. When these were secure and they had a clear role within these networks (as a partner, brother, mother for example) they had been sure of 'who they were'. However when these networks were negative, such as being in an abusive relationship, this could lead to a time of crisis and breakdown in this role. Therefore it could also be that moving away from the threat others posed to them, and having the capacity to manage their own space, was tied to this sense of control over their 'selves' that they felt they had. This was often what was cited when people explained why 'now' was the most settled and secure they had felt. However to regain a sense of 'who they were' once more they had to enter into and develop new relationships with people. Otherwise they faced intense isolation and lacked a role, constructed through the relationships they had with others.

Secondly, when asked to describe themselves before being homeless all just said 'normal'. What being 'normal' actually constitutes is not the issue here. They had all had different experiences over their life course. The point is that most people see themselves in this way, however many of those studied here felt they had ceased to be seen as 'normal' once they were homeless. Obtaining this 'normality', a 'normal' day-to-day existence once more, was also what they aspired to in the future. This was what would lead to their sense of having made a 'real' transition out of homelessness, whatever their material housing circumstance.

Thirdly, they recognised that it has been a crisis point – a going over the edge – that had led to their separation from an externally 'normal' status. As they recalled their life and how they felt about it, it was when they identified their edgework going 'over the edge' into addiction and homelessness that they felt their identity and ontological security had been ruptured. They began to feel they were losing their 'selves' as this process occurred (and often they suffered anguish and depression at this point). They then had to try to regain some sense of ontological security and a foot hold in the world once more. They identified that they did indeed need to find some way to bring themselves back over the edge – both subjectively and materially. This was their 'fateful moment' (Giddens, 1991), but only one they retrospectively recounted as such, once they had gone over the edge, and that they may not have reflexively at the time realised would have had such a damaging impact. Indeed as explored throughout, at the time they may have had clear rationales for this action and often were still engaging in edgework.

Lives and transitions, and the sense of security people have within them are complex and subjective. Elizabeth's ongoing process of negotiation across her life course is used to illustrate this.

Elizabeth's story

Elizabeth was 41 years old when she was took part in the first interview. She was living in supported accommodation. Elizabeth had had a relatively stable childhood and her life had initially taken integrative passages. As the quote below describes, she had been employed, married and had obtained her own housing:

All my life I've stayed in [the same area]. I've not moved out of it. [I lived with] my mum and my dad [growing up]. We all got on...it was fine, and everything was alright. I was 16 when I left school. And I got a job as a machinist, on sewing machines, in a factory. I got married. This was when I was about 19, 20 years old. We got a council flat.

(Elizabeth, 41)

Elizabeth did not have access to a high level of economic or human capital through her education or employment, but she experienced degrees of security, and was integrated into the community she lived in. Over time however Elizabeth's life became characterised with insecurity, and traumatic incidents. Due to domestic violence, she left the flat she had with her husband and returned to her mother's home:

I stuck that [house with my husband] about eighteen months and then I was hospitalised. I used to get beating's. Until I got up, and just left one day and then I moved back in with my mum.

She then obtained her own tenancy once more, but continued to experience domestic violence from new partners over the next ten years. She had a breakdown and returned to living with her mother at one point.

Although she had experienced periods of what may be defined as hidden homelessness (staying with her mother, for example) these times of living with her family also provided her with important sources of social support and security. She only *identified* her first episode of homelessness occurring once she was in her 30s, after she became addicted to heroin (she began using heroin with a partner) and had to leave the flat she was living in. By now she had become estranged from her family due to her drug use:

> *I was on the drugs and I had to leave [partner's house]. It was about then that I had nothing, no where to go.*

She began to sleep rough, before entering a rehab. She then moved into the supported accommodation, where she was living at the time of the first interview. Below she describes how she felt about this process:

> *In the space of a year I lost everything, my children, my house, everything had just went and here I was an addict at six stone and …I still see, it's like drugs, it wasn't anything about us, it was always like film stars or rock singers or pop groups. I didn't associate hard drugs with anybody that was just, a little normal woman with two children and a crap life, and I ended up injecting when I was 35 years of age.*

Elizabeth thought of her life as 'normal' up to this point, she was just a 'little woman' with a 'crap' life. Then it had been ruptured by her drug use and homelessness. However she had also experienced intense trauma and difficulty prior to this. She had experienced repeated abusive relationships and a mental breakdown. When she was asked when she had been most settled, she said 'now', living in supported accommodation. Below, she describes why this was:

> *[I am most settled] here. Because all my adult life, between one thing and another, even before the drugs, I've never, ever been safe. Just going to your bed – every time I used to shut my eyes and sort of, is he going to batter me? What's going to happen? It's the safest…. I'm 41 this year… this is the safest I've felt. Ever.*

So her sense of ontological security was tied to her sense of being secure in the actual environment she lived in. She was controlling the voluntary and involuntary edgework in her life, and due to this control felt settled. A sense of control (or 'mastery' as it is referred to) over housing, circumstances and treatments has been identified as key to how successfully people can make transitions out of disordered circumstances and manage the related problems they have, such as mental illness (Greenwood, Shaefer-McDaniel, Winkel & Tsemberis, 2005). This is reiterated once more as key. At this stage, Elizabeth was not worried about being assaulted by her partner; she was controlling her drug use; her mental well-being was improving due to this sense of security she had. She then moved into her own housing – a Housing Association tenancy – and continued negotiating her identity and sense of ontological security in this next stage. This next stage in Elizabeth's life is discussed in Section 4 of this chapter. What her experiences also illustrate is the constant negotiation that people make, over time, with their circumstances and lives. Elizabeth has been, and was, many things in her life – mother, addict, daughter, machinist, wife, victim of violence. But essentially to her and the people who knew her she was just a person, none of these 'markers' alone could begin to illustrate or explain her life.

3. Being homeless

In this section how the people studied described 'being homeless' is explored. From this situation, they had to regain a sense of ontological security once more, a sense of their place in the material space they were in and compatibility with their narrative identity. Once this resocialisation had occurred, it could be that for some people, making a transition *out* of homelessness also then involved another crisis of selfhood.

'The slow grind' – Homelessness and day-to-day life

Claire's case can be used to illustrate how being homeless and accommodated in temporary accommodation was experienced. Claire had experienced repeated homelessness throughout her life. She had lived in many different forms of temporary accommodation and her own tenancies. Here she describes a typical day for her in temporary accommodation:

> *I get up, go downstairs, get something to eat, go back up and watch the telly. If I'm staying in I'll stay in my room and watch the telly all day. I'm thinking about going back to [counselling] cause it gets me out of here. Time is my biggest problem actually. Too much time to sit and think, play with my mind.*

Time itself, and the boredom that accompanied having nothing to do and no role within the time-space they inhabited, could be a serious problem. This was life as a 'homeless person' when they were living in hostels or supported accommodation. They had few resources, little to do to occupy their time, or opportunity to change this. They were in a social context where the majority of the social interactions they engaged in involved people in the same situation as them. Alongside this, they were attempting to emotionally deal with and manage a range of traumatic and risky events that had occurred in their life, such as violence, addiction, and mental illness, sometimes compounded by the environment they are in (Hutson, 1999). The quote from Frank, below, highlights the effect this life could have, ontologically. They felt they were 'going nowhere', they faced the 'slow grind' of this day-to-day life. Using substances to escape this 'horrendous repetition' was one means of escape, of 'mindscaping' themselves away from this reality (Cohen & Taylor, 1992):

> *I think even if somebody went into a hostel clean [not using alcohol or drugs] and they didn't have any support base round about them, they would just be washed up in a big cloud of negativity in a hostel because it's just – nowhere in there – nobody in there going anywhere in a hurry. It's just a slow grind.*
>
> (Frank, 39)

The alternative to interacting with others in the same situation as they were was to 'hide' away and isolate themselves. However with few alternative means to occupy their time available to them, this isolation could lead to intense loneliness and more difficulty in their live as they became increasingly disembedded from 'normal' social interactions. Many described being homeless as a time they lost a sense of self:

> *It's as if you are a nothing, a no one. That's how homelessness makes you feel.*
>
> (Rachel, 46)

In the face of this they had to find the means to cope with this day-to-day existence or face the anomie of 'nothingness', of being nothing (the ontological crisis of Somerville's (1992) last indicator of homelessness). They had to try to regain a sense of ontological security, resocialise themselves (Giddens, 1984) as a homeless person, within the environment they were in. This process may be what underpinned the actions and interactions they then engaged in.

Homelessness, actions and interactions

In the following quote Claire describes this tension inherent when living in temporary accommodation:

> *[In homeless accommodation] you want to shelter yourself ... hide away, 'I'll just get through it, keep your head down' but then you end up, it could be drinking or it could be taking drugs... just to escape it [the experience of homelessness].* People do turn to the streets, and the drugs, because they're meeting other people who don't care about themselves, because they've been in that situation for a long time, you're swept up with anybody and everybody.

(Claire, 26)

On the one hand Claire had wanted to 'deny' her homelessness and avoid the 'risks' that this environment could bring. Claire's comment also illustrates, however, that as a social 'being' she had to interact and engage with others in whatever material situation she was in. The social interactions and social networks that people have once they become homeless is often with people in the same circumstance. This meant the people studied here felt they could get 'swept up' in what was now 'normal' behaviour, within this social setting. And if, as was argued earlier, this setting and the structural position these people were in can be understood as a trigger for their edgework, as a form of escape and taking control, then it is logical that a concentration of people in this setting together may further exacerbate this concentration of edgework. Once again an interplay of emotional and material factors provide a rationale for what may appear irrational behaviour – such as ongoing alcohol or drug use, violence, or sleeping rough to be with friends who had been evicted from supported accommodation. On a micro-level these actions were described as the only means they had to operate on a day-to-day basis, to cope, to 'exist'. They were therefore rationale actions given the circumstance they were in, as noted in other studies on deviant behaviour (Craine, 1997) and assimilation (Young, 2006).

This edgework was not only a way to escape the situation they were in, or to interact with others. It may also have been a way to take control over the situation they were in, and ontologically resist the potentially dehumanising experience of being accommodated in institutions such as hostels, rehabs, or supported accommodation. This dehumanising effect was first highlighted in Chapter 4, as the quote from Francesca illustrated – *'that homeless hostel broke me....they are hell on earth... ramming all of the chickens into one building...these are people with feelings and emotions, and a lot of them may not act like it, but at the end of the day they are'.* It may be that in the face of being homeless, a new day-to-day routine, and sense of identity as a 'homeless person' had to be developed to regain ontological security. The alternative faced was the horrific anomie of being 'nothing', over time.

Being homeless and regaining ontological security

Most of those studied had experienced being homeless for many years. Some had been living precariously on 'the edge' of society all their lives. They were used to living in hostels, being in prison, and rehabs, for example. The accommodation people who are homeless can access changes regularly (Fitzpatrick, 2000; Anderson & Tulloch, 2001), and each time they entered a new form of accommodation, their environment and day-to-day life changed. Often these moves were not something they had 'control' of. They either moved there as it was deemed more 'appropriate' for them by their support workers, or because they had to leave the accommodation they were in due to time constraints on how long someone could stay there, or they were evicted for not abiding by the rules. Sometimes they chose to stay with friends for short periods, or to sleep rough. These patterns of change became 'normal' life for them, although they were also aware that it was not the 'ideal' – that they were not taking integrative passages and remained 'outside'.

It could be argued that, over time, to regain their sense of ontological security, many had internalised this life and the identity of being homeless. This was who they were, in their narrative identity (Ricoeur, 1991a). Being homeless may have been difficult at times, but had come to constitute their day-to-day reality and routine. As a means to 'cope' with the lack of control they may have felt they had, within the material reality they operated within, they may have emotionally internalised the identity and lifestyle that they had, conciled it with the person they perceived themselves to be and acted accordingly. In this way they managed to maintain some ontological security and take some 'control' back over their life course.

Claire's case can be used once more as an example to illustrate this point. Below she describes how she felt she should be 'institutionalised' after the history she had had:

I was in care all my life, and then I was through all the hostel systems, I should be institutionalised, and that's what I thought, that once I got a house my life would fall apart and I would be back on the streets, doing drugs and all that.

(Claire, 26)

However negative being homeless could be, the alternative – of obtaining her own tenancy – also carried risk. This brought the risk of losing it all again, going through difficult spirals of divestment once more. These actions were part of 'being homeless' and similar processes of the self fulfilling prophecy of making transitions out of homelessness reported in other studies – that people feel they cannot do it and so set themselves up to fail (Dix, 1995).

In Claire's case she was living in her own flat at the end of the research. Transitions out of homelessness can be made when the material resources of housing and support are provided. However what this study highlights is that this often provided a precarious security. Many had few other 'possible selves' (Markus & Nurius, 1986) to fit into the narrative identity they had. They remained flip-flopping on the edge, materially and emotionally. Claire had had tenancies previously and had become homeless again each time. She spoke in the interviews about how difficult integrating into 'mainstream' society was after a life of institutionalisation and homelessness:

I have worked, you know, like jobs in shops and that. It's a lot better when I am working you know, but then the people you're working with, they've all got their families, they've got this, they're doing that, but I've not got that, I can't put anything towards it, when they're all talking, and I find that difficult, I just don't know how to make conversations.

(Claire, 26)

Some, such as Claire, had been in this cycle of homelessness and institutionalisation throughout their life. They had always had close contact with institutions of the state. This contact was bound up within the structural conditions they existed within and the social and cultural conditions of late modernity. Perhaps an unintended consequence of the welfare state that has developed throughout this time, has been to create this group of 'outsiders'. Claire did not feel she could 'put anything towards' the normal lives others around her had. Being 'outside' had become normal life for her. So once embedded in this welfare system, it can be particularly difficult to reintegrate once more (as studies into the experiences of drug users (Buchanan, 2004) and sex workers (McNaughton & Sanders, 2007) have also noted).

Homelessness as normal life

For some their homelessness now constituted not 'being homeless' but just 'being' – this was their 'normal' life, as Margaret discussed:

> *See, you get used to it [homelessness], even though you hate it, you still get used to it, you get used to the people, to being there and the people there. It becomes normal; normal life.*

(Margaret, 43)

Those who remained homeless by the end of the study had all experienced long-term and repeated homelessness over their life course. For some of them their social networks consisted almost entirely of people in the same situation as them. Often they shared a lack of resources, and experiences of poverty, trauma and vulnerability. They also often engaged in forms of edgework, such as alcohol or drug use together. The following quote from Gary, who had spent 20 years rough sleeping and living in temporary accommodation, gives resonance to this:

> *When you're on your own just staring at four walls, you know, you've nobody to talk to, just listening to your watch, I mean you're just living your life away to nothing.....but the friends I've all got, they're just in the same boat as myself, alcoholics.*

(Gary, 52)

What option did Gary face than engage in these interactions, this 'lifestyle'? He faced intense isolation and loneliness, leading to a sense of non-existence. He had poor physical health and suffered from chronic alcoholism. The *stigma* of homelessness and of the 'lifestyle' associated with it meant that other people in the same situation (often for the same reasons) were the only source of social networks where they could interact with people on 'equal' terms some had – just as the quote from Goffman earlier in this chapter articulated.

Interactions and social networks remained key mechanisms affecting lives when they were homeless. On a subjective level, it is entirely rational that people seek out relationships and interactions with others, yet when these people occupy the same low social status and also have few resources, this network can act to exacerbate this situation and the problems and risk inherent (as studies such as Alexander & Ruggieri, 1998, also note). In Chapter 3 the concept of the rationale

of irrational behaviour was introduced. Social networks and the interactions people engage in within these networks also generate this rationale. To be normal, to 'fit in' in this reality of being homeless may
be to act in ways that can also exacerbate or maintain a negative
situation.

Ontological crisis and transitions out of homelessness

For some, homelessness had become normal life, and so to change this
and make a transition out, then also involved ontological crisis. To
'move on' from being homeless usually required them to reject contact
with the people that they knew whilst being homeless and resocialise
in a new landscape of settlement. However risky or violent these relationships had sometimes been, these were people they had developed
close emotional ties with over time. Homelessness was part to their
identity and deeply imbued in their day-to-day life, to change this,
may have involved a rejection of the individual they were, if they were
to develop a 'new self'. This may provide a subjective emotional reason
for why it did not always occur.

So ontology and identity impacts on actions and transitions. Eddie's
quote (from Chapter 4) can be used once more to illustrate this – *'I was
getting there...I was progressing, maybe that frightened me, I don't know'*.
Eddie remained homeless throughout the research. He was evicted
from hostels and supported accommodation for continuing to use
drugs. However to cease using drugs and 'move on' meant facing up to
the abuse he had suffered previously, something that led to a intense
psychological and ontological crisis. In the face of this, it may indeed
be more rational, on an individual micro-level to remain homeless,
and to continue using drugs. They had to 'pull apart their past', and
face the ontological crisis of doing so, before they were able to 'move
on' in their transitions. And this could be intensely difficult even if the
material resources they required to obtain their own tenancy had been
provided by the state.

Once more it is clear that transitions out of homelessness require a
myriad of support, that cannot be prescriptive, but that Pleace (1995)
notes is likely to include some of the following five issues: housing;
support; living skills; finance/income, and positive social networks.
These mirror the different resources that have been identified here as
key to providing a foundation for resilience. Lacking these can remove
the 'safety net' that may prevent people becoming homeless when
something 'goes wrong' in their life. In the case of the people studied
here mechanisms of the welfare state and support services it funds then

had to step in to plug this gap, which was achieved with differing levels of success.

People making a transition out of homelessness are active participants in this however, and despite some of the difficulties they faced in obtaining access to some of the support they needed (be it social or financial for example) another key point to emphasis is that most *did* continue to attempt to make these transitions. They continued to attempt to survive, to change their circumstances, and to integrate into a society they had often been 'outside' of for long periods of their lives. Nineteen had their own housing at the end of the research. They may still have been experiencing problems in their lives, but this was often a more integrative phase. What requires further understanding however is how to cease the triggering of the individual actions that led to their homelessness – that led to lives going over the edge.

4.   Lives after homelessness

So the majority of the people whose transitions through homelessness were studied had their own housing (in the form of socially rented tenancies) by the end of the research. However it has also been identified that many were flip-flopping between integration and divestment. They were no longer homeless but many of the factors that had led to their homelessness had not fundamentally changed. However some did experience more positive, integrative transitions and in this section lives, beyond homelessness, are explored.

Integration, interactions and social networks

As these 19 of the 28 made their transition out of homelessness, some had made contact with relatives or old friends, sometimes through a process of mediation between them, their family, and their support workers. This could improve their social networks and increase their social capital. Due to these relationships they were also able to reintegrate more, to *feel* ontologically like a 'normal' person, operating within mainstream society, again. The social identity of being 'homeless' could begin to be superseded by other forms of identity they had, due to the interactions with others they were now engaging in. Continuing the cases of Elizabeth and Tommy illustrate this.

Elizabeth's life beyond homelessness

Elizabeth moved into her own housing during the research and had began to spend time with her mother and family again. They had lost contact when she became homeless. Below she describes the effect regaining this contact had:

> *I'm going on holiday with my mum soon, I'm looking forward to that, see when you met me a year ago who would have thought I'd be going on holiday with them, they weren't even speaking to me then, it is such a difference when you get your family back.*
>
> (Elizabeth, 41)

Elizabeth had made contact with her mother before moving into her own tenancy, when she was living in supported accommodation. This was after she had stopped using heroin, and had been through a period in a residential rehab. They now regularly visited each other, went shopping together, and spoke on the phone. Sometimes she phoned her mother for advice on how to do things around her house.

If the people who obtained their own housing were able to make contact with other people they knew, such as their family and friends from before being homeless, they described this as an important aspect of their transition out of homelessness. This aspect of transitions remained one highlighted in research but approaches to actually promote them are undeveloped despite this (Fitzpatrick et al, 2000). The people studied here were able to develop a status as a 'normal person' once more if they managed to reconnect with positive social networks. This 'feeling' of normality did not come about just because they gained their own housing, this was a much longer process, tied to these other factors. The interactions they engaged in, regardless of whether they were housed or not, were pivotal to the sense of identity and security they felt. So mirroring classic work such as that by Maslowe (1987; 1999) their transitions had to be made on material, emotional, and social levels. This can be conceptualised that three levels of the social world had to come together for this to be achieved – the structural (the actual real world they were in, and how it is constructed), the social (their family, friends, interactions, networks) and the individual (their own internal senses, identity, agency). These relate to the key causal mechanisms discussed in Section 3 of Chapter 2, foregrounding this analysis – economic and housing structures, interpersonal and socio-structural forces, and the individual. Their resilience and ability to develop integrative passages over their live course will be underpinned by a triangulation of these structural forces. In turn this resilience and the individual acts that stem from it will affect the circumstance that people have – the material reality, and how they experience it subjectively – in a dynamic, feedback loop, incorporating each strata, over time (Fitzpatrick, 2005).

Clearly social networks and the interactions they allow people to engage in are crucial for them to generate integrative passages over the life course. When things have 'gone wrong', this is a particularly important mechanism to assist people come 'back' into society. Tommy's experiences illustrate this further.

Tommy's life beyond homelessness

Tommy had a small group of close friends he had lost contact with as his mental health deteriorated and he became homeless. He made contact with them again after he moved into his own housing. Here he explains how this support was crucially important to assist him feel integrated once more, and to cope with his ongoing mental illness:

> You've not got markers around you [when you are homeless]. I mean things like, if I'm feeling paranoid I can take out a couple of my mates and they might say 'I don't think so somehow,' you know, have a talk about it. I think support can come in many shapes and forms, going for a pint with your mate, talking about football.

Obtaining housing was an important outcome required to make a transition out of homelessness, triggered essentially by the housing structure – the supply available, where and how it can be accessed, with which resources. However social contacts were then a key mechanism that then acted to assist people continue to make integrative passages (and these are embedded within interpersonal structures). These networks provide the markers required to maintain and develop a sense of (ontological) security within a new 'phase' in life on an individual level. Making contact with positive social networks was sometimes facilitated and encouraged by support workers as part of their 'recovery' out of homelessness. When this was successful it meant people could develop a support network, and access resources, outside of the welfare system. Opportunities to allow people to develop these independent sources of support and resources are key, if transitions out of homelessness are to be made – on all the structural levels discussed above, releasing resources of social, economic and material capital. Yet this interpersonal level is particularly complex to address due to the subjective nature of such relationships. Once again resilience (as discussed in Chapter 3) may actually be the crucial mechanism that can act to allow people to develop integrative passages over their life course wherever they start from. Yet this resilience is deeply undermined by poverty, trauma, and a lack of resources, generated on multiple causal levels. Furthermore whilst there may be recognition that resilience is a crucial mechanism to foster in people, how to go about doing so remains unclear. It may be that it is at the interpersonal level that this is most important as it does not appear that economic and material resources alone necessarily provide it. In a time of when people are relatively richer in material terms than ever before, it does not follow that they are happier, stronger or more secure in their world (Dorling, 2007; Layard, 2006). Instead the diseases of excess – often forms of edgework – appear all the more endemic (Patton & Viner, 2007). Certainly it remains that informal sources of support are important and as Hutson (1999:223) argues *'informal or 'private' pathways and networks should be acknowledged by, incorporated into and strengthened by public policies'.* How to successfully do so appears to be the challenge.

There are also some important qualifications that have to be made about the positive effect social networks can have. Some of the people studied here did not have any positive social networks they could re-contact. They had few means to meet new people, or to develop new social networks once they were living alone in their own housing. They may have been in care as a child, and had a history of abusive family relationships and friendships. The only people they knew may have been people who had been or were still homeless. They may have been trying to avoid people who had once been abusive or violent towards them. Relationships also carry risk. Social networks can generate negative as well as positive effects. And for those with no sources of positive social networks, how could the positive effects of these networks be obtained?

In other cases, material and economic resources were required to be able to engage successfully in interpersonal relationships – going for a drink, going on holiday. Therefore these resources need to be available for people to live relatively 'normal' lives relative to the consumerist context or relative affluence they operate within (Dorling, 2007).

Putting homelessness in the past

It is important to highlight that some of the people studied were beginning to move on, along more integrative emotional and material passages in their life course, beyond just moving into housing. Bess's story is an example of this.

Bess's life beyond homelessness

Bess was living in her own housing (a socially rented tenancy) by the end of the research. She had moved there from supported accommodation. At the third interview she had recently started a new relationship, and was thinking about trying to access a college course in the future. In the quote below she describes some of these positive developments:

> Things have been brilliant, I've started going out with a man. My confidence has gone up, I've been getting out more....getting up, cleaning, going to the shops, going into town. And that's good, I feel my time is filled up, and also now, I feel as if I can relax, whereas before I always felt I had to get up and do something. I saw [housing support] worker for a while, and it was good, but I've stopped seeing her now. That was my decision, well to get on with my life, not put my problems onto someone else. I have the strength to do that now, I don't need other people to do it.
>
> (Bess, 25)

She was reducing contact with her support workers and had increased the contact with her family. They had become estranged when she was homeless. So her resilience and resources had improved. However as the following comment also highlights she still worried that problems she had had in the past would recur. She felt unable to tell her family about having been homeless. She had worked in prostitution whilst homeless and had experienced violence (including being raped) from partners and other men. She did not feel able to enter paid employment because of the 'benefits trap':

> Sometimes I think like I'm still making the same mistakes though, like having a boyfriend again, and a year ago I was like 'I hate all men!' But I know I've developed my own sense of well-being. So maybe it is different, maybe I'm not making the same mistakes. I saw my mum last week. I saw them after I spoke to you last and that was a bit scary. But everything is fine now. I haven't told them though about like being homeless and those things, I keep that quiet. (...) I have been put off considering getting work because of the whole benefits thing, I mean the money, and covering everything, but I would like to eventually, it would be nice to rely on my own money.
>
> (Bess, 25)

As Bess story illustrates, transitions out of homelessness can be made, but this is not without challenges. It requires both material and emotional outcomes to develop, such as access to reasonable housing, and opportunities to negate the stigma of having been homeless and the trauma and vulnerability that had often accompanied it. The opportunity to reintegrate fully into society remained limited for many of the people studied. They were flip-flopping close to the edge. They lacked opportunities to develop a new social role or new social identity – and once again this particularly related to the social interactions (or lack of) they now could engage in. And in turn this may have related to the economic and housing structures they were embedded within – for these constrained or enabled where they could live, with whom, and how they could spend their time.

Isolation and stigma – After homelessness

All of those who moved into their own housing could describe the intense difficulties they faced as they made this critical transition. Many were scared that they would not be 'able to cope', and would 'lose everything again'.

Overwhelmingly those who had gained their own housing cited isolation, loneliness, and boredom as key problems they were now experiencing. This is a common complaint made by participants in studies of transitions out of homelessness (Alexander & Ruggieri, 1998; Fitzpatrick, 2000). They still often 'felt' 'outside' of society. Once they had sorted the legal aspects of their tenancy, moved in and obtained the basic household goods they required, usually with the assistance of their housing support worker, they said they had 'nothing' to occupy their time and few means to interact with others, or get to know new people. It may be that for anyone making a transition to a new living arrangement or area there may be periods of isolation or loneliness (or indeed for people who are settled and without problems). It is in exploring issues such as this that a longer period of tracking the sample, had it been possible, could have been very illuminating. However it may also be that there is something distinct about making a transition out of homelessness (or other disordered circumstances (Buchanan, 2004; McNaughton & Sanders, 2007)) that makes isolation particularly problematic. For example, many were unsure whether they would be able to tell new people that they met about their 'past'. However this meant they were inhibited from developing new relationships or contacts. The following comment from Ann illustrates this:

Well I'm not going to tell them [neighbours] anything about my past. I just don't want them to know that I was a drug addict and that I had been through the homeless system. I just don't want them to get that impression of me.

(Ann, 26)

Therefore the stigma attached to homelessness was also a key mechanism that could go on affecting their transitions, even after they were homeless. New people that they met may or may not have actually been judging them in negative ways due to them having been homeless. The point is that they did not want people to know this about them. This could reflexively inhibit their actions and their ability to interact with others in the future. The following comment from Keith, who was living in his own tenancy throughout the research, after a history of repeated homelessness and drug addiction, further highlights this ongoing isolating affect of a past of homelessness, and also how this interacted with edgework:

I keep myself to myself, I've got no friends at all. I don't want my friends to be ex-addicts and I don't want 'clean' friends 'cause I'm hiding the past from them, that I used to be an addict. So I don't have any choice

(Keith, 34)

Keith's comment also illustrates a paradox. He too wanted to avoid people who may be considered deviant or risky, due to past acts they had engaged in and the risk they posed to him – such as 'ex-addicts'. But in this way he was trapped – he felt other people would not want to know him, or that he would have to lie about his past. He felt who he had been and the identity he had had over time, could not now be reconciled into a narrative identity acceptable to mainstream society. The experience of having been homeless was something that had to 'fit' into their sense of narrative identity, over time. The inability to do so could act as a barrier to being able to move on in the future. One way it could act as a barrier was that it went on providing a rationale for edgework. This edgework was the only way to escape this reality, or assert their 'selves', from this trapped and isolated situation.

Self-actualisation, edgework, and isolation

Boredom and loneliness was often cited as the reason for relapse. Substance use was a form of escape from this ennui and a wall of exclusion (Buchanan, 2004) brought about by the duality of edges (subjective stigma and material poverty) discussed in Chapter 3. So the stigmatised identity, attached to them due to the past of homelessness, addiction, mental illness, that they had experienced, operated as a barrier to developing positive social identities and networks in the future. William describes this effect, below. William moved into his own housing over the course of the research. By the last interview he was relatively settled there but was concerned because he had recently started to use heroin again, with people he knew:

Well staying on my own, has been problematic, I kind of miss the company [I had in supported accommodation], I've not got that now, if I'm not careful about the kind of company I keep, I'm with addicts, whatever, people to spend time with.

(William, 29)

Intense social isolation could be the rationale for spending time with people that had brought risk in the past. Even once housed, the people studied here could continue to experience the tension encapsulated in the rationale of irrational behaviour identified earlier. It may appear 'irrational' to take the risk of drug use or addiction by entering a social context and interacting with people where this activity is the 'norm' – the action required to 'fit' in. This may seem particularly irrational when these same factors had initially appeared to have led to them becoming homeless, and they had recently resolved this. However on a micro-level, the alternative – the intense boredom, loneliness, and isolation – faced after homelessness, provided a rationale for this. Through this edgework they could retain some escape and some sense of identity, against the 'nothingness' they faced in their day-to-day life.

Using the findings from this section, and on the 'flip-flopping' effect in their transitions routes, outlined in Chapter 4, it is asserted here that these were people becoming 'trapped individuals'. Elizabeth's comment, describes this process. Despite her contact with her mother, and relative integration, she also felt isolated, depressed, and could see little opportunity for her life to change in the future. This sentiment was something repeatedly brought up – once they were living in their own housing, had gone through being homeless, they felt they had 'nothing':

Once you've gone through the whole system, and you've got your little house and then you've done all that and everything's fine, there's nothing to do. I think that's how a lot of people end up going back on drugs. There's nothing then, nothing at all. And there must be thousands like me. They've got to the point, they're clean, they have their own little

place, starting to get a little bit of pride back in themselves, starting to feel
good, and there is just, nothing.

(Elizabeth, 42)

Once settled in their own tenancies all were still relying on the state for
income and housing. They were in 'limbo'. They often felt they had
'nothing' then not even a focus of making a transition out of homelessness or contact with support workers. They could see few opportunities
for this to change. The subjective anomie of life on the edge of society in
the structural conditions of late modern society had not been resolved by
their homelessness being resolved, although undoubtedly their material
situation and security had improved. They still lacked access to resources
that could allow them 'full' integration to society and they lacked a new
day-to-day routine from which to develop a sense of ontological security,
well-being, and identity, emotionally. In the final section, Brian and
Margaret's cases are used to develop this concept of 'trapped individuals'
further.

5. Becoming trapped individuals?

So these people may have been becoming trapped individuals, within
and due to the structural conditions of late modernity, including the
liberal individualism inherent to this. In the previous section social
networks and emotional experiences were focussed on to illustrate this.
In this section, the material outcomes they were attempting to gain to
increase the level of resources they had is used.

Material resources and life beyond homelessness

Paid employment may be perceived to be the 'ultimate' route to integration that could have been experienced. In this way the people studied
here would no longer have had to explicitly rely on the welfare state for
housing and subsistence, they could be active citizens, and consumers,
engaging in social interactions with the identity of 'normal' integrated
individuals. They would not longer be the 'failed individuals' they felt
they had become as they became homeless.

However the majority did not think they could access employment,
or other legitimate forms of activity to occupy their time, such as education. The reasons cited for this were: poor health; old age; lack of
qualifications or experience; discrimination they faced due to having
been homeless or an addict; and because they would not be able to
afford to work – the level of income their benefits generated was higher

than any amount they could make through legitimate paid employ-ment. Therefore they would be unable to afford to continue to live in their tenancy if they worked. Many were on Incapacity Benefit (often due to addiction) and by definition, were therefore not supposed to be capable of work.

Brian and William did start to work in paid employment over the course of the research. However when these cases are explored in more detail the integrative nature of this is not as it may first seem.

Brian's life beyond homelessness

Brian had worked for many years before becoming homeless in a rela-tively skilled service sector job. Over the last seven years of his life, he had been homeless, repeatedly, due to a combination of drug addic-tion, being in prison, and debt. After going through rehab, he had moved into supported accommodation and then into his own housing (a socially rented tenancy). A few months after moving there he started to work as a security guard. Below he describes how once he had housing, he felt this work assisted him to 'move on' from the experi-ence of being homeless. This was on both material economic (his income increased) and emotional individual levels (he felt he had control, something to occupy his time, a role):

> *I mean at the beginning when I moved into my flat, I was just like sitting staring at the four walls, it took a while, I was 'happy as' straight away but it takes a few months for it all to sink in, that it was real, that I was secure. I think it was when I went back to work that I started to feel I had control over my life, because I had control over my money.*
>
> (Brian, 35)

Again structural mechanisms (economic and housing) converged to create a greater sense of resilience, and well-being on the individual level. This also highlights how important employment could be to assist people to integrate into society and develop a sense of ontological security. In this way they could feel 'secure', have some control over their life and identity, beyond their reliance on the state. However Brian (and William) were working irregularly in the informal economy. They said this was due to the fact that they could not afford to pay their rent if they were working legitimately in the low paid sectors they could access employment in, as they would lose welfare entitlement. In this way they were also committing benefit fraud however, and had not moved far from the insecure 'edges' of society. Their social status could take a divestment passage if they were convicted of fraud, perhaps leading to them becoming homeless again. However this risk was created by the very same actions they were engaging in as individuals to try to gain more security and more resources. They actually were constrained by their lack of resources, and their reliance on the welfare system to maintain their housing, to remain at the 'edge'. They were negotiating with what appeared to be voluntary risks, such as working illegally. However these risks may also be understood as being something they engaged in to improve their situation as individuals, with few other more 'rational' choices available. This is the thin rationality (Somerville & Bengtsson, 2002) of the rationale of irrational behaviour, contingent on agents' contexts, motivations and social circumstance. Brian and William had no legal employment rights, but given the intense bureaucracy and difficulty they may have faced if they attempted to enter the formal economy (such as criminal record checks, and a lower net income) then it may also actually be a rational, individual act, to work in this way, as other studies into the counter-rationale of deviant 'careers' and interactions with welfare services have shown (Craine, 1997).

They were therefore trying to negotiate the best outcome and situation for themselves, as individuals and as liberal ideology would promote (Cohen & Taylor, 1992). In doing so however they were also continuing to recreate risks that could lead to a spiral of divestment and were not legitimately engaging in society. They also continued to potentially recreate the subjective stigma they faced from being 'outside' of mainstream society – either as benefits cheats, or as those who remained unemployed – 'poor' with no role. This 'hidden' world of the reality of life on the edge – the many means to generate incomes, find meaning, and occupation that people adopt are important for considering the reality of people's lives (Craine, 1997) and how they are actually being lived (Hutson, 1999). Many people engage in acts of edgework at times, and return from the edge. The motivation for this exists in many people. For those trapped by the structural edge, and that have at some point in their lives gone over the edge, how could they move on from this marginal structural position within the many layers of structure they were embedded in? Margaret's story further illustrates this bind.

Margaret's life after homelessness

Margaret had a history of chronic alcoholism. She had been in care as a child, and then spent her adult life moving between hostels, her own tenancy's, staying with friends, sleeping rough, and always having contact with welfare services. In some ways, her transition through homelessness had this time been a 'success'. At the final interview she had her own housing, and had been living there for a year. She now had little contact with support workers. But she also felt she had 'nothing', that something acute was missing in her life:

> *You're stuck in a house, nobody to talk to, apart from four walls, I mean you've got your telly, music centre, I've got all that, but there is something missing. Because there is nobody there. And that is why a lot of people give up their houses, you're sitting like that, 'what do I do now?'.*
>
> (Margaret, 42)

Margaret had attempted to attend a college course once she moved into her own housing but had been unable to due to her health, and the cost. She did not know what else she could do and remained with a low level of human, social, and economic capital. She consumed alcohol heavily and said in the final interview that she sometimes felt she could just leave her tenancy, and enter the 'system' she had spent most of her life being accommodated within, once more. This system may have been, to her, a more 'normal' and emotionally fulfilling life than the one she now had, given the isolation, and lack of identity, she was experiencing. Being homeless had exposed her to many risks and to living in poor material conditions. However all she now faced beyond this was the 'horrendous repetition' of the new day-to-day life she had as an 'ex-homeless' person, once she was housed.

Boredom and loneliness have already been highlighted as key factors affecting people's lives once they move out of homelessness. This lack of contact with other people was often cited as a trigger for ongoing substance use. This was either to cope with this isolation, or because to interact with other people they knew involved using substances. Despite their transition out of homelessness, and lack of any absolute poverty, 'something', as Margaret discussed, was missing. But what was that 'something'?

Becoming trapped individuals?

Both Brian's and Margaret's experience highlight, in different ways, a key assertion made here. This is that some of the people studied were becoming trapped as individuals within the structures of late modernity – trapped on the edge. Once they were no longer homeless they did not appear to be making further transitions, or see how they could. Once they had their own housing they became trapped between either the purgatory of day-to-day isolation and loneliness, or in engaging in edgework activities (drug use, alcohol use, working illegally) as a way to escape or remedy this, that then only exacerbated their marginality further. These actions had also underpinned their initial transition into homelessness. In this way some were also trapped in a destructive cycle of going over the edge once more and becoming homeless, in a repeating cycle.

Either way, many remained reliant on the social welfare system, and had few opportunities or resources with which to develop a new routine or identity. Despite the positive 'surface' outcomes that many experienced, what was also apparent was the *lack of opportunities* to 'move on' beyond this situation that most now faced. This lack of opportunity could be experienced both materially and emotionally. Materially they lacked opportunities to generate more resources of social, human, and (legitimate) economic capital, and emotionally, they had few opportunities to leave behind the stigmatised identity they had, or to find a 'role', and greater ontological security in the social structure of late modernity. Some faced having few means to escape the repetition – escape the anomie and 'nothingness' – of their day-to-day life, even once their homelessness was resolved. Their homelessness may have been a marginalising situation, one that was more emotionally fulfilling, and 'alive' than the situation they were now in. To remain 'safe' and housed, they were trapped on the edge of society, not going over, but not able to move any further, with their life becoming stuck in this situation, this day-to-day repetition – a limbo space between integration and divestment, inclusion and exclusion, belonging and being 'cast out', being nothing. Perhaps it could tentatively be suggested that the welfare system of homeless policy and services is working to provide housing to those in need, in quicker or more enabling way than other economic, interpersonal and socio-structures are operating to enable the other resources required for successful integration to be generated. Pleace (1995) identified five levels of need that may need to be addressed when people are experiencing homelessness, housing, support, finance, life skills and social. If only one or some of these are addressed and others are lacking then perhaps people and their individual transitions are stalling. It may also be that the trauma and difficulty that the people studied here have experienced has undermined their resilience to the extent that their individual actions – edgework – will continue to mire them in this circumstance, in an ongoing structurated cycle.

By obtaining housing many had only moved into a more secure position along a continuum whereby they were still lacking a role, on the edge of society. They were no longer perceived to pose a risk to others or themselves but were trapped in the situation they were in, with few opportunities to move on beyond. They had clear ideas about the sort of identity they wanted to have, and the actions they should engage in to be a 'proper' 'normal' member of society – someone in employment, in a relationship, a *consumer* – as the following comment from Keith illustrates:

> *It feels as if I'm a taker, you know, a sponge. I feel other people think that as well. A lot of people look at me and say to me, 'why are you not working?' and stuff like that. I do have mental health issues, you know. But working would help, if I could, it would help. Maybe get a car again, and get another relationship, be a proper member of society. When I walk along the street, I feel as if people are staring at me, as if to say, 'scumbag'.*
>
> (Keith, 34)

But they also often felt that this 'normality' was something they could not attain. Being able to negotiate these outcomes – employment, successful relationships, certain consumer possessions such as a car – was viewed as the indicators of someone who has 'successfully' negotiated a positive life course through integrative passages. Without these trapping of consumer success, they felt they were doomed – to remain 'failed' individuals, flawed consumers, on the edge. Yet the lack of resources they had, meant that obtaining the ideal consumer outcomes may be distant goals for them, and many people. And resources are underpinned by the structural context of an increasingly globalised, late modern society, where resources and life chances are unequally distributed and inequality, as well as wealth, is on the increase (Dorling, 2007).

They faced the knowledge that they may never attain what they perceived to be this 'normal life' within the social context they were in. This may actually be the reality many people now face – no longer living in a work society, or a risk society, but in a society of unattainability, of the mirage of lifestyle consumerism (Cohen & Taylor, 1992). When someone has nothing to lose, they have nothing to value, nothing to care about (Bauman, 1998). Edgework may be the manifestation of this – an attempt to gain, where there is felt to be nothing. And in these cases, this edgework occurred as part of a life course imbued with extreme trauma and difficulty, with mental illness, institutionalisation, addiction, and of having few resources to act as a buffer to the effect of this. These were lives that on an individual level appeared to have little left to lose, and they often felt, little they could gain – that they were trapped in the circumstance they were in, on the edge.

7
Conclusion: Lives on the Edge

1.   Understanding transitions through homelessness – In a risk society

The transitions into homelessness studied here occurred in a complex process involving an interrelation of three key factors: edgework, a lack of resources of different forms of capital, and the influence of social networks.

To reiterate, edgework refers to voluntary risk taking (such as drug use) actions that involve negotiating the edges of normative behaviour and trying to manage the risk these acts involve (Lyng, 2005a). The concept has also been used here as a way to understand involuntary risk situations also – being assaulted, mental illness, for example. These situations also require that individuals find some way to physically and emotionally manage risk, and return from the edge of normative behaviour these events have brought them too – or face the consequences of going over. Both forms of edgework carry the risk of going over the edge, they involve a rupture in the day-to-day reality people operate within, and involve episodes of 'real' extreme risk that has to be managed and over-come. However this may also be part of their appeal, as this 'rupturing' also provides 'escape' on an ontological level.

Homelessness is attributed to an interrelation of structural forces, and individual factors (often relating to personal pathology, such as addic-tion, deviance) (Fitzpatrick, 2005). Prevalent constructions of homeless-ness refer to minimalist account of homelessness as being without shelter, and the homeless person as someone outside of society (Jacobs et al, 1999; Fooks & Pantazis, 1999).

This minimal account appeared initially evident in the narratives of the people studied here. They all described the cause of their homelessness as individual events, such as drug and alcohol use, relationship breakdown, and mental illness. However it has been asserted here that these events and actions all encapsulate a need to negotiate the edges of normative social behaviour – they are edgework, motivated from within the structural reality individuals operate within. That they led to homelessness also related to broader structural context whereby the people studied had relative low levels of resources. Resources of human, social, material, and financial capital provide a buffer to the negative effects of such events, and are something accessible (or not) due to structural mechanisms.

On an individual level it was often due to a combination of traumatic events, interacting with relationship breakdowns, that led to the people studied here going over the edge, and their resources eroded until they had few options but to rely on state funded agencies for accommodation (and sometimes social support) provided for people within the 'homeless system'. In this way, they became defined as homeless, by both themselves and others. Another issue that has been identified from this study however, and that requires further research, is a consideration of *why* and *how* these *individual problems* and the edgework that led to homelessness are generated.

The rationale of irrational behaviour

The motivation for the edgework that was engaged in was generated through an interaction of three key factors. These factors were: social networks and social interactions; traumatic experiences; and the resources that the people studied here had access to. These three factors, combined, create the material and emotional reality that these people operated within. The resources that people have access to can be understood as relating to social, human, financial, cultural and material capital. Each was once again found to be important mechanisms that intersect to create or constrain outcomes and transitions over the life course, alongside the social networks that people had, and their individual experiences and attributes. This recognition reiterates work by Fitzpatrick (2005) arguing that four key causal mechanisms have to be explored to understand homelessness – housing structures, economic structures, interpersonal structures and individual attributes. It has been articulated here that socio-structural forces also operate alongside these other structures, in a complex web involving multiple casual mechanisms. Economic, housing, interpersonal and socio-structures (relating to culture and lifestyles) act to constrain or enable the access to resources of economic, material, social and human capital an individual has, and their ongoing development of individual attributes (Fitzpatrick, 2005). These resources will underpin their resilience and opportunities, and therefore impact upon their actions and the outcome of these actions, in an ongoing structurated praxis.

How this material and emotional reality generated actions that appeared irrational as a means to avoid risk, has been encapsulated here as the 'rationale of irrational behaviour'. Actions that may appear irrational as a means to avoid risk could be understood as rational when the micro-level reality they occurred within was taken into account, uncovering the 'thin rationality' (Somerville & Bengtsson, 2002). It may be that the actions that led to these people's homelessness and other related problems in their lives were also a way they could self-actualise (Lyng, 2005b) as individuals, from the micro-level they operated on.

Social networks and the interactions that people engage in on a day-to-day basis constitute an important part of, and are embedded in, the material reality they operate within. Whilst these can be important sources of social capital and ontological security (Giddens, 1984) they can also underpin negative actions and outcomes. If the people that those studied here had contact with as peers, were people also engaging in similar actions or experiencing similar problems – such as extreme drug or alcohol use, criminal acts – then these actions became fairly normal. Not only that, engaging in them may have provided the means to inter-act and 'fit in' with these peers. Furthermore these actions may also have been motivated by the desire to escape the material reality they were in, transcend it, or to take some control over the lack of agency they felt they had (Cohen & Taylor, 1992).

The paradox of the edgework the people studied here experienced is that, whilst it may have been a way to self actualise and escape (Lyng, 2005a) engaging in it further desecrated and destroyed their lives. They did not have access to the resources of different forms of capital they needed to manage this 'work' or the resilience to avoid it. It could lead them to be so consumed by their need to assert their 'selves' from within the position of relative powerlessness they operated, that they attempted to destroy themselves, through suicide. This became the only act some felt they could engage in as an individual, to escape or break free from the destructive cycle their lives were in.

Understanding edgework

These acts of edgework, the motivation or trigger for which has been conceptualised here in this rationale of irrational behaviour, did often bring negative outcomes – such as addiction, assault, imprisonment, homelessness. These people had gone over the edge and were unable to engage in this edgework effectively. They had no buffer to return from the edges they were negotiating with – to 'hide' the actions they engaged in that appeared deviant and outside of normatively accepted social actions. This was particularly exacerbated by them becoming visibly homeless. They became identified and labelled as a range of deviant characters – 'addicts', 'alcoholics', 'homeless people'. They also had to rely on the state to access resources, or face destitution. In this way they were indeed constructed as homelessness people (as Jacobs et al, 1999) argue, however this construction occurs within and due the intersection of many social structures, thus further asserting the ortho-doxy of homelessness and causation (Fitzpatrick, 2005) into a critical realist account. These individual acts did occur, they were real, and did lead to homelessness, but only due to the broad structural reality they occurred within and the relative lack of resources of those who went on to become homeless due to them.

So as they became homeless, the social, human, and financial capital they had increasingly eroded. They faced being dually 'over the edge' for being homeless. They were 'over the edge' in a (often traumatic and difficult) material situation due to their homelessness, but also had the identity of someone who could not 'manage' their own life in the con-ditions of late modernity.

Within these structural conditions it has been argued here, we may all be becoming edgeworkers, and many are going over the edge. Everyone may engage in 'individual' acts that appear irrational as a means to man-age risk – the current panics over obesity and binge drinking for example, and ensuing figures that illustrate they are on the rise due to lifestyle factors, are evidence of this. From what to have for breakfast, to whether to have wine with a meal at night, we all make choices, and now, in this liberalised era have to negotiate many edges as individuals, every day. This edgework may not be as extreme as that experienced by the people studied here, or some people may have more resources to hide the effects of this, but most of us are 'deviant' sometimes, it appears. Indeed this may be due to the very acts that we adopt to try to escape or transcend the ennui and inequality (Dorling, 2007) that can be wrought from life in late modernity (Cohen & Taylor, 1992), and the suspended animation of the constant lifestyle cycle of ongoing individualised transitions and choices that the structures of modernity promote (Furlong & Cartmel, 1997; Patton & Viner, 2007).

Stressed perspective on homelessness and causation

Anyone may experience a traumatic incident, or use drugs or alcohol excessively. However if this occurs whilst they retain an outward appearance of integration to mainstream normative ideas and actions, their lives remain integrated to mainstream society. These actions can be conceptualised as an attempt to transcend or escape, and therefore as the outcome of, life in late modernity – a life increasingly bureau-cratised, disenchanted, and where inequality is widening. Constraint and inequality occurs alongside discourses of individualisation being promoted – the individual, their actions, and choices being celebrated and highlighted as what defines them. But the ability that someone has to negotiate their life course will be underpinned by the access to resources – of social, human, and financial capital that they have, which is structurally enabled or constrained. Therefore, avoiding home-lessness, both in 'reality' (due to the housing situation someone is in) and as a subjective identity (being labelled as a homeless person) is tied to the access to resources someone has over their life course rather than the actual actions they engage in. The individual actions and problems that lead to homelessness are real, they do occur, and could occur in anyone's life. Therefore this perspective relates entirely back to structural explanations for homelessness but one that ties the indi-vidual pathology associated with minimal accounts directly to struc-tural mechanisms also.

Traumatic events and problematic actions influence people's lives, and how their actions are perceived, in profound ways. Anyone may become an addict, mentally ill, or suffer emotional trauma and this will be exper-ienced as 'real' not just as a construct. Anyone may become homeless, but the *chance* of this homelessness occurring when something goes wrong in their lives (and perhaps the chance of these other divestment events occurring) is related to the different levels of resources they have. How they can then constitute themselves, and are perceived by others, will be affected by this, and they can enter into spirals of increased alienation and isolation. Social policy and an adequate supply of housing is impor-tant to address homelessness on a material level, but is not enough alone. Other complex individual factors – trauma, edgework, emotional contexts – and why these occur or can be managed, have to also be taken into account. Because these factors also underpin who is likely to become homeless and how their homelessness is conceptualised. There is now a greater emphasis on the support needs of people who are vulnerable and excluded (Pleace, 1995). However this still acts to segregate, places the focus of these problems onto the individual (Hutson, 1999) and avoids addressing the structurally generated pressures that may lead to anyone, having the same 'pathological' problems, just not the means with which to buffer them.

Transitional phases through homelessness

As, once the people studied here entered the 'homeless system', they became primarily defined as a 'homeless person'. The majority of the social interactions they could engage in were with others in the same situation as them, or professionals whose relationship with them was defined by their need to be assisted to resolve their homelessness, or related individual problems such as addiction. They often became increasingly alienated and isolated from mainstream society and the resources of social capital that 'normal' social relationships can provide, such as accommodation, financial, emotional or social support.

At the outset of the research, the majority of the people studied were lacking their own housing. Some had recently moved into their own housing after being homeless. All were accessing services specifically developed to assist homeless people. Over the course of the year they were researched, half of those that were homeless at the outset moved into their own housing, and half remained without it.

The transitional routes of those that remained homeless throughout the research particularly encapsulated what are termed here as spirals of divestment. Despite some short-term improvements having occurred at some points, such as moving into supported accommodation, their situation and the resources they had, continued to erode and deteriorate. Some of these people represented the most marginalised and excluded individuals in late modernity, intensely isolated, stigmatised, and often engaging in real problematic behaviour, unable to interact with others, and barred from accommodation and support services due to this. In this way they were caught on the very edge of society, unable to even access services that may have assisted them – 'cast' out, in purgatory. This group represents a key challenge and problem yet to be resolved (Fitzpatrick & Jones, 2005).

However many of the people studied did make a transition out of homelessness – at least as it is minimally defined. The majority were living in their own housing by the end of the research. Analysing the qualitative accounts of these transitions, and by taking account of other factors that were occurring in their lives simultaneously, it was clear that these transitions did not occur as ongoing integration. Their lives were characterised by a flip-flopping effect, in a constant struggle between integration and divestment passages, as they attempted to make ongoing transitions. Having their own housing clearly indicated that their surface situation had improved. However they then had many new challenges and risks to face, and previous trauma to reconcile.

Many felt acutely isolated once they obtained their own housing and still faced intense difficulties, for example, drug or alcohol use, and chronic physical or mental health problems. They all also still had limited access to resources. They were caught in the space on the edge of society.

Even once housed, their situation was still precarious, and rather than taking clearly integrative passages, their lives continued to flip-flop in a constant struggle to maintain the precarious security that they currently had. Their housing status may have changed but not the fundamental structural context that they operated within, intersecting between many different factors. And from this context they had to overcome the new individually experienced problems in their lives (due to obtaining housing) – such as budgeting, meeting new people, and the isolation of living alone. It has been recognised that support to address this is a key aspect of transitions out of homelessness (Franklin, 1999). On a micro-level support staff and services that worked with them provided a critical resource that assisted the people studied here to maintain this precarious security. However until other fundamental structural factors, that are outside of the control of any one organisation or individual, are addressed, then this could only ever be a surface-level effect. Creating a society whereby people and communities have the capacity for high levels of resilience in the face of risk, may be a much greater structural change that is required to address homelessness and generate the informal support that is also so crucial to these transitions (Franklin, 1999).

The universality of risk and transitions

On an individual level ongoing risk is hard to avoid as people continue to make transitions over the life course. We all have to negotiate new outcomes at times. People may enter into relationships that carry the risk of breaking down, may use drugs or alcohol – some may have the resources to engage in sky-diving, as a form of escape from the pressures of late modern society, and the process of individualisation embedded within it, as Lyng's theory initially recognised – many will not. As was highlighted in the stressed perspective on homelessness and causation articulated here, if people have the resources to 'negotiate' and return from the edge, they remain integrated into society, despite the *same processes* actually being played out. In this way the *difference* between people who go on to become homeless and those who never do, are *both* imagined and real. They are imagined in that people who experience 'homelessness' due to what appear to be individual pathological actions may subjectively be no different to those who do not. We are all affected by the same processes of life in late modernity and may engage in actions that are irrational as a means to avoid risk.

The differences are real, in that the key cleavage of difference that exists is the access to resources that we have, within the structural context of late modernity. These resources may or may not act as buffer to the risks that the process of increased individualisation and late modern capitalist society has exposed us to and generate more or less resilience that then feeds back into the individual problems and characteristics, so apparent in 'the homeless' that often defines how 'they' are perceived. And this is a process that may keep on going in spirals, as inequality increases. Some people's lives may continue to spiral into further divestment passages once an initial divestment has occurred, or are trapped in this space on the edge, rather than ongoing integration developing. These people may then become actually, materially and emotionally isolated and alienated – actually become the imagined 'outsiders' they encapsulate, damaging to both themselves and others. The fundamental motivations for their actions, and the outcomes they wish to achieve, may not be so different from the 'insiders', however – pleasure, escape, self-actualisation, some meaning in life.

2. Individualisation and the unintended consequences of the welfare state

Each of the people studied here had, at some point in their lives, experienced spirals of divestment. As they became homeless they had accessed the services of the social welfare system to assist them regain housing and resolve the other problems they were experiencing. This system is part of what is identified here as a reflexive system of governance (Dean, 1999), with services that now focus on the individual needs and risks posed by the citizens it governs, and how they can reflexively manage themselves, working in partnership with government agencies, services and support workers. Collectively experienced social problems may now be conceptualised as the problems of individuals and their actions. Groups of individuals experiencing these problems become targeted populations (Dean, 1999) – targeted to assist them manage or resolve these problems, through specialist government agencies, education and programmes, that have proliferated to address such issues as homelessness, addiction, exclusion and poor health in recent years as part of this reflexive mode of self governance.

The role of the social welfare system to transitions through homelessness

Almost all of the people studied here had experienced living in large-scale hostels for the homeless, and other forms of temporary accommodation such as Bed & Breakfasts. This was often an acutely negative experience, leading to further divestment passages, as the situation they were in (and how they emotionally responded to this) continued to deteriorate. Two key sources of support they accessed when they began to take more integrative positive transitions once more were entering supported accommodation, and being allocated a specialist housing worker. As homeless services in the UK increasingly shift from temporary accommodation to models of floating support and prevention in the community (Fitzpatrick et al, 2000) the focus on these two sources of support could be used to unpack the relative merits of both in Chapter 5.

The people studied were often able to gain some stability and a reasonable quality of accommodation in supported accommodation. They were assisted by specialist housing workers to access material resources, and support and advice – such as how to apply for housing and how to get grants for furniture. So in this way they were assisted to access some of the economic and material resources they were entitled to through the current welfare system, to assist them 'rebuild' their lives, to become increasingly integrated once more. They were able to access Housing Association tenancies – showing that for some the housing structures operated to provide them with accommodation. However they also remained 'reliant' on the support and resources they could access through this system even once they had lived in their own housing, for long-periods. This may highlight a critical unintended consequence of this welfare system – it creates a rationale for dependency. It then also has to continue to develop, reflexively, to meet the needs of those who had been rendered reliant on it (Dean, 1999). Yet this reliance was also due to the structural reality they now operate within and how this is underpinned by the structures of contemporary society.

Once they had come to rely on the system for support and income, they often had to continue to. They had no other source of social support or resources with which to continue integrating. They accessed training courses, drop-in's, continued to have contact with their individual support workers (often in the face of having few other sources of positive social support) and were involved as volunteers, or in forums, consulted on as 'ex-homeless people'. In this way they did continue to have support and access to resources that assisted them to maintain some stability in their lives, and avoid becoming homeless once more. Their fundamental structural situation had not changed, and it was this that had led to their homelessness in the first place. This led to their reliance on welfare services and caught them, close to the edge, but the structural complexity that generated this reliance is obscured by the focus on individual problems. Longitudinal research covering a much longer term in the lives of people who are homeless or at risk of homelessness is required to further elucidate on this, and the extent to which this may be a short- or long-term affect.

Even for those who appeared to reject the influence of this targeting – that continued to use alcohol or drugs for example – their rejection only continued recreating the need for services to continue targeting them, to manage the 'risk' they may have posed.

The services of the social welfare system do at times 'work' on some levels to assist people resolve their homelessness. Recent policy changes have led to a development in how these services and accommodation projects operate (such as programmes of hostel reprovisioning in the UK and homeless strategies (Fitzpatrick et al, 2000). This may have assisted in triggering these positive individually experienced outcomes. These objective aspects to making a transition out of homelessness, underpinned by policy, such as housing supply, the condition of housing, welfare entitlement, support services, and advice and information being available, remain important mechanisms to solve the problem of homelessness. However it is also important to highlight once more that making a transition out of homelessness is about more than objective material outcomes and being provided with housing. Support needs often have to be addressed that relate to housing, life skills, social networks, and financial income (Pleace, 1995). Yet as this study has shown, addressing these needs can also draw people into the life of homelessness.

So a transition out of homelessness has to be about integration, social cohesion, and involves intense ontological processes. These were the barriers many of the people studied here faced in making their transitions out of homelessness. These subjective aspects need to be acknowledged and understood, to understand the intense difficulty of making a transition out of homelessness, and to begin to understand why homelessness endures in some people's lives, despite policy changes that appear to provide mechanisms that resolve it. Many mechanisms – economic, interpersonal, social – that lead to resilience (or not) need to be triggered, to not constrain people into a life of poverty or limbo. Repeatedly mental illness and addiction are the problem factors that interrelate with this homelessness. These are symptoms perhaps of much wider malaise and suffering. They lead to homelessness, in some cases, when experienced by those with few resources in the risk society. This wider malaise is the key issue that needs to be addressed.

Identity and ontological security – Making transitions

The internal, psychological, emotional processes that some of these people went through as they attempted to negotiate a route out of homelessness could act as a barrier to making their transitions. The very experience of being targeted, the pressure of having to 'move on', address their past and take 'control' of their future, as liberal *individuals,* could be the trigger for some of their ongoing divestment passages, and problems in their life. All at some point had experienced some intense trauma – violence, suicide attempts, sexual abuse and mental breakdown. They had to try to manage this from within the social and material context they operated within. The example of Eddie illustrated this – *'the drugs are like a shield, I was getting there…I was progressing, maybe that frightened me'.* By becoming homeless, they experienced an intensely difficult material reality, and also had the stigma of the social identity of a homeless person, of someone reliant on the state, lacking a role, a 'failed self' (Bauman, 1998) in late modernity, attached to them. They then had the problem of reconciling this with their sense of narrative identity (Ricoeur, 1991a/b), and the roles they could play in the day-to-day interactions they engaged in as a 'homeless person'. They had been 'cast out', over the edge of society both objectively and subjectively, and this had become their life, their position within the social structure. They were not entirely 'outside' however, as the ongoing targeting of services continued to feed them back into this system and in this way they were circularly trapped in this situation (Dean, 1999).

For some, homelessness, reliance on the state and being accommodated within institutions had become 'normal life', they were socialised into this. This may also have provided them with the internal process required for them to maintain their ontological security (Giddens, 1984) – their foothold in the world – homelessness became their day-to-day life; being homeless their narratable identity.

Some had been in care as children and then had spent their entire lives moving between supported accommodation, hostels, prisons, staying with friends, sleeping rough, occasionally having a tenancy of their own, and moving on again. Their lives were immersed in 'being homeless' and by being targeted by the state – this was their 'normal' life. The interactions they engaged in within this setting constituted their social networks and to change this, could involve intense ontological crisis. This involved a rejection of the individual they were, and the people they knew, if they were to develop a 'new self' beyond being homeless. This could be intensely difficult, especially as their fundamental structural situation did not change when they moved into a tenancy. They still lacked resources, experienced extreme forms of edgework, and had much trauma and isolation to reconcile with in their lives, and the context of a late modern liberal individual consumerist, capitalist society, creating the structures they were embedded in (Young, 2006).

What is important to highlight however is that they *did continue to strive* to make integrative transitions, despite this intense difficulty. Their acts of agency (attempts to assert their sense of individuality) occurring within the structural context of them having to rely on the state to access resources, could operate to trap them in this situation. Even those who had made a transition out of homelessness remained in this space on the edge, (in their own housing; in supported accommodation), perhaps rendered 'safe' through the targeting of the state, so long as they adhered to behaving in ways that continued to indicate their 'responsibility'. But this 'safe' life was also often a life in limbo: of isolation, of boredom, of 'nothingness' – as is often found to be the case when people make a transition out of homelessness (Alexander & Ruggieri, 1998).

Understanding transitions through homelessness in late modernity

The welfare state as a universal provision for all may be receding, but there is also a proliferation of services for people experiencing individual social problems (Dean, 1999). It has been asserted here that society may be becoming increasingly stratified, culturally and materially, along lines of those who are, and those who are not, perceived to be able to 'manage' their lives and resources without explicit state intervention (Dean, 1999). This intervention is encapsulated by reliance on benefits, and the social support of specialist professionals, such as resettlement, addiction or social workers, that act together to 'case manage' individuals' lives. This intervention may well relate to needs that have to be addressed (Pleace, 1995). However, it has also been argued here, that the ability people have to avoid this labelling – of the social identity of a 'homeless person', or a 'junky', for example – is of course stratified along lines of those who have to rely on the state to obtain resources and support for their problems through services of the state, and those who do not. This is despite the actions they have engaged in, or the motivation they have for doing so, actually being *the same* as those who do not have to. Some people do not have to rely on the state, or will not face such extreme risks, due to the buffer they are provided with through the access to different forms and levels of capital they have.

There may be more fluidity, more choice, in this than in previous eras, and this may bring increased risk for all. People may fall *'further and faster'* (Marsh & Kennett, 1999) when things 'go wrong' in their life course, however the chance they have to negotiate with risks will still be stratified unequally. The only escape or resistance from poverty, from the day-to-day struggles and traumas people face, may be through edgework deemed illegitimate (Katz, 1988). These acts (drug use, violence) are damaging, and are real, they do occur, but by not addressing or acknowledging the broad structural underpinnings that motivate and trigger them, and the emotional dimensions that are also inherent, they will only continue to do so (Buchanan, 2004). Socio-structural forces may motivate and create more opportunities for the 'individual' problem factors that can lead to homelessness – addiction, relationship breakdown, depression, the breaking away from the unbearable 'stress' that people were experiencing. Structural conditions generate individualised problems, in a feedback loop. As has been repeatedly asserted here both minimalist and maximalist accounts of homelessness can be mutually inclusive and are interlinked at root source by structural forces.

A concluding comment from one of the people studied sums up this duality of agency and structure explored here, and how irrational actions – edgework – may be understood as a rational response to the situation people are in:

> *The root problem [in society] could be having the class system, the rich and the poor, I think the root problem is, if you're poor, your life is a struggle, you know, if you are poor, people are not caring about what you say, people have less opportunities, and the more you struggle, the more stress you have to live with.*

(William, 29)

As William notes, the root problem remains embedded in structural factors, and in how these structural factors affect the lived individual reality of people. The more they attempted to struggle, to escape this structural context, as individuals, the more 'stress' they had to live with, and this context was recreated, all the worse.

The space between them and us in late modernity

To move on and to integrate may only be done at the risk of losing it all over again. This risk was particularly due to them lacking resources that could act as a buffer if something went wrong in their lives or they engaged in edgework. They were rendered 'safe', if they adhered to the conditions of the liberal welfare state – safe to themselves, as they gained housing, and safe to others, as to maintain this housing they had to act 'responsibly'. However they were also marginalised and trapped due to this reliance. In exchange for this security from the state they had to surrender actions they engaged in to assert their individuality. These may be actions (alcohol or drug use for example) other people with enough resources can engage in, safely. When the people studied here engaged in edgework, they risked losing this security they gained through the state – for if they appeared to be acting in unruly, irresponsible ways they would be targeted and drawn back into the institutions of this system once more. They may lose the tenancies or support they had been provided with in this way, and have to enter rehabs, hostels, or hospital, for example. The structural conditions that actually underpinned these actions remained the same however. Therefore individuals only have the opportunity to develop their own 'biographies' – to be the 'authors' of their lives (Giddens, 1991) – when they have enough resources to do so.

To assert individuality, celebrated among those with resources to do so, becomes distorted in the lives of those who lack resources and have to explicitly rely on the state. They become viewed as threatening, and a drain on resources. Indeed it may be that sometimes they become so, as their lives take increasing spirals of divestment, and they become increasingly de-socialised and de-humanised by processes of institutionalisation.

Is it not just fear, as Young (2006) would argue, but also possibly envy of the escape and freedom from the ongoing rationalisation of modern life these stigmatised groups represent, that generates this revilement? To remain integrated is to continue constantly negotiating new options and risks – the need to constantly gain employment and maintain security as individuals, constant edgework, but without the hedonistic escape or self actualisation – only constant repetition. Young (2006) argues that 'outsiders', the underclass, are a source of resentment for 'respectable' responsible citizens, whose individuality and actions are constantly curtailed by their avoidance and management of risk in the conditions of late modernity:

[T]he bank manager could not countenance being a street beggar (...) for both real and imagined reasons, the lives of such disgraced 'Others' are

impoverished and immiserised. (...) But their very existence, their moral intransigence, somehow hits all the weak spots of our character armour. Let us think for one day of the hypothetical 'included' citizen on the advantage side of the binary: the traffic jam on the way to work, the hours which have been slowly added to the working day, the crippling cost of housing and the mortgage which will never end, the need for both incomes to make up a family wage (...) the temptations and fears of the abuse of alcohol as a means of enjoyment, in the time slots between the rigours of work... [The underclass] set of every trigger point of fear and desire.

(2006:25)

This stigma, this fear of the 'other' (or perhaps resentment and pity towards them) then generates the need to contain and control them also, through the mechanisms of the state. Above all they are the 'them' not the 'us' – making this constant empty edgework justifiable. Are we all becoming increasingly trapped individuals within the reflexive individualised conditions of late modernity, trapped by our need to constantly negotiate new outcomes, transitions and 'lifestyles' as individuals? Are we all unable to actually move far from our own edges, of birth, culture and education, but in a constant battle to do so, facing the risks of constant transitions, and the suspended animation of a pluralistic and individualised society? Some may have less resources than others, and have more suffering for it, but also more freedom? These could be central questions to end this book on. However another more positive interpretation of these findings, can also be offered.

3. The power of the individual in society – Agency, structure and risk in late modernity

In relative terms, we may be getting richer, and living potentially more enriched lives through the opportunities, technologies, and social change that has been brought about through the process of modernity (Dorling, 2007). And we *all* face potential risks and trauma over our life course. However the outcome of our negotiations with these risks, and the extent to which we may enjoy the benefits of modernity, are still affected by the resources we have. And these resources are distributed through the structural institutions and cultural ideologies of our society.

A key institution through which some resources are distributed is the social welfare system. It has been shown here that in relation to homelessness the social welfare system and services that are funded through it, can operate effectively to assist people resolve material problems in their lives, such as access to housing. However that these problems occurred in the first place, and that people have a stigmatising social identity attached to them due to these problems, remains tied to social structures and ideologies, and also have a profound emotional impact. In this way a vicious circle of structuration exists – that the outcome of the *actions* to escape this, recreate the very structural reality that generates these problems – problems such as social isolation, trauma, poverty, homelessness or addiction. For some people, through this process, life in late modernity may be a life becoming increasingly trapped. The transitions they make, the actions they engage in, only lead back to this situation once more, due to their ongoing attempts to both face up to, and manage, the risks they face. This is in the face of negotiating what is perceived to be an individualised life courses, but an 'individuality' still bounded by their place in the structured reality they exist within.

'*The poor will always be with us*' (Bauman, 1998:1), as will the question of '*how the poor are made to be poor and come to be seen as poor, and how much the way they are made and seen depends on the way we all live our daily lives and praise or deprecate the fashion in which we and others live them*'. The poor then will always be with us – must always be with us? – the by-product of the struggle between different groups over finite resources within the structural 'reality' created by the conditions of global capitalism. There are always winners and losers in this ongoing struggle for resources, with the poor encapsulating those who have lost. Yet it is also this struggle that continues to create, transform, and generate the structural and material reality, and emotional landscape that we operate within.

And herein lies another more positive interpretation of the findings of this study. We are all essentially the same, and all have some power as individuals in society. *Despite* the poverty, trauma, stigma, and intense difficulty they had experienced, they all continued to strive to assert themselves, to survive, to find some meaning, pleasure and escape in their lives. They all continued to resist becoming trapped – despite the hardship they experienced. As the opening quote conveyed, we all continue to negotiate outcomes as individuals – 'the dance on the periphery' may not be leading anywhere, but what it does celebrate is a 'refusal to sleep, a resistance to arrest, a mode of motion'. The people studied here all refused to sleep. And in this refusal, in the continued assertion of agency, lies power. This is the power of every individual in society. We all must continue to negotiate new outcomes as individuals within the conditions of late modernity. For those on the periphery, for many of us, this dance may not be leading far, but it does illustrate power, and an ongoing mode of motion. And it is this motion that continues to generate ongoing transitions, actions, and society. People continue to try to escape, resist, or transcend the structural reality they are in, and in doing so sometimes may transform structures, may become more trapped within them, but always are celebrating the power that exists, of the individual, within society – and are illustrating the role we all play in constituting and recreating our society.

So despite the pessimistic view of trapped individuals and flip-flopping transitions presented here, it is also important to highlight that each of these individuals were survivors. And in their ability to survive and to go on, lay their power. Through this power of individuals, transformation and change can be galvanised on both individual and structural levels – leading to a different material reality and a different social context coming into being. We may be the products of our society, but we also produce it. Our material reality, the structures we operate within, exist independently of any one individual. However it is through the power inherent in each individual, to survive, to act, and to go on, that this reality is collectively generated. The future therefore is in all our hands – we all do have some power, however small this may be. The key issue then for civil society is to ensure that people have the capabilities to implement this power in positive ways, to live and develop lives that they and others value and enjoy.

So one final similarity that all the people studied here shared can be identified, and this was their refusal to sleep, each one a survivor, continuing to strive to engage with others, and with society, however difficult this may have been. Some were coming back over the edge and their lives and well-being had tangibly improved. The stigma and alienation that accompanies the problems they had faced must continue to be acknowledged, assessed, and challenged. Because stigma and discrimination are mechanisms that act to prevent integration and generate isolation. Furthermore, how and why individual problems (such as addiction, isolation, violence, mental illness) that cause such damage and suffering, occur and *can be addressed* must continue to be explored, in new ways. This constant dance on the periphery may not lead far, but we hope at least, it leads us home.

Whatever risks society may face, however uncertain about the future we may be, one thing we can be sure of – for now, life goes on, societies continue to be recreated and transformed, transitions are made – and so too must our efforts to understand this, and to bridge the spaces in between, to celebrate our ongoing motion.

Appendix

List of Research Sample

			Slept rough?	Repeat homeless?
Ann	26	Female	No	Yes
Bess	25	Female	No	No
Claire	26	Female	Yes	Yes
Dee	26	Female	No	No
Elizabeth	41	Female	Yes	No
Francesca	28	Female	Yes	Yes
Gary	52	Male	Yes	Yes
Henry	48	Male	No	No
Ian	33	Male	No	No
Jane	29	Female	No	No
Keith	34	Male	Yes	Yes
Lorna	42	Female	Yes	Yes
Margaret	43	Female	Yes	Yes
Ollie	60	Male	No	Yes
Pat	47	Female	Yes	Yes
Quinn	52	Male	No	No
Rachel	46	Female	No	Yes
Steven	51	Male	Yes	Yes
Tommy	33	Male	Yes	No
Allan	58	Male	No	No
Val	59	Female	No	No
William	29	Male	Yes	Yes
Brian	35	Male	Yes	Yes
Connor	47	Male	Yes	Yes
David	38	Male	Yes	Yes
Eddie	42	Male	Yes	Yes
Frank	39	Male	No	Yes
Helen	35	Female	Yes	Yes

References

Alexander, K. & Ruggieri, S. (1998) *Changing Lives* (London: Crisis).

American Psychiatric Association (2000) *Diagnostic and Statistical Manual of Mental Disorders* (Washington: APA).

Anderson, A., Kemp, P. & Quilgars, D. (1993) *Single Homeless People* (London: HMSO).

Anderson, I. (1999) 'Social Housing or Social Exclusion? Non-access to Housing for Single Homeless People', Hutson, S. & Clapham, D. (eds) *Homelessness: Public Policies and Private Troubles* (London: Cassell) 155–172.

Anderson, I. (2004) 'Housing, Homelessness and the Welfare State in the UK', *European Journal of Housing Policy*, 4:3, 369–389.

Anderson, I. & Tulloch, D. (2000) *Pathways Through Homelessness* (Edinburgh: Scottish Homes).

Baker, L. (1997) *Homelessness and Suicide* (London: Shelter).

Ball, S., Maguire, M. & Macrae, S. (2000) *Choices, Pathways and Transitions Post-16: New Youth, New Economies in the Global City* (London: Routledge-Falmer).

Baron, S., Schuller, T. & Field, J. (eds) (2000) *Social Capital: Critical Perspectives* (Oxford: Oxford University Press).

Bassett, K. (1999) 'Is there Progress in Human Geography? The Problem of Progress in the Light of Recent Work in the Philosophy and Sociology of Science', *Progress in Human Geography*, 23:1, 27–47.

Bauman, Z. (1998) *Work, Consumerism and the New Poor* (Buckingham: Open University Press).

Bauman, Z. (2000) *Liquid Modernity* (Cambridge: Polity Press).

Beck, U. (1992) *Risk Society: Towards a New Modernity* (London: Sage).

Beck, U. (1999) *World Risk Society* (Cambridge: Polity Press).

Beck, U. (2000) *The Brave New World of Work* (Cambridge: Polity Press).

Bhaskar, R. (1979) *The Possibility of Naturalism: A Philosophical Critique of Contemporary Human Sciences* (Brighton: Harvester).

Bines, W. (1994) *The Health of Single Homeless People* (York: Centre for Housing Policy, University of York).

Bourdieu, P. (1986) 'The forms of Capital', Richardson, J. E. (ed.) *Handbook of Theory and Research* (New York: Greenwood) 241–258.

Bramley, G. (1988) 'The Definition and Measurement of Homelessness', Bramley, G., Doogan, K., Leather, P., Murie, M. & Watson, E. (eds) *Homelessness and the London Housing Market* (Bristol: SAUS Publications).

Breen, R. & Rottman, D. (1995) *Class Stratification* (Hemel Hempstead: Harvester Wheatsheaf).

British Crime Survey, Walker, A., Kershaw, K. & Nicholas, S. (2006) *Crime in England and Wales* (London: Home Office).

Buchanan, J. (2004) 'Tackling Problem Drug Use: A New Conceptual Framework', *Social Work in Mental Health*, 2:3, 117–138.

Buchanan, J. & Young, L. (2000) 'The War on Drugs – a War on Drug Users?', *Drugs: Education, Prevention and Policy*, 17:4, 409–422.

Buhrich, N., Hodder, R. & Teesson, M. (2000) 'Lifetime Prevalence of Trauma Among Homeless People in Sydney' in *Australian and New Zealand Journal of Psychiatry*, 34, 963–966.

Burchard, T., Le Grand, J. & Piachaud, D. (2002) 'Introduction', Hills, J., Le Grand, J. & Piachaud, D. (eds) *Understanding Social Exclusion* (Oxford: Oxford University Press) 1–12.

Burrows, R., Pleace, N. & Quilgars, D. (eds) (1997) *Homelessness and Social Policy* (London: Routledge).

Clapham, D. (1999) 'Conclusion', Hutson, S. & Clapham, D. (eds) *Homelessness: Public Policies and Private Troubles* (London: Cassell), 226–235.

Clapham, D. (2002) 'Housing Pathways: A Post Modern Analytical Framework', *Housing, Theory and Society*, 19, 57–68.

Clapham, D. (2003) 'Pathways Approaches to Homelessness Research', *Journal of Community and Applied Social Psychology*, 13, 119–127.

Clapham, D. (2005) *The Meaning of Housing* (Bristol: Policy Press).

Cohen, S. & Taylor, L. (1992) *Escape Attempts: The Theory and Practice of Resistance to Everyday Life* (2nd edn) (London: Routledge).

Coleman, J. S. (1988) 'Social Capital in the Creation of Human Capital', *American Journal of Sociology*, 94, s95–s120.

Collins, M. & Phillips, J. (2003) *Disempowerment and Disconnection: Trauma and Homelessness* (Glasgow: Glasgow Homelessness Network).

Courtney, D. (2005) 'Edgework and the Aesthetic Paradigm', Lyng, S. (ed.) *Edgework: The Sociology of Risk Taking* (London: Routledge) 89–116.

Craig, T., Hodson, S., Woodward, S. & Richardson, S. (1996) *Off to a Bad Start: A Longitudinal Study of Homeless Young People in London* (London: The Mental Health Foundation).

Craine, S. (1997) 'The "Black Magic Roundabout": Cyclical transitions, social exclusion and alternative careers', MacDonald, R. (ed.) *Youth the 'Underclass' and Social Exclusion* (London: Routledge).

Crane, M. & Warnes, A. (2006) 'The Causes of Homelessness Among Older People in England', *Housing Studies*, 21:3, 401–421.

Dean, M. (1999) *Governmentality: Power and Rule in Modern Society* (London: Sage).

Dench, G., Gavron, K. & Young, M. (2006) *The New East End: Kinship, Race and Conflict* (London: Profile Books).

Depres, C. (1991) 'The Meaning of Home: A Literature Review & Directions for Future Research and Theoretical Development', *The Journal of Architectural and Planning Research*, 8, 96–115.

Dix, J. (1995) *Assessing the Housing, Health and Support Needs of Single Homeless People Living in Hostel Accommodation in Cardiff* (Cardiff: City Housing).

Dorling, D. (2007) 'For What We Dream Of: Identity, Poverty, Wealth and Politics in Britain', Paper Presented at *CASE Welfare Policy and Analysis Seminars* (London, LSE: 14 November).

Durkheim, E. (1952) *Suicide: A Study in Sociology* (London: Routledge & Kegan Paul).

Easthope, H. (2004) 'A Place Called Home', *Housing, Theory and Society*, 21:3, 128–138.

Edwards, R. (1996) 'An Education in Interviewing: Placing the Researcher and the Research', Lee, R. & Renzetti, C. (eds) *Researching Sensitive Topics* (London: Sage) 181–195.

Edwards, B. & Foley, M. (1998) 'Civil Society and Social Capital Beyond Putnam', *American Behavioural Scientist*, 42:1, 124–139.

Evans, A. (1999) 'Rationing Device or Passport to Social Housing? The Operation of the Homeless Legislation in Britain in the 1990s', Hutson, S. & Clapham, D. (eds) *Homelessness: Public Policies and Private Troubles* (London: Cassell) 133–154.

Ezzy, D. (2001) *Narrating Unemployment* (Aldgate: Aldershot).

Fitzpatrick, S. (2000) *Young Homeless People* (Basingstoke: Macmillan Press Ltd).

Fitzpatrick, S. (2005) 'Explaining Homelessness: A Critical Realist Perspective', *Housing Theory and Society*, 22:1, 1–17.

Fitzpatrick, S. & Clapham, D. (1999) 'Homelessness and Young People', Hutson, S. & Clapham, D. (eds) *Homelessness: Public Policies and Private Troubles* (London: Cassell) 173–207.

Fitzpatrick, S. & Jones, A. (2005) 'Pursuing Social Justice or Social Cohesion?: Coercian in Street Homelessness Policies in England', *Journal of Social Policy*, 34:3, 389–406.

Fitzpatrick, S. & Kennedy, C. (2000) *Getting By: Begging, Rough Sleeping and the Big Issue in Glasgow and Edinburgh* (Bristol: The Policy Press).

Fitzpatrick, S. & Pawson, H. (2007) 'Welfare Safety Net or Tenure of Choice? The Dilemma Facing Social Housing Policy in England', *Housing Studies*, 22:2, 163–182.

Fitzpatrick, S. & Stephens, M. (1999) 'Homelessness, Need and Desert in the Allocation of Council Housing', *Housing Studies*, 14:4, 413–431.

Fitzpatrick, S., Kemp, P. & Klinker, S. (2000) *Single Homelessness: An Overview of Research in Britain* (Bristol: The Policy Press).

Flemen, K. (1997) *Smoke and Whispers: Drug Use and Youth Homelessness in Central London* (London: Hungerford Drug Project).

Fooks, G. & Pantazis, C. (1999) 'The Criminalisation of Homelessness, Begging and Street Living', Kennett, P. & Marsh, A. (eds) *Homelessness – Exploring the New Terrain* (Bristol: The Policy Press) 123–159.

Forrest, R. (1999) 'The New Landscape of the Precarious', Kennett, P. & Marsh, A. (eds) *Homelessness – Exploring the New Terrain* (Bristol: The Policy Press) 17–36.

Franklin, B. (1999) 'More than Community Care: Supporting the Transitions from Homelessness to Home', Hutson, S. & Clapham, D. (eds) *Homelessness: Public Policies and Private Troubles* (London: Cassell) 191–207.

Furedi, F. (2006) *Taking the Social Out of Policy: A Critique of the Politics of Behaviour*, Paper presented at: Diverse Britain: Social Practice and Social Policy Conference (Keyworth Centre, London South Bank University, September 8th 2006).

Furlong, A. & Cartmel, F. (1997) *Young People and Social Change – Individualisation and Risk in Late Modernity* (Buckingham: Open University Press).

Furlong, A. & Evans, K. (1997) 'Metaphors of Youth Transitions: Niches, Pathways, Trajectories, or Navigations', Bynner, J., Chisholm, L. & Furlong, A. (eds) *Youth, Citizenship and Social Change in a European Context* (Aldershot: Avebury) 17–44.

Gibb, K. & Maclennan, D. (2006) 'Changing Social Housing: Economic System Issues', *Public Finance and Management*, 6:1, 88–121.

Giddens, A. (1984) *The Constitution of Society* (Cambridge: Polity Press).

Giddens, A. (1990) *The Consequences of Modernity* (Cambridge: Polity Press).

Giddens, A. (1991) *Modernity and Self-identity: Self and Society in the Late Modern Age* (Cambridge: Polity Press).

Giddens, A. (1992) *The Transformation of Intimacy* (Cambridge: Polity Press).

Giddens, A. (2002) *Runaway World* (London: Profile Books).

Giuliani, M. (1991) 'Towards and Analysis of Mental Representations of Attachment to Home', *The Journal of Architectural and Planning Research*, 8:2, 133–146.

Goffman, E. (1963) *Stigma: Notes on the Management of Spoiled Identity* (London: Penguin).

Goffman, E. (1969) *The Presentation of Self in Everyday Life* (London: Allen Lane).

Goodwin, J. & O'Conner, H. (2005) 'Exploring Complex Transitions: Looking Back at the "Golden Age" of "From School to Work"', *Sociology*, 39:2, 201–220.

Greenwood, R., Schaefer-McDaniel, Winkel, G. & Tsemberis, S. (2005) 'Decreasing Psychiatric Symptoms by Increasing Choice in Services for Adults with Histories of Homelessness', *American Journal of Community Psychology*, 36:4, 223–238.

Greve, J. & Currie, E. (1990) *Homelessness* (York: Joseph Rowntree Foundation).

Gulcur, L., Stafancic, A., Shinn, M., Tsemberis, S. & Fischer, S. (2003) 'Housing, Hospitalization, and Cost Outcomes for Homeless Individuals with Psychiatric Disabilities Participating in Continuum of Care and Housing First Programmes', *Journal of Community and Applied Social Psychology*, 13, 171–186.

Hall, T. (2001) *Better Days than This: Youth Homelessness in Britain* (London: Pluto).

Halpern, D. (2005) *Social Capital* (Cambridge: Polity Press).

Harocopos, A. & Dennis, D. (2003) 'Maintaining Contact with Drug Users over an 18-month Period', *International Journal of Research Methodology*, 6:3, 261–265.

Harvey, B. (1999) 'Models of Resettlement for the Homeless in the European Union', Kennett, P. & Marsh, A. (eds) *Homelessness – Exploring the New Terrain* (Bristol: The Policy Press) 267–292.

Holland, J., Thomson, R. & Henderson, S. (2004) *Feasibility Study for a Possible Qualitative Longitudinal Study: Discussion Paper* (ESRC, www.esrc.ac.uk (Home page) on 17/04/05).

Homelessness Monitoring Group (2004) *Helping Homeless People: Delivering the Action Plan for Prevention and Effective Response* (Edinburgh: Homelessness Monitoring Group First Report, Scottish Executive).

Hutson, S. (1999) 'The Experience of "Homeless" Accommodation and Support', Hutson, S. & Clapham, D. (eds) *Homelessness: Public Policies and Private Troubles* (London: Cassell) 208–225.

Hutson, S. & Clapham, D. (eds) (1999) *Homelessness: Public Policies and Private Troubles* (London: Cassell).

Hutson, S. & Liddiard, M. (1994) *Youth Homelessness: The Construction of a Social Issue* (London: Macmillan).

Hutton, N. (1995) *The State We're In* (London: Cape).

Hyde, J. (2005) 'From Home to Street: Understanding Young People's Transitions into Homelessness', *Journal of Adolescence*, 28:2, 171–183.

Jacobs, K., Kemeny, J. & Manzi, T. (1999) 'The Struggle to Define Homelessness: a Constructivist Approach', Hutson, S. & Clapham, D. (eds) *Homelessness: Public Policies and Private Troubles* (London: Cassell) 11–28.

Jenks, C. (2003) *Transgression* (London: Routledge).

Jones, G. (1995) *Leaving Home* (Buckingham: Open University Press).

Jones, A., Quilgars, D. & Wallace, A. (2001) *Life Skills Training for Homeless People: A Review of the Evidence* (Edinburgh: Scottish Homes).

Katz, J. (1988) *The Seductions of Crime: Moral and Sensual Attractions in Doing Evil* (New York: Basic Books).

Kearns, A., Hiscock, R., Ellaway, A. & Macintyre, S. (2000) '"Beyond Four Walls". The Psycho-Social Benefits of Home: Evidence from West Central Scotland', *Housing Studies*, 15, 387–410.

Kemp, P., Lynch, E. & Mackay, D. (2001) *Structural Trends and Homelessness: A Quantitative Analysis* (Edinburgh: Scottish Executive).

Kennett, P. (1999) 'Homelessness, Citizenship and Social Exclusion', Kennett, P. & Marsh, A. (eds) *Homelessness – Exploring the New Terrain* (Bristol: The Policy Press) 37–60.

Kennett, P. & Marsh, A. (eds) (1999) *Homelessness – Exploring the New Terrain* (Bristol: The Policy Press).

Lash, S. (1994) 'Reflexivity and its Double', *Reflexive Modernisation: Politics, Tradition and Aesthetics in the Modern Social Order*, Beck, U., Giddens, A. & Lash, S. (Cambridge: Polity Press) 110–173.

Layard, R. (2006) *Happiness: Lessons from a New Science* (London: Penguin).

Le Grand, J. (2003) *Motivation, Agency, and Public Policy* (Oxford: Oxford University Press).

Lee, B. (2005) 'Danger on the Streets: Marginality and Victimization among Homeless People', *American Behavioural Scientist*, 48:8, 1055–1081.

Lemos, G. (2000) *Homelessness and Loneliness* (London: Crisis).

Liddiard, M. (1999) 'Homelessness: The Media, Public Attitudes and Policy Making', Hutson, S. & Clapham, D. (eds) *Homelessness: Public Policies and Private Troubles* (London: Cassell) 74–88.

Lukes, S. (1974) *Power – A Radical View* (London: Macmillan).

Lyng, S. (1990) 'Edgework: A Social Psychological Analysis of Voluntary Risk Taking', *American Journal of Sociology*, 95:4, 851–886.

Lyng, S. (2005a) 'Edgework and the Risk-Taking Experience', Lyng, S. (ed.) *Edgework: The Sociology of Risk Taking* (London: Routledge) 3–16.

Lyng, S. (2005b) 'Sociology at the Edge: Social Theory and Voluntary Risk Taking', Lyng, S. (ed.) *Edgework: The Sociology of Risk Taking* (London: Routledge) 17–28.

Mallet, S. (2004) 'Understanding Home: A Critical Review', *The Sociological Review*, 51:2, 62–89.

Mallett, S., Rosenthal, D. & Keys, D. (2005) 'Young People, Drug Use and Family Conflict: Pathways into Homelessness', *Journal of Adolescence*, 28:2, 185–199.

Marcus, A. (2005) *Where Have All the Homeless Gone? The Making and Unmaking of a Crisis* (New York: Bergham Books).

Markus, H. & Nurius, P. (1986) 'Possible Selves', *American Psychologist*, 41, 954–969.

Marsh, A. & Kennett, P. (1999) 'Exploring the New Terrain', Kennett, P. & Marsh, A. (eds) *Homelessness – Exploring the New Terrain* (Bristol: The Policy Press) 1–16.

Martijn, C. & Sharpe, L. (2006) 'Pathways to Youth Homelessness', *Social Science & Medicine*, 62:1, 1–12.

Maslowe, A. (1987) *Motivation and Personality* (3rd edn) (New York: Harper and Row).

Maslowe, A. (1999) *Towards a Psychology of Being* (3rd edn) (Chichester: John Wiley & Sons).

May, J. (2000) 'Housing Histories and Homeless Careers: A Biographical Approach', *Housing Studies*, 15:4, 613–638.

May, J., Cloke, P. & Johnsen, S. (2005) 'Re-phasing Neoliberalism: New Labour and Britain's Crisis of Street Homelessness', *Antipode*, 37:4, 703–730.

May, J., Cloke, P. & Johnsen, S. (2006) 'Shelters at the Margin: New Labour and the Changing State of Emergency Accommodation for Single Homeless People in Britain', *Policy & Politics*, 34:4, 711–729.

McNaughton, C. C. & Sanders, T. (2007) 'Housing and Transitional Phases out of "Disordered Lives": The Case of Leaving Homelessness and Street Sex Work', *Housing Studies*, 22:6, 885–908.

Molnar, B., Shade S., Kral, A., Booth, R. & Watters, J. (1998) 'Suicidal Behaviour and Sexual/Physical Abuse among Street Youth', *Child Abuse & Neglect*, 22, 213–222.

Mullins, D. & Murie, A. (2006) *Housing Policy in the UK* (Basingstoke: Palgrave Macmillan).

Mythen, G. (2005) 'Employment, Individualization and Insecurity: Rethinking the Risk Society Perspective', *The Sociological Review*, 53:1, 129–149.

Neale, J. (1996) *Supported Hostels for Homeless People: A Review* (York: Centre for Housing Policy, University of York).

Neale, J. (1997) 'Theorising Homelessness: Contemporary Sociological and Feminist Perspectives', Burrows, R., Pleace, N. & Quilgars, D. (eds) *Homelessness and Social Policy* (London: Routledge) 35–49.

Newburn, T. & Rock, P. (2005) *Living in Fear: Violence and Victimisation in the Lives of Single Homeless People* (London: Crisis).

O'Connell, M. E. (2003) 'Responding to Homelessness: An Overview of US and UK Policy Interventions', *Journal of Community & Applied Social Psychology*, 13, 158–170.

Padgett, D. (2007) 'There's No Place Like (a) Home: Ontological Security Among Persons with a Serious Mental Illness in the United States', *Social Science & Medicine*, 64, 1927–1936.

Padgett, D., Gulcur, L. & Tsemberis, S. (2006) 'Housing First Services for People Who are Homeless with Co-concurring Serious Mental Illness and Substance Abuse', *Research on Social Work Practice*, 16:1, 74–83.

Patton, G. & Viner, R. (2007) 'Pubertal Transitions in Health', *Lancet*, 369, 1130–1139.

Pawson, R. & Tilley, N. (1997) *Realistic Evaluation* (London: Sage).

Pickering, K., Fitzpatrick, S., Hinds, K., Lynn, P. & Tipping, S. (2003) *Tracking Homelessness: A Feasibility Study* (Edinburgh: Scottish Office Central Research Unit).

Pleace, N. (1995) *Housing Single Vulnerable Homeless People* (York: Centre for Housing Policy, University of York).

Pleace, N. (1998) 'Single Homelessness as Social Exclusion: The Unique and the Extreme', *Social Policy & Administration*, 32:1, 46–59.

Pleace, N. (2000) 'The New Consensus, the Old Consensus and the Provision of Services for People Sleeping Rough', *Housing Studies*, 15:4, 581–594.

Pleace, N. & Quilgars, D. (2003) 'Led Rather Than Leading? Research on Homelessness in Britain', *Journal of Community & Applied Social Psychology*, 13, 187–196.

Pleace, N., Burrows, R. & Quilgars, D. (1997) 'Homelessness in Contemporary Britain: Conceptualisation and Measurement', Burrows, R., Pleace, N. & Quilgars, D. (eds) *Homelessness and Social Policy* (London: Routledge) 1–18.

Plumridge, R. & Thomson, R. (2003) 'Longitudinal Qualitative Studies and the Reflexive Self', *International Journal of Research Methodology*, 6:3, 213–222.

Portes, A. (1998) 'Social Capital: Its Origins and Application in Modern Sociology', *Annual Review of Sociology*, 24, 1–24.

Quilgars, D. & Pleace, N. (1999) 'Housing and Support Services for Young People', Rugg, J. (ed.) *Young People, Housing and Social Policy* (London: Routledge) 109–126.

Randall, G. & Brown, S. (1995) *Outreach and Resettlement Work with People Sleeping Rough* (London: DoE).

Randall, G. & Brown, S. (1996) *From Street to Home: An Evaluation of Phase 2 of the Rough Sleepers Initiative* (London: HMSO).

Randall, G. & Brown, S. (1999a) *Homes for Street Homeless People: An Evaluation of the Rough Sleepers Initiative* (London: DoE).

Randall, G. & Brown, S. (1999b) *Ending Exclusion: Employment and Training Schemes for Homeless Young People* (York: York Publishing Services).

Reith, G. (2004) 'Consumption and its Discontents: Addiction, Identity and the Problems of Freedom', *The British Journal of Sociology*, 55:2, 227–246, 383–300.

Reith, G. (2005) 'On the Edge: Drugs and the Consumption of Risk in Late Modernity', Lyng, S. (ed.) *Edgework: The Sociology of Risk Taking* (London: Routledge).

Ricoeur, P. (1991a) 'Life in Quest of Narrative' in Wood, D. (ed.) *On Paul Ricoeur* (London: Routledge) 20–33.

Ricoeur, P. (1991b) 'Narrative Identity' in Wood, D. (ed.) *On Paul Ricoeur* (London: Routledge) 188–200.

Ricoeur, P. (1992) *Oneself as Another* (London: University of Chicago Press).

Rosengard, A. with Scottish Health Feedback (2001) *The Future of Hostels for Homeless People* (Edinburgh: Scottish Executive).

Rosengard, A., Laing, I., Jackson, A. & Jones, N. (2002) *Routes out of Homelessness* (Edinburgh: Scottish Executive).

Rosengard, A. & Ogg, J. (2004) *Improving Homelessness Services and Service User Involvement* (North Lanarkshire: NLC).

Sassen, S. (1991) *The Global City: New York, London, Tokyo* (Chichester: Princeton University Press).

Saunders, P. (1990) *A Nation of Home Owners* (London: Unwin Hyman).

Sayer, A. (2000) *Realism and Social Science* (London: Sage).

Sevenhuijsen, S. (2003) 'The Place of Care: The Relevance of the Feminist Ethic of Care for Social Policy', *Feminist Theory*, 4, 179–197.

Smith, J. (1999) 'Gender and Homelessness', Hutson, S. & Clapham, D. (eds) *Homelessness: Public Policies and Private Troubles* (London: Cassell) 108–132.

Smith, S. J. (2005a) 'States, Markets and an Ethic of Care', *Political Geography*, 24, 1–20.

Smith, C. W. (2005b) 'Financial Edgework: Trading in Market Currents', Lyng, S. (ed.) *Edgework: The Sociology of Risk Taking* (London: Routledge) 187–202.

Smith, S. J., Easterlow, D., Munro, M. & Turner, K. M. (2003) 'Housing as Health Capital: How Health Trajectories and Housing Paths Are Linked', *Journal of Social Issues*, 59:3, 501–525.

Somerville, P. (1992) 'Homelessness and the Meaning of Home: Rooflessness or Rootlessness?', *International Journal of Urban and Regional Research*, 16:4, 529–539.

Somerville, P. (1997) 'The Social Construction of Home', *The Journal of Architectural and Planning Research*, 14:13, 226–245.

Somerville, P. (1999) 'The Making and Unmaking of Homelessness Legislation', Hutson, S. & Clapham, D. (eds) *Homelessness: Public Policies and Private Troubles* (London: Cassell), 29–57.

Somerville, P. & Bengtsson, B. (2002) 'Constructionism, Realism and Housing Theory', *Housing Theory and Society*, 19:3, 121–136.

Speak, S. & Tipple, G. (2006) 'Perceptions, Persecution and Pity: The Limitations of Interventions for Homelessness in Developing Countries', *International Journal of Urban and Regional Research*, 30:1, 172–188.

Taylor, D. (1998) 'Social Identity and Social Policy: Engagements with Post Modern Theory', *Journal of Social Policy*, 27:3, 329–350.

Thomson, R. & Holland, J. (2003) 'Hindsight, Foresight and Insight: The Challenges of Longitudinal Qualitative Research', *International Journal of Social Research Methodology*, 6:3, 233–244.

Tipple, G. & Speak, S. (2005) 'Definitions of Homelessness in Developing Countries', *Habitat International*, 29, 337–352.

Tsemberis, S. & Eisenberg, R. (2000) 'Pathways to Housing: Supported Housing for Street-Dwelling Homeless Individuals with Psychiatric Disabilities', *Psychiatric Services*, 51:4, 487–493.

Tsemberis, S., McHugo, G., Williams, V., Hanrahan, P. & Stefancic, A. (2007) 'Measuring Homelessness and Residential Stability: The Residential Time-Line Follow Back Inventory', *Journal of Community Psychology*, 35:1, 29–42.

Tyler, K. & Johnston, K. (2006) 'Pathways Into and Out of Substance Use Among Homeless Emerging Adults', *Journal of Adolescent Research*, 21:2, 133–157.

Van Der Poel, A. & Van De Mheen, D. (2006) 'Young People Using Crack and the Process of Marginalization', *Drugs – Education Prevention and Policy*, 13:1, 45–59.

Vizard, P. & Burchardt, T. (2007) *Developing a Capability List: Final Recommendations of the Equalities Review Steering Group on Measurement* (London: CASE, London School of Economics).

Watson, S. & Austerberry, H. (1986) *Housing and Homelessness: A Feminist Perspective* (London: Routledge and Kegan Paul).

Webb, S. (1994) *My Address is not my Home: Hidden Homelessness and Single Women in Scotland* (Edinburgh: Scottish Council for Single Homeless).

Weber, M. (1930) *The Protestant Ethic and the Spirit of Capitalism* (London: Allen & Unwin).

Wilcox, S. (2002) *UK Housing Review 2002/2003* (York: Joseph Rowntree Foundation, Chartered Institute of Housing and Council of Mortgage Lenders).

Yanos, P., Felton, B., Tsemberis, S. & Frye, V. (2007) 'Exploring the Role of Housing Type, Neighbourhood Characteristics and Lifestyle Factors in the Community Integration of Formerly Homeless Persons Diagnosed with a Mental Illness', *Journal of Mental Health*, 16:6, 703–717.

Young, J. (1999) *The Exclusive Society* (London: Sage).

Young, J. (2006) *Crossing the Borderline: Globalisation and Social Exclusion: The Sociology of Vindictiveness and the Criminology of Transgression*, (http://www.malcolm-read.co.uk/JockYoung/crossing.htm on 09/05/2006).

Zetter, R. with Griffiths, D., Sogona, N., Flynn, D., Pasha, T. & Beynon, R. (2006) *Immigration, Social Cohesion and Social Capital* (York: Joseph Rowntree Foundation).

Index

CPSIA information can be obtained at www.ICGtesting.com
Printed in the USA
LVOW011154051011

249191LV00003B/1/P